Microeconomics of Money and Banking and Other Essays

Microeconomics of Money and Banking and Other Essays

Boris P. Pesek

Professor of Economics
University of Wisconsin-Milwaukee

NEW YORK UNIVERSITY PRESS
Washington Square, New York

First published in the U.S.A. by
NEW YORK UNIVERSITY PRESS
Washington Square
New York, NY 10003

LIBRARY OF CONGRESS
Library of Congress Cataloging-in-Publication Data

Pesek, Boris P.
  Microeconomics of money and banking and other essays / Boris P.
Pesek ; two essays coauthored by Thomas R. Saving.
    p.   cm.
  Bibliography: p.
  Includes index.
  ISBN 0-8147-6607-2
  1. Money. 2. Monetary policy. 3. Banks and banking. I. Saving,
Thomas Robert, 1933–   . II. Title.
  HG221.P384 1988
  332.1—dc19   88-17840
                                                                    CIP

61,958

I dedicate this book to

the next generation of monetary, banking and *credit* theorists

Contents

List of Figures

List of Tables

Special Acknowledgment to Thomas R. Saving

THOMAS R. SAVING is the co-author of two essays in this volume. One I consider to be a major contribution to the micro analysis of money and banking. While our exposition there leaves much to be desired, it was robust enough to become the basis of much of my future work.

I came to know Tom in 1960 when we were both teaching at the Michigan State University. After tentative explorations, cooperation started to appear to both of us as highly desirable. Both being nurtured by the (then) unorthodox Chicago School, and by the superlative microeconomic rigour of Milton Friedman, we were convinced that it is microeconomics on which all applied fields must build. We were especially dissatisfied with the total absence of price theory in texts from which we had to teach our money and banking students. And we realized that our professional characteristics are strongly complementary. I do have a tendency to rush to where the angels of analysis fear to tread. Tom is a meticulous craftsman who will look at every proposition from all possible—sometimes even impossible—angles, strive for rigour, and search for holes, inconsistencies and just plain errors. And, he was more often right than not.

After having written two books, our cooperation ended. Barbara's and Tom's allergy to pollen has made it imperative for them to move south, while Milena's and my allergy to the absence of four seasons (Wisconsin blizzards included) has made it impossible for us to look in the same direction. Upon separation by almost one thousand miles we have discovered that there is—in our case—no substitute for vigorous hour-by-hour, day-by-day verbal exchanges.

To me, however, this separation represented sorrow, personal loss and—I am sure—professional loss.

Introduction

If I had not read in a major review article the following statement, I could have spared myself for the next quarter of a century much work, grief—and fun:

If this logic applies to interest-bearing money, why should it not apply to the limiting case of non-interest bearing government debt [currency], which is equally the debt of the public to itself, and to commodity moneys, which are the same thing though based on custom rather than law?[1]

First, I have never met in my price theory a debt by "custom," only debts that arise from past borrowings of some assets. And "law" may enforce such price-theoretic debts, but it cannot create them. A "debt" by law alone—unproven by microeconomic analysis—must be called deferred taxation or expropriation. Second, the idea that a ton of either steel or gold produced and sold by a miner is an asset of the buyer and a debt either of the miner or of "the public to itself" seemed to me too silly to contemplate. That ton must be a part of wealth. But since gold money, fiat money, and bank money yield the same flow of services to their owners, it struck me like a thunderbolt that this seminal chain of reasoning by analogy should probably be reversed:

Since gold money is nobody's debt, why shouldn't logic tell us that the same is true about fiat money and bank money that perform the same service to their owners? The last two may be debts by law (which, Dickens teaches us, is an ass) but surely not by price theory.

In the case of fiat money it was supremely easy to prove to myself this counterproposition. The Federal Reserve System sells currency for the public's assets: "all sales are final." All that it promises to do for its "creditors" in the future is to exchange on demand one $5 bill "debt" for five $1 bill "debts'. To become satiated with such "debts" is my notion of Paradise. Fiat money must be a productive asset in its own right, for which the public is willing to sacrifice some other assets. In 1967 Thomas R. Saving and I published a book contradicting the then and now ruling dogma.

The response of the establishment represented by Don Patinkin was amazing. This author in his key book has mirrored the current orthodoxy by analyzing repeatedly fiat money as a government debt or "bond" (on pp. 173, 288, 213, 216, 219, 229, 276, 290, 295, 307, 339, 364 and in T-accounts on p. 296, and in section heading on p. 288).[2] Yet, his answer to us was that the above quotation represents "an isolated view in the literature."[3] And, he added:

> Needless to say, [Pesek and Saving] *also* regard fiat money ... as part of the net wealth of the community. I think it can, however, safely be said that they recognize that this is *also* the accepted view of the matter. In any event, the *only* [emphases added] example of a contrary view that they are able to cite (and they do so repeatedly) ... is [the above] rhetorical question ...[4]

Rarely have so many read so much nonsense on so few lines. We have quoted with admittedly tiresome repetitiveness (but, obviously, not often enough) James Tobin's and Don Patinkin's not rhetorical questions but an explicit contrary view. And, even funnier is the fact that from the moment this disclaimer has been offered until today, fiat money is treated—as it has always been treated—as a debt of the government. This is done in all texts[5], in professional wealth accounts, and in the Federal Reserve System's T-accounts and Flow of Funds accounts. Armed with foresight, a defending mumpsism[6] could have improved on Patinkin's statement: "You two know that we all have never done it, and we all shall continue doing it." Is there any wonder that in one of my major articles (Chapter 7) I have claimed that monetary theorists live in an Alice-in-Wonderland Era?

Bank money has represented a much more difficult nut to crack. There *is* the banks' legal liability to exchange bank money on demand for some different asset: currency. Thus, the appearance of a deposit-asset of the holder and deposit-debt of the banker is very strong. Yet in the above-mentioned book we have attempted to point out that when a monopolist (found in many texts) borrows $100 of currency, uses it as reserves, and lends $900 of bank money, it is price-theoretically impossible to prove that he or she borrowed $100 + $900; that the latter is her or his debt. Given the usual simplifying assumption of a zero-cost banker, he or she has one positive income stream ($900 times the interest rate r), and one negative income stream ($100 \times r$). The discounted present value of these streams is $+ \$900$ (Net Worth) and $- \$100$ (Liabilities). With positive costs, the factors he employs share this Net Worth with him (Chapters 2, 3, 4, and 7).

James M. Buchanan has courageously jumped to our defence against some pretty fierce attacks. He has pointed out[7] that if there is, say, a hundred per cent probability that a debt will not be called—that the right to obtain currency will never be exercised by bank depositors acting as a group—there is a legal liability but no price-theoretic debt. In price theory, debts are valued not by their legal or nominal values. They are measured by the discounted present value of their future repayments (see note 13). The discounted present value of the future repayment of $0 is $0. It should be entirely immaterial for economists that a lawyer will disagree.

While reading Buchanan's paper I was reminded of a touching novel I once read. A man gives to his beloved a signed blank cheque and goes away to amass a fortune. When the lady dies, among her effects they discover it filled out as follows:

"I OWE TO MISS JONES *my heart* $X"

This man's lawyer would have prepared during his life a T-account showing zero Net Worth. His price theorist—if familiar with the lady—would have prepared a T-account showing zero Liabilities. Our money and banking theorists prefer being para-lawyers to being economists. This elegant defence by Buchanan has been left to expire through neglect.

I would have preferred to offer a different defence. Instead of basing my case on mathematical probabilities that a genuine debt will not be called—impeccable as that case is price-theoretically—I would have preferred to continue basing my case on a different price-theoretic argument: that in the above monopolistic case there is no genuine $900 debt to start with. If one borrows $100, one doesn't borrow $1,000—period. However, despite fairly massive attacks by the prominent of the profession on the new analysis of the nature of money and the nature of banking, no reply by those attacked has been permitted.

This is not surprising because doubts about—or even overturning of—*the two key dogmas on which rests our modern banking and monetary theory* (that all monies are debts, and that each bank is a mere intermediary) would constitute a serious blow to the vested interests of all those who have published texts and advanced monetary treatises. They have spent their lifetimes elaborating these two propositions, and have been basing on them their policy-recommendations. So, ignoring or silencing counter-arguments must have seemed to be the best defence.

As T. S. Kuhn put it, "Might makes right" in sciences.[8] In 1968 Harry G. Johnson took me aside at a reception in London and in a most fatherly fashion (for which I will be forever grateful) advised me to drop the issue. "Boris," said he, "you will not destroy monetary theorists[9]. They will destroy you." However well-meaning that advice was, I just could not follow it, for two reasons. First, I have survived as a former European two far nastier establishments; that gets to be habit-forming. And, in any establishment, a professor who abstains from professing is a corrupt fraud. Second, I really had nowhere to go. I could not accept the two key dogmas of modern monetary and banking theory. The magnificent theoretical edifice built on top of these two cornerstones just cannot last. Sooner or later it must crumble. For me, trying to adorn it by carving curlicues (depicting ever more esoteric and untestable theories) into its walls would be Sisyphus' labour.

OTHER PROBLEMS WITH OUR CURRENT THEORY

So, for the next two decades I kept searching for more persuasive arguments. And, in the performance of my duty to teach the future generations I have based my lectures on the original rather than on the secondary sources. What made me wary was the old parlour game: a person whispers an item of gossip to his or her neighbour at the table. Experience shows that after the gossip is repeated for the tenth time, it bears no resemblance to the initial version. Keynes had experienced it, and so have—I discovered—both Fisher and Pigou. My readings have caused me to conclude that the two dogmas do not represent an isolated theoretical aberration:

Item.   In all texts and treatises the two distinct and famous Quantity Theories of Money are depicted as being merely one single theory, expressed by different symbols. In fact, those who have read Irving Fisher and A. C. Pigou would know that these theories have absolutely nothing to do with each other. Fisher focuses on flows and media of exchange, while Pigou focuses on stocks and stores of value. (Chapters 1 and 8)

Item.   To foster the notion that we face one single theory in two different garbs, many a modern text and several celebrated treatises claim that Pigou's proportion k of resources held in the form of money and Fisher's velocity V are related by the formula $k = 1/V$. Oscar Morgenstern once said that we have exchanged our ambition to be first-rate economists for the ambition to become second-rate mathematicians. But, even a third-rate mathematician would instantly reject this equation. The former term is a ratio at a point of time; the latter is a rate per unit of time. As such, the two are incommensurate; they cannot be related by any formula.

Our senses have become so dulled by infinite repetition in our texts that a parable may be useful: I used to sink a k-proportion of my total wealth into my car, so that I used to drive it at the average velocity $V = 1/k$ (per day? per hour?). Recently I let some of my real assets depreciate, so that k has increased. The inevitable consequence of this is that I now drive my car at a proportionately smaller velocity V. Would you not say that this is too silly for words? (Chapters 1, 4 and 8)

Item. All texts and advanced treatises claim that Fisher predicted that velocity V and transactions T are constants in the short run, from which it follows that he has expected proportional changes in money M and prices P. Many a text offers a graph of two time series depicting money and prices, and thereby gleefully contradicts Fisher's alleged prediction. Yet, should anybody read Fisher, she or he would discover that he has devoted the whole of Chapter IV to explain that all four variables are constantly in a state of flux, *all mutually interact*, and come to rest—perhaps—every ten years. (Chapter 4)

When last summer I pointed out all the above Items to an author of a textbook, he wrote back with disarming frankness that he is sorry to have been wrong, but that he never read either of the two authors (remember the old parlour game). I wonder if many writers of texts—and advanced treatises—would so freely and honestly admit the same.

Item. All texts raise the spectre of an unlimited demand for money at some low rate of interest, and they devote several pages to an exploration of the dire consequences of this for the monetary policy maker. Yet, the inventor of "the liquidity trap" had suggested this notion most casually, and on p. 207 claims that it has never been seen before. Inevitably so. The notion that people may be supplied with up to an infinite quantity of money and not spend any of it—waiting for a bargain on bonds—is too silly for words. (Chapters 1 and 7). I, for one, spend it on goods and services faster than it comes in.

Item. All texts and advanced treatises devote substantial space to discuss equations—in fact, accounting tautologies—specifying "The Proximate Determinants of the Stock of Money".[10] Not one of them mentions or quantifies bank resource costs. Yet, commercial banks alone in the US spend around $100 billion each year (and Mutual Savings Banks, Savings and Loan Association, and Credit Unions must be spending a similar amount, for a total amounting to some 5 per cent of our GNP). For all we teachers and our students are told, these resource costs could double or triple, and neither the size of banking nor the stock of bank money would be affected. Empirical analysis of banking is made to seem superfluous. (Chapters 2, 4, 5, 6 and 7)

In genuine economics, neglect of the firms' production functions and cost functions is inconceivable. Could (say) transportation economists adopt our standard "simplifying assumption of zero-cost banking"— assume that freight levitates by itself from place to place—and make policy recommendations on this basis? Surely that would be too silly for words.

Item. A chapter in a major book, reprinted in numerous books of readings, bases its "Critique of Neoclassical Monetary Theory" on the claim that this theory has failed to integrate the real and the money sectors. The rest of the book (as its subtitle Integration of Value and Monetary Theory indicates) is then devoted to the correction of this error. It turns out that the entire "Critique" stands or falls on one single assertion, hidden in a geometrical (mis)interpretation of the neoclassical theory: an assertion that our predecessors did not know that everybody's spending is limited by her or his budget constraint. That they have believed that everybody will purchase a fixed quantity of goods, irrespective of their prices. Surely, that is too silly for words. (Chapter 8)

Item. Just recently I read an article evaluating Keynes after fifty years. It claims that

But in this admirable attempt at formal theory, Keynes failed. His top-priority goal of articulating model with an unemployment equilibrium ... foundered on the Pigou-Patinkin real balance effect. [11]

However, I am sure that Pigou would refuse to take bows for this neoclassical self-declared victory. He has described what later came to be called "The Pigou Effect" as a mere toy, based on so "extremely improbable assumptions" as to never be played "on the checkerboard of actual life." [12] However, even with these extreme assumptions met (which, Pigou correctly claims, governments would not permit) the Patinkin Effect would still not work in any except the most formal version of a most naive model.

Consider (a) deflation-caused bankruptcies and (b) expected further price decreases that keep increasing the demand for money (M. Friedman and Chapter 1), and keep reducing the demands for consumption and investment goods. Both are forces with which Keynes was quite familiar: two chapters in his General Theory have "Expectations" in their title. While the Patinkin Effect requires the economy to move towards full employment along any given aggregate demand function—*ceteris par-*

ibus is crucial—simultaneous bankruptcies and deflation keep shifting both the LM and IS functions, and therefore the aggregate demand function, towards the origin. The result is much more likely to be a depression than full employment. (Chapters 1, 5 and 8)

Keynes wanted government to fix expenditures so as to enable us to reach full employment. The neoclassical theory, relying on the Patinkin Effect, shows that a drop in prices will enable the free market to do that job. And so it would, provided that the government would first fix overnight a new full-employment-equilibrium price level, and so prevent step-by-step price decreases and their catastrophic consequences. That appears to be a Pyrrhic victory of the free-market forces over Keynes's model. (Chapter 1)

Item. A major economist had proposed that we obtain optimum money through a permanent deflation equal to the rate of interest. It is embarrassing to remind that economist about permanent income, but it cannot be helped. Any price theorist or accountant would point out that every new permanent future income stream will become capitalized "forthwith" (Keynes's term), so that the recommended deflation is impossible to obtain. Fully expected deflation is an oxymoron. (Chapter 1)

Item. All theoretical analyses of money come up with negative interest elasticity of demand; the validity of the Keynesian IS-LM framework depends on it. Yet, "the empirical approach to money" permits inclusion of assets with both positive and negative interest elasticities. In the last decade, the former predominate. But then, the LM function has a negative slope.

If it intersects the IS function from above, we get the strange conclusion that an increase in the supply of money will increase the rate of interest at any given level of income. And, if the intersection is from below, such an increase in money will also reduce the demand for goods and services and thus cause deflation. (Chapters 1 and 4) With this definition of money, speeding up the printing presses would be the best defence against an inflation. Is this not just too silly for words?

Item. The modern (and new) belief that the competitive ideal is applicable to money and banking led in the US to a drive for deregulation. As a result, the concept of money has been changed. Previously, banks have been forced to offer only two distinct assets: chequable non-interest bearing deposits with a huge velocity and non-chequable interest-bearing deposits with a negligible velocity. One was akin to Scotch, and the other to soda. Now, each bank is permitted to supply its own numerous mixes of these two: some with plenty of Scotch, some so-so, and some with plenty of soda. The alcoholic (inflationary) content of these innumerable cocktails is inscrutable. To measure the aggregate gallons supplied—"the stock of money"—is not very helpful (Chapters 1, 4, 11, and 12). Monetary theorists should have tried to block this "reform" instead of fostering it. Because of it, we do not have a definition of our subject matter—"money."

E. H. Phelps-Brown said in his Presidential address that economics is now where natural sciences were in the seventeenth century. (Chapter 4) I am convinced that monetary theory and banking theory lag by a similar margin behind the rest of economics. Given the above sampler, the reader should not be surprised that I am ashamed to be known as a monetary theorist, and to feel duty-bound to teach our undergraduates the current orthodoxy. (Of course, I feel free to spare my graduate students.) An isolated blunder may be expected to be found in any discipline. But a massive and interlocking conglomerate not just of blunders with respect to most fundamental issues, but also of transparent arithmetic nonsenses causes me to believe that monetary and banking theory is to economic theory as astrology is to astronomy.[13]

This was bound not to be—and was only briefly and naively expected by me to be—a popular view. As a result, the publication of some of my articles has an air of a Byzantine intrigue. In one case an editor has been able to secure one additional favourable review, from a quite prestigious upper-rank economist, by giving a him a promise that the review and its author will not be revealed unless this editor's job became endangered.

Fortunately, as the above example out of several I could mention shows, there are some colleagues of mine who share Harry Johnson's opinion of me, as it was recounted to me in 1968 in the early hours of the morning by Karl Brunner and Allan Meltzer over a delicious French dinner: "Boris may be wrong, but he is one the few who don't play games." That, to me, was and remains to be a treasured and supreme accolade: we should first worry about the fundamentals before offering prestigious esoteric models—resting on crumbling foundations—that have no relationship to reality and can never be tested or applied empirically (*e.g.* and only *e.g.*, Chapter 10). If I ever get to rest under a tombstone of my own, I do hope that Johnson's comment will be carved there as my epitaph.

MY LAST TWO DECADES

For two decades, the leaders of the University of Wisconsin-Milwaukee kept me patiently in the style to which I have become accustomed.

I suspect that they were disappointed that I have not become a star overnight by disposing of the two dogmas—as they must have hoped when they have hired me in 1967. Like myself, they have failed to realize just how fiercely people will protect their turf: but they have tolerated and even generously rewarded my nonconformity.

However, I could have been less fortunate elsewhere, and probably would have had less reason to be so very grateful. I may also say that as a young and naive young academician I had little use for tenure. By now, I have comprehended our criminologists: it is better to let ten lazybones go fishing than to have one creative professor bite the dust. Tenure protects those who point out that the Emperor has no clothes. [14] As a result, the Emperor is not able to take away "the bully pulpit" (to quote Teddy Roosevelt). And, with this bully pulpit goes the likelihood that some editor will be open-minded.

In the last few years I think I became luckier than I had any right to be. As far as the first dogma is concerned, I believe I finally became able to construct a microeconomic theory of money as a productive asset in its own right (not only a debt) that is—I believe and hope—rigorous enough to withstand even the most hostile scrutiny. (Chapter 1) I do not apologize for my previous tries: they mark my unaided and solitary struggle (Chapters 4, 5 and 6) and contain some interesting analyses of other issues.

As far as the second dogma ("all banks merely intermediate") is concerned, a referee for the American Economic Review had unwittingly furnished me with a major lead. With the hauteur typical of that genus he asked why, if I so much disagree with the notion that our banks are mere intermediaries, I do not attack directly Chester Arthur Phillips who is the celebrated father of it. Willing to take advice, I read Phillips's *Bank Credit* (1921) (to my shame) for the first time. While doing so I have discovered that my colleagues have not read Phillips's book either. Had we done so, we would have all discovered that some miscreant, lost in history, put Phillips's theory on its head. Phillips's key point is that dishomogeneous banks usually—not always—lend more than they borrow; in our modern theory, homogeneous banks always borrow more than they lend. Phillips's theory has a tremendous advantage over modern theory in that he puts his empirical facts where his mouth is. He has undertaken a unique and extremely sophisticated research into the microeconomic activities of a broad sample of banks covering the eastern half of our continent (Chapter 2).

I must admit that it was sobering to realize that in the past quarter of a century I was trying to repeat Columbus's feat of discovering America. However, it became a source of my added confidence in my writings to realize that another banking theorist had not only proposed that same theory but had also confirmed it by his solid empirical research; something that never crossed my mind. That was foolish of me. Theorizing cannot match the impact of measured facts.

THE EUROPEAN CONNECTION

While working in two extremely difficult topics—and on some embarrassingly easy ones for those few who do happen to read (rather than read about) the Old Masters—I was also lucky to find a warm reception, often critical but always open-minded, at a number of European universities. My colleagues in Namur, Wien, Modena, Milano, Venezia, Firenze, and Giessen (listed in chronological order) will always be in my most respectful, grateful, and affectionate memory. They have helped me immensely by noticing major holes in my analyses; and, by causing me to recognize places where what seemed clear to me actually required careful, sensitive, and rigorous persuasion.

I can only speculate why European universities have proved to be so hospitable and so stimulating to my work. I venture to share with my readers my guess: in a highly competitive American society, science is for the participants a zero-sum game, and the tempo is too hurried and too much focused on the short run. To reconsider the simple foundations of our theories just may not pay, while something new and elegant is likely to do so. So, ever-new untestable theories keep bursting upon us, become fashionable for a few years, propel their authors to fame, get mummified and entombed in ever-growing textbooks, and are never seen again in advanced professional work. American academia is a mirror image of our corporations: it's the quarterly dividend that counts, however ephemeral its source. In a more secure and relaxed (professionally, not intellectually) European environment, economic science seems to be a positive-sum game, among a band of brothers seeking not only personal advancement (of course they do), but more durable truths. A convergence of the two systems might prove fruitful.

I am extremely grateful to Wheatsheaf Books Ltd., (Brighton, in off-shore Great Britain) for enabling me—nay, asking me—to put under one roof my various essays. Many of my articles have been scattered among many journals, often with circulation so small as not to be generally known to my profession. Here they will be available to the next generation of monetary and banking theorists.

CONCLUSION

Monetary theory has been in a most sorry state for decades. A year ago the President of the American Economic Association, Alice M. Rivlin, said that "no one seems to know what money is anymore".[15] This has been a permanent state of affairs. In 1962 Harry G. Johnson wrote: "Obviously, there is no point in monetary theory if we cannot define what it is that we are theorizing about".[16] Since then, banking "reforms" have made the situation much worse. Monetary theory is the only branch of economics which admittedly is unable to quantify its subject any better than to say that it lies somewhere between $M1 = \$693$ billion and $L = \$4,061$ billion (see any issue of the *Federal Reserve Bulletin*). Does a discipline that cannot even define its subject matter have a right to exist?

It is inconceivable that any other field of economics would claim for itself even one tenth of so many degrees of freedom. With them, one may prove any monetary theory under the sun. We theorize *ex ante* that money determines economic activity, without specifying what money is. If something within the above huge range does happen to correlate best—*ex post*—with economic activity, well then: that's what money is. (As Abba Lerner is claimed to have said, "that" could turn out to be peanuts.) And if that concept of money should happen to make nonsense of the standard Keynesian analysis found in all texts? Well, that's no problem, because nobody notices it.

As always, the more nebulous the doctrine, the more vigorous its defence. Lord Acton wrote: "There is no error so monstrous that it fails to find defenders among the ablest men." In this case the defenders are indeed formidable because of their vested interests, skills—and power. For bringing monetary theory out of the mess it is in we must look to our successors, to whom I have dedicated this book. I find much hope for monetary and banking theory in the claim of one of the greats in physics, Max Planck: "science progresses from funeral to funeral".[17]

NOTES

1. Johnson, Harry G., *Essays in Monetary Economics* (London: George Allen & Unwin, 1967; p. 25).
2. Patinkin, Don, *Money, Interest, and Prices* (New York: Harper and Row, 1965).
3. Patinkin, Don, "Money and Wealth: A Review Article", *Journal of Economic Literature*, Dec. 1969, p. 288.
4. *Ibid.*, p. 288.
5. I happen to have eleven money and banking texts in my library; they *all* say the same thing. (List on request.)
6. I owe this word to Joan Robinson. My *Webster's Third New International Dictionary* defines it as "A bigoted adherent to an exposed but customary error."
7. Buchanan, James M., "An Outside Economist's Defense of Pesek and Saving", *Journal of Economic Literature*, Sep. 1969.

8. Kuhn, T.S., *The Structure of Scientific Revolution* (Chicago: The University of Chicago Press, 1962, p. 167).
9. Actually, he used a proper name; however, I am (almost) sure he meant it in a generic sense.
10. Friedman, M. and Schwartz, A.J., *Monetary History of the United States, 1867–1960*. Princeton, NJ: Princeton University Press, 1963, pp. 776–808.
11. McCallum, Bennett, "The Development of Keynesian Macroeconomics", *American Economic Review*, May 1987, p. 125.
12. Pigou, A.C., "Economic Progress in a Stable Environment," in F.A. Lutz and L.W. Mints (eds) *Readings in Monetary Theory*. (New York: Blakiston, 1951).
13. Strong statement, that. Let me support it with one more Item. In an acclaimed book Don Patinkin wrote:

    > For the government's issuance of money in this case is essentially an exploitation of the private sector's willingness to hold increasing real balances so as to "float" an interest-free [interest $i = 0$] "loan" [government bond or debt $D > 0$] in perpetuity [principal $P = 0$]. (1965, pp. 363–4)

    For a quarter of a century monetary theorists have failed to object to this sentence. Nay, most have made the book a required reading. Yet, every economist (as well as every accountant or business person) would substitute the above three variables into the orthodox formula

    $$0 < D = i/(1 + r) + i/(1 + r)^2 + \ldots + i/(1 + r)^{n-1} + P/(1 + r)^n = 0$$

    shrug her or his shoulders, and start reading something worthwhile. A macroeconomic model that confuses productive assets with offsetting loans-debts cannot merit attention.
14. A distinguished friend of mine who kindly read this Introduction strenuously objected to my phrase about the "naked Emperor". One should never, never, say such a thing if one wants to remain a member of the establishment (*Genossenschaft* was his alternative term), and not be viewed as an "eccentric". My answer was that, at my age, I have no ambition with respect to the former, and no objection to the latter.
15. Rivlin, Alice M., "Economics and Political Process", *American Economic Review*, March 1987, p. 5.
16. *Op cit.*, p. 95.
17. Professor Swanrnjit S. Arora, in charge of our Social Science Research Facility, has been extremely helpful in the preparation of this manuscript. One student (James Piekarski) whose intellect makes me wish to be his contemporary—we could produce some good stuff together—took upon himself the boring task of proofreading the whole thing and of taking care of the innumerable editorial details: I am most grateful to him.

And, my treasure beyond compare—MILENA—took exceptions to my last sentence, and has asked for my permission to express here her loving hope that our science will not progress *too* fast. I understand and reciprocate her hope: my own life without her would be grim. She is my umbrella on (many) a rainy day, and a brilliant sunshine on good days. As the old Roman saying puts it, *Sine Mila non est vita.*

Part One:
Microeconomics of Money and Banking

1 Microeconomics of Money*

Several distinguished economists have persuaded the profession to accept the doctrine of optimum money. If it costs nothing to produce, it should cost nothing to hold: it should pay the equilibrium rate of interest. Very few monetary theorists—including Robert W. Clower, Jerome Stein, C. S. Tsiang, and myself—have expressed opposition. I believe I can now show that the verdict does not depend on superior theorizing but on facts. Each side starts with its own empirical assertions of facts about money's production function. Each deems them so self-evident that they need not be explicitly spelled out and defended by empirical evidence.

Each of the two—seemingly conflicting—analyses of two different sets of facts is correct. But, with empirical assertions concealed in the wings, and with the protagonists on the stage looking only at their own assumptions across each other's shoulders, each side is persuaded that the other fellow must be making theoretical errors. I will show that only a strictly empirical decision as to which of the two competing production functions applies to money may settle the controversy, the resolution of which is of major policy-making importance.

1. MANY FACTORS' BELL-SHAPED FUNCTION

According to Milton Friedman, "the fundamental production function of money" is its service of facilitating transactions (1969, p. 3). He—along with several other economists—has devised a policy designed to maximize this function:

If deposits transferable by check pay interest equal to the market rate, people will indeed be induced to hold an amount such that, at the margin, an additional

* From: *Giornale degli Economisti e Annali di Economia*, November–December, 1986, pp. 595–616.

dollar will render no additional services in facilitating transactions. The transaction services ... have become a free good, available without cost to the holders of demand deposits. (Friedman and Schwartz, p. 114)

It is clear that they are asserting here as an empirical fact that the transaction service is related to money by a bell-shaped production function, which becomes at some point horizontal and yields a zero marginal product. Elsewhere Friedman claims that this is "natural to assume" (1969, p. 18). Let me start with the standard production function one finds in any price theory text:

$$x = g(f_1, ..., f_n) \qquad (1)$$

where x denotes one unit's output and f's denote factor inputs. Suppose that one factor, f_n, is varied while all others are kept constant. To cover all possibilities, all texts (e.g., Friedman, 1976, p. 132) offer a function that increases at a decreasing rate and ultimately becomes horizontal and starts to decline. In the relevant range

$$\partial x / \partial f_n \geqslant 0 \text{ and } \partial^2 x / \partial f_n^2 < 0. \qquad (2)$$

The production function of the sector to which the unit belongs exhibits the same characteristics. If we denote sectoral output by an X and sectoral inputs by Σf's, we may write

$$X = h(\Sigma f_1, ..., \Sigma f_n), \qquad (3)$$

$$\partial X / \partial \Sigma f_n \geqslant 0 \text{ and } \partial^2 X / \partial \Sigma f_n^2 < 0. \qquad (4)$$

It should be stressed that not every factor needs to have a function with this generalized shape, which has been artificially designed to account for all possibilities. For instance, it would be most unnatural to impute it to a catalyst, which has a function that is a ray passing through the origin until the cooperating chemicals are exhausted; thereafter, it becomes horizontal. When discussing any specific factor—say, money—one must not blithely assume that it does fall under the scope of the generalized function. One should—one must—offer empirical evidence proving which segment or segments of the generalized function do apply.

What is the demand for the factor f_n? Let P_f denote the price of the factor, s its marginal product *per annum*, and p the value assigned to this product. If we assume depreciation away, we may use the market interest rate r to capitalize this permanent income flow:

$$P_f = sp/r. \qquad (5)$$

The resulting demand functions in Figure 1.1 intersect the axis either when $p = 0$ or when $s = 0$. Friedman is convinced that optimum quantity of money will obtain when sp (which he splits into two parts, MVP and

MNVP) is made equal to zero through interest payments (Friedman, 1969, pp. 18 and 20). If money is depicted by Figure 1.1, he is right:

Consider this policy in the case of any factor to which the production functions in equations 1 and 3 do apply. Start with a positive price and assume that some discovery causes the supply price of the factor to fall to

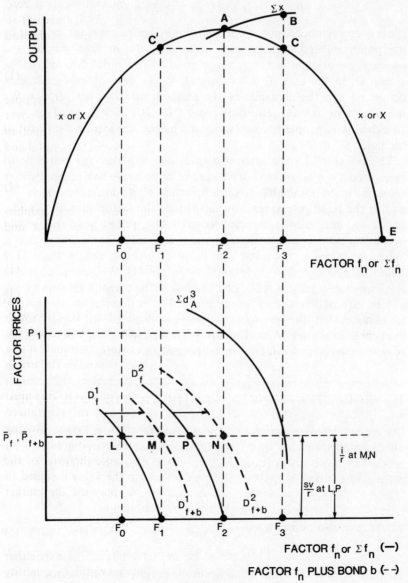

Figure 1.1

zero. Suppose, however, that the policy maker for some valid reason does not want to permit this, but still wants to allocate resources correctly. Zero holding costs, achieved through interest payments i, seem to be a perfect substitute for the zero price. To analyze this case, we must revise equation 5:

$$\bar{P}_{f+b} = sp/r + i/r, \ sp \geqslant 0, \ i/r = \bar{P}_{f+b} \tag{6}$$

(Bars over a symbol denote a variable that is either a constant, or fixed by the policy-maker.) The function represents *the demand for a joint product*: the original factor f_n plus a bond b. The initial demand for the factor D_f^1 in the case of $p = 0$ (or, D_f^2 in the case of $s = 0$) becomes converted into the demand for the factor-bond D_{f+b}^1 (or, D_{f+b}^2). We move from the initial equilibrium point L (or P) to the point M (or N)[1]. In either case, people become satiated with the services of the factor at the point C' (or A).

The policy of paying interest applies the orthodox key principle of price theory—which I shall try to prove erroneous—that a competitive solution, when obtainable, assures optimum allocation of resources. By adding the bond component, we have made the factor (almost [2]) a free good, without pushing its price to zero. The welfare gain that would benefit the holders of the money-bond is claimed to be most impressive. When measured as a capital sum in 1986 prices, it ranges from $134 billion to $1,842 billion (Friedman, 1969, pp. 44). Who could object to the impeccable analysis replicated here, or to the magnificent gain? I will object, instead on empirical grounds. I will show that it is most unnatural to assume that the production function depicted in Figure 1.1 is applicable to money. And, I will offer in section 7 what I believe to be conclusive empirical evidence in support of this claim.

2. PRODUCTION FUNCTION IN THE CASE OF SOME GOODS

Let me first prepare the ground for my analysis. When Friedman takes off his monetarist hat and dons his price-theorist hat, he rejects the production function in equation 1 as a special case by offering a more general one (Friedman, 1976, p. 127):

$$x = g(f_1, \ldots, f_n; X) \tag{7}$$

which may also be written as

$$x = h(f_1, \ldots, f_n; \Sigma f_1, \ldots, \Sigma f_n). \tag{8}$$

He points out (p. 93) that a change in the output X of the sector (in our case, due to an increase in inputs Σf_n) may unleash *external technical economies or diseconomies*, internal to the sector but external to each part of it:

$$\partial x/\partial f_n \geqslant 0 \text{ and } \partial X/\partial \Sigma f_n \gtrless 0. \tag{9}$$

One factor's "quasi-marginal product" may be perceived to be positive (because each unit is able to observe only its own part of equation 7) even though the true marginal product of the entire sector is a negative one. Friedman then introduces the analysis of this phenomenon into the discussion of the cost function (pp. 92–102), derived from the production functions. Strangely enough, he pays no attention to it in his discussion of the production function itself (pp. 130–8). To my knowledge, no other price theorist has done so. Let me fill this lacuna.

Assume that the function in Figure 1.1 now depicts the production function of the factor f_n employed by the entire sector (equation 8). And, assume that the sector is in equilibrium at the point A. If we add up the increments to output that each unit expects from its own increment to inputs, we get the function Σx. I call it "*the quasi-production function*", aping Friedman's term (pp. 92–102) "quasi-supply (of the product) function", which is derived from it. If demand for the product of the factor exists, so will the quasi-demand Σd_A^3 for the factor itself. I (call it "quasi", because it is derived from the quasi-production functions Σx passing through the point A.) This is something that obviously would be impossible at the point A in the case of the production function in equation 1. Let the price of the factor fall from P_f^1 to P_f. All units will buy $F_2 F_3$ quantity of this factor, in the expectation that they will reach the point B. In fact, the sector will end up at the point C. Should the price of the factor become zero, it will end up at the point E^3.

Examples of external technical diseconomies are to be found everywhere:

(1) The demand for two-way radios may be positive even though increased quantities—stimulated either by a lower price or by an interest income subsidy—may cause a reduction of the number of messages transmitted.

(2) Faced with road congestion caused by their own trucks, firms may increase their purchases of cheaper or subsidized trucks.

(3) The index of the quantity of the store-of-value service of non-industrial gold may be deduced from the demand function: multiply each pair of prices and quantities, and their products will serve as an index of the quantity of the store-of-value service of gold[4]. Suppose that we are at its peak at the point A in Figure 1.1, where the elasticity of demand for gold is equal to minus one, so that the production function starts to be negatively sloping. However, the quasi-production function has a positive slope: each demander believes that, with a slightly lower price, he or

she could afford to add to the store of value and so move collectively to the point *B*. In fact, increased output of gold will push them to the point *C* in Figure 1.1. Instead of employing more of cheaper gold miners, the sector would allocate resources much more efficiently if it would employ a few safe-crackers who would steal enough gold so as to move us to the point *C'*.

Under the scope of this analysis fall also rarities of all kinds (satiation with rarities is an oxymoron), valuable goods with Veblen's "snob appeal", and income-generating assets like nobility titles, Nobel Prizes, and probably others. Let any such good—say, rarities—become available at zero production cost. The resulting increase in the number of these goods will not increase the quantity of rarities; it will merely convert the initial quantity of treasured "assets" into "rubbish". As Max Weber and Karl Marx have pointed out, in some cases a quantitative change turns into a qualitative change. The declared goal of price theory—to bring us closer to satiation with everything—is in these cases a path not to Paradise (Friedman, 1976, p. 1) but to Hell.

3. EXTERNALITIES AND EXTERNAL TECHNICAL DISECONOMIES

External technical diseconomies are completely different in nature from externalities, and so are the policies needed to cope with them. Unfortunately, one is frequently confused for the other (e.g. Mansfield, pp. 427–9 or David D. Friedman, pp. 412–26). With externalities, sectoral output may remain constant. All that happens is that one unit wrongfully removes from its production function in equation 1 some factor f_a (e.g., smoke scrubbers) necessary to protect the rest of the economy. It thereby forces other units—probably in a completely different sector—to insert into their production function some superfluous factor f_b to repair the damage. Externalities are not a problem for economic analysis; they are a problem for the police (like theft or vandalism). Fines, court-imposed cease and desist orders, judgements for damages are some of the tools needed to correct the wrongdoing.

In the case of external technical diseconomies all units in the sector respond—in good faith—to market determined lower factor costs and try to expand their outputs along their own production functions because their quasi-marginal product is perceived to be positive. To send the police after them would be unjust. In some cases, the increment to output may be merely smaller than expected. But, in some cases it may be a negative one (equation 9). By increasing factor inputs, the sector reduces already existing wealth instead of adding to it. Willy-nilly, additional workers become modern Luddites.

Orthodox price theory notwithstanding, the only way of preventing destruction of wealth is to prevent competition. Government minimum price legislation, quotas, retail price maintenance, licenses, monopolies or cartels become essential tools for optimizing society's allocation of resources—in fact, for prevention of the destruction of already existing resources—in the case of goods subjected to external technical diseconomies leading to a negative sectoral marginal product.

It is peculiar that the supporters of optimum money have not tried to prove empirically that the bell-shaped production function is applicable to money. They have also failed to prove empirically that money belongs among those goods in the case of which the competitive solution is desirable. Operating in a vacuum, they have simply taken for granted (Meltzer, p. 300) these empirical facts, even though both are crucial for the validity of the theory of optimum money.

4. MONEY'S PRODUCTION FUNCTION

Let me now consider the production function that relates the aggregate of money to the aggregate transaction service of money. According to Irving Fisher, the volume of transactions T that the society wants to undertake is determined by the real forces of the economy (pp. 74–5) such as resource endowments, division of labour, and organization of markets. Transitional disturbances aside, it is said to be "... independent of the quantity of money." (p. 155). And, it goes without saying, independent of the rate of interest that measures the cost of holding money; a factor he must have viewed as so minor as not to be even worthy of consideration. In fact, in a different context the author argues on the basis of his analysis and empirical evidence that interest payments on one of several monies will actually reduce its use in transacting (p. 9). In section 8 I shall argue that in the case of deflation this is true in the general case as well. However, at the moment I will lean backwards and merely assume that interest payments have zero effect on the quantity of transactions. The equilibrium quantity of transactions measured in real terms (as Fisher does) may be specified as

$$T = f(f_a, f_b, ..., M; p_a, p_b, ..., p_M),$$ (10)

$$T/M > 0, \ \partial T/\partial M = 0, \text{ and } \partial T/\partial p_M = 0.$$

where f's denote all the factors that must cooperate with money M in the transacting activity, and p's denote the costs of using these factors. In section 7 I shall offer strong empirical evidence in support of Fisher's verbal analysis and of the second part of equation 10.

Given that fact, *the sectoral production function* that relates money to the transaction services of money is a horizontal line shown in Figure 1.2. I admit that I ignore the function close to the origin. Shortages of monies with denominations small enough to meet the needs of trade (such as they existed in American colonies) have prevented many desired transactions from occurring and thus have resulted in a production function with a positively sloping segment, prior to its becoming horizontal. Similarly, it might be that an insufficient stock of nominal money in an economy with price rigidities will prevent the desired level of trading and lead to a less-than-full-employment equilibrium (Fisher, p. 69). For my analysis these two ills (and thus the positively sloping production function to which they lead) are irrelevant, because the theory of optimum money is not designed to cure them, but to accomplish a completely different purpose in a full employment economy.

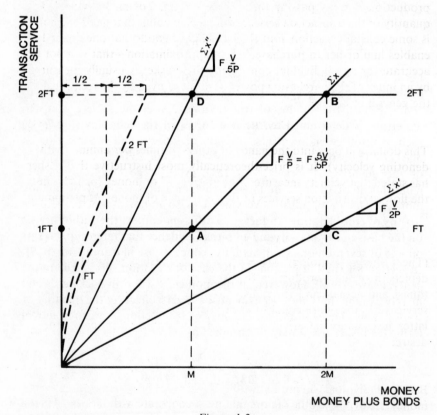

Figure 1.2

The horizontal production function yields an average product that is always positive, and a marginal product that is always zero, at every quantity of nominal or real money. A policy of optimum money is not needed to accomplish what already exists. However, this zero marginal product has no effect on the purchasing power of money, because that is determined by each individual's perception of money: by the quasi-marginal product of money.

5. MONEY'S QUASI-PRODUCTION FUNCTION

How does the relationship between money and its transaction services look to each individual? It certainly would be most unnatural to depict it by the bell-shaped function in Figure 1.1, leading to a zero marginal product. Every five-year old knows that his or her first nickel will purchase one candy exactly like the tenth nickel. Money's quasi-production is a ray passing through the origin. For an individual, the quantity of the transaction service of a specific dollar that he or she holds is some constant fraction F of the basket B of goods that one dollar $1M$ enables him or her to purchase. As an approximation—that will not be accurate for any individual consumer—this basket is usually measured by an index of the purchasing power of money, given by the reciprocal of the general price level P:

$$x = FB1M = F1/P1M. \tag{11}$$

This dollar will pass into the hands of others V-times per annum (with V denoting velocity). It is price-theoretically most instructive that Fisher has stated that velocity measures "the efficiency" of money (p. 14). Thus, the flow of transaction services of the total stock of money M per annum is

$$\Sigma x = FV/PM = F\Sigma q. \tag{12}$$

(The Fisherian tautology $MV = P\Sigma q$ yields the last term.) Figure 1.2 depicts this "quasi-production function" by the function x. The average (quasi and actual) and the quasi-marginal quantity of the transaction services of money are equal to each other and are always positive. The latter just cannot be driven to zero, as the optimum money theorists desire:

$$\partial \Sigma x/\partial M = \Sigma x/M = F\Sigma q/M = FV/P > 0. \tag{13}$$

Because individuals do not know the true sectoral production function of money, it is the "quasi-marginal product" that co-determines their valuation of money in the demand for money function.

In Friedman's general production function, equation 7, external technical economies may be specified only in general terms; by any coefficient that may be attached to X. In the case of money and the function in equation 11 it is possible to offer a specific measure (V/P) of this coefficient:

1. Should the quantity of money double, the public will irrationally expect to move on its quasi-production function from the point A to the point B in Figure 1.2, doubling its purchases of goods. With the volume of goods traded fixed, prices will double and thus halve the physical ability of a unit of money to help to transfer assets. We move along the aggregate production function to the point C. The quasi-production function $\Sigma x'$, now determined by $FV/2P$, shifts to intersect that point.

2. Or, suppose that with the fixed quantity of M the public decides to double the quantity of goods traded. Prices fall, and each unit of money becomes able to transfer twice as many baskets as before; we move to the point D. The quasi-production function $\Sigma x''$, now determined by $FV/.5P$, shifts accordingly.

3. Or, suppose that the demand for money as a store of value (or, a temporary abode of purchasing power) doubles. Velocity falls to $0.5V$ which shifts the new quasi-production function $F0.5V/P$ to the right. With purchases cut, prices then fall to $0.5P$, and this causes the new quasi-production function given by $F0.5V/0.5P$ to replace the former function given by FV/P.

This, of course, is standard macroeconomic analysis of money expressed in terms of price theory. T. R. Saving and I have been closer to pure price theory than we have realized when we spoke in this connection about "the special technical property of money" (pp. 60 ff., 135, 246 ff). The fact that my above micro-analysis mirrors orthodox macro—analysis strengthens my confidence in it.

6. THE DEMAND FOR MONEY FUNCTION

Let me now use this analysis of the production function of money to derive the demand for money function. The price or "purchasing power" of money is determined, like the price of any other factor, by the marginal product or (if it exists) the quasi-marginal product. And it is also determined by the value p per unit that the consumers assign to this product. That is in this case easy to specify. With the total quantity of transactions T unchanged, the value p must also remain unchanged. (Of course, an increase in the valuation of some other service of money—such as is the numismatic service—will both permanently reduce velocity and transitionally increase the opportunity cost of using money for transactions and thereby increase p.) The demand function reads

$$P_M = (\bar{F}\bar{p}\bar{V}/P)/r = (\bar{F}\bar{p}\Sigma\bar{q}/M)/r \qquad (14)$$

where P_M measures the number of the baskets of resources that people must pay for one unit of money. It is actually a connection of the only attainable point on each of the innumerable negatively sloping quasi-demand for money functions (e.g., such as the function Σd_A^3 in Figure 1.1) that intersect from below the above demand function.

This function is, of course, a rectangular hyperbola D_M asymptotic to both axes (Figure 1.3). Thus, it agrees both with (a) Keynes's full employment function (p. 209), and with (b) the function yielded by both the Cambridge and Fisher's versions of the quantity theory (Patinkin, p. 179). It should be stressed, however, that the microeconomic function yielded by equation 14 and the orthodox macroeconomic functions have merely the same mathematical properties, but do not have the same

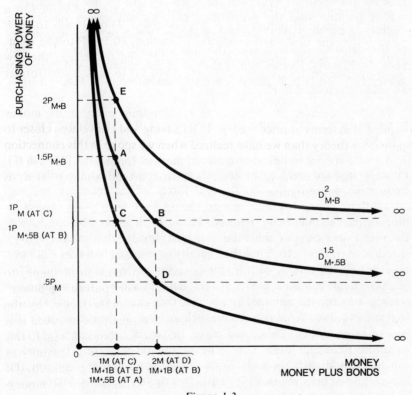

Figure 1.3

analytical standing. The former employs price theory's orthodox "value of the marginal product" $\bar{F}_p\Sigma\bar{q}/M$ approach, and it is based on empirical facts (see section 7): in contrast with monetary theory, no other branch of economies would consider specifying the empirical properties of the demand function covering their subject on the basis of armchair theorizing. The latter is yielded by price-theoretically *ad hoc* constant ratios $\bar{T}/\bar{V}$ (Fisher) or $k\bar{R}$ (Pigou). Like myself, Fisher chose to focus on the transaction service of money, with the asset demand subject to the *ceteris paribus* assumption. (To that service one may add, *e.g.*, the numismatic service or the interest income). In contrast, Pigou chose to focus on the asset demand (or, store of value service) in the context of a balanced portfolio, with the transaction and other services subject to the *ceteris paribus* assumption. Analytically, both approaches are valid; empirically, only facts may determine which one fits reality better. Or, they may tell us that both the left asset side and the right transaction side of the equation must be considered simultaneously. It is a pity that so many monetary theorists view the two sides of the equation as additive; view the transaction service and the store of value service as additive.

It is peculiar that the proponents of optimum money have never considered the need to reconcile their theory (which requires an intercept of the demand function with the quantity axis in Figure 1.1) with Fisher's, Pigou's, Keynes's, and their own macroeconomic demand for money function (which cannot have such an intercept in Figure 1.3).

7. EMPIRICAL SUPPORT FOR MY SECTORAL PRODUCTION FUNCTION

Fisher's reasoned and lengthy analysis according to which the volume of transaction depends only on the real forces of the economy and not on anything connected with money should have been given respectful hearing, rather than being ignored. However, it cannot be conclusive. Empirical foundations must be provided for the partial derivatives specified in equation 10. That the quantity of nominal balances will have no effect on the volume of transacting seems obvious (Friedman, 1976, p. 284). Real balances are passively determined by the volume of transactions and the nominal money. So, they cannot increase the desire to transact either. What could have such an effect is the reduction of the cost of using money. This could make the partial derivative $\partial T/\partial P_M$ in equation 10 bigger than zero. The horizontal aggregate production function could shift up and so—in a way not foreseen—confirm the expectation of Friedman and Schwartz that optimum money will increase transacting to the satiation level.

What is the elasticity of the demand for transactions in the case of the factor money? In general, the only way to settle this issue is to go out and measure it. However, Alfred Marshall has shown that in a very few, extreme, cases we may make empirical conclusions based not on laborious econometric investigations of laboriously collected empirical data, but on some very rudimentary empirical evidence. He has enumerated several empirical conditions which must cause the demand for the product of a factor, and thus the demand for the factor itself, to be extremely or perfectly inelastic with respect to the cost of using that factor. Friedman has summarized Marshall's conditions for a highly or perfectly inelastic demand for the factor—and thus, for the product of the factor—as follows:

1. the more essential the factor in question—this condition is guaranteed in an extreme fashion by fixed proportions ...;
2. the more inelastic is the demand curve for the final product;
3. the smaller the fraction of the total cost that goes to the factor in question ... (Friedman, 1976, p. 158)

Money meets all these conditions in a *very extreme* manner:

(1) Money is not only an *essential factor* but an indispensable factor. In Keynes's terms, its special characteristic is an elasticity of substitution in consumption equal, or nearly equal, to zero (p. 231). One must have money to buy anything. It meets Marshall's criterion of "fixed proportions."

(2) Transactions are an absolutely *essential product* in an exchange economy. (Barter or self-sufficiency are not viable alternatives.) The demand for them, and thus the demand for transaction balances, must be extremely inelastic with respect to all the costs of using money.

(3) The *absolute cost* of money's transaction service is microscopic. In 1977 (one of the last years preceding deregulation, which makes data hard to interpret) the cost of using demand deposits to facilitate $1's worth of transactions has amounted to $0.0007[5].

(4) The microscopic absolute cost of using money represents—in turn—an absurdly *microscopic fraction of the total cost of transacting*. Let me consider some of the factors $f_1, ..., f_n$ that enter equation 10: Besides the cost of using money, there are also the substantial costs of time and transportation spent on shopping. Even the negligible costs of cashing a check in my supermarket ($0.005 per $1), of the sales tax ($0.05 per $1), or of a postage stamp ($0.04 per $1) needed to pay for delivery of my Sunday paper each separately dwarfs the cost of using my money. In all non-trivial transactions—which dominate the total—we must add the very substantial costs of brokers, real estate agents, shippers, lawyers,

insurers, tax advisors, and purchasing agents. Finally, transportation costs are a major part of any transacting activity: many are the goods that I have failed to buy at garage sales because the cost of dragging the goods home would have exceeded the advantage of a low price. Frequently, potential buyers and sellers live on different continents. As far as these forces are concerned, the derivative $\partial T/\partial P_M$ in equation 10 must be equal to zero.

It is peculiar that nobody notices that absolute costs and the share of money in the total cost of transferring assets from person to person is well-nigh invisible. To those who do not operate in an empirical vacuum it must be obvious that the likelihood that a zero cost of employing money in transactions will increase the level of transacting to the satiation level is a good deal smaller than is the likelihood that free salt will result in gluttony.

8. THE POLICY OF OPTIMUM MONEY: AN EVALUATION

We now have a microeconomic theory of money. And, we do have empirical evidence on which to base our evaluation of the policy of optimum money: of paying interest on money. That policy is based on the orthodox (and erroneous) rule of price theory according to which every asset that may be produced at zero cost should be available at a zero price. Monetary theorists do not dare to follow the adherents of the theory of free money; to accomplish zero price directly. So, they have tried to accomplish this through a subterfuge: interest income on a positive price. Three allegedly alternative—but, in fact, vastly different—methods have been proposed. Let me consider them one by one.

1. Fixed price level, increase in real and nominal balances
One method, proposed by Johnson (p. 535), requires that explicit interest to be paid on money, while the purchasing power of money is kept constant. If I substitute my equation 15 for the optimum money theorists' equation 6 I get

$$\bar{P}_{M+B} = (\bar{F}\bar{p}V/\bar{P})/r + i/r = (\bar{F}\bar{p}\Sigma\bar{q}/M)/r + i/r \tag{15}$$

$$(\bar{F}\bar{p}V/\bar{P})/r = (\bar{F}\bar{p}\Sigma\bar{q}/M)/r > 0 \text{ and} \tag{16}$$

$$i/r = \bar{P}_{M+B}. \tag{17}$$

It should be noted that inspection of this equation reveals that it is true that the more there is of the second term, the less there is of the marginal product in the first term (see Friedman and Schwartz, p. 116). As far as interest payments are concerned, it would be nice if we could satisfy optimum money theorists' desire for equlibrium interest income (equation 17). With equation 16 always positive, this is an arithmetic impossibility. Any attempt to satisfy it would result in a violation of the equilibrium conditions and cause an explosion of the nominal and real stock of money.

However, let us satisfy ourselves with (say) half of the loaf, and see what happens. Let us pay only one half of the equilibrium rate shown by equation 17. With a fixed quantity of nominal money, the purchasing power of money in Figure 1.3 would increase by the discounted present value of these payments, to 1.5 P_{M+B} on the new demand function $D_{M+B}^{1.5}$. This function approaches asymptotically the price line drawn at 0.5 P_M. To keep the price level constant, we must double the nominal quantity of money and move to the point B. This halves the productivity, the efficiency, or the velocity of money to 0.05 V. The public has now doubled its "real balances", but derives no benefit from this:

(a) Previously it had to sacrifice $OMCP_M$ quantity of resources to obtain pure money. It has been free to buy or not to buy pure bonds separately.
(b) To get to the new position, it has to sacrifice in addition $M2MBC$ quantity of resources. This done, the public now holds the money component of the joint product worth $O2MD0.5P$ $(=OMCP_M)$ of resources. And, if it wants to use money, it *must* hold $0.5PDBP_M$ (equals the additionally required investment $M2MBC$) of its resources in the bond component.

An exact equivalent of this policy of optimum money would be the following: (a) Double nominal money by giving it away (point D), and (b) force the public to buy bonds of equal value and to attach them permanently to each unit of money (point B). The first measure would double the price level, the second would restore it. There is no accounting benefit. But, there is a welfare.loss: the loss of choice of buying money and bonds separately, or of not buying bonds at all.

2. Fixed stock of money, increased purchasing power
As an alleged alternative Johnson proposes (p. 535) that we hold the nominal quantity of money the same and pay interest:

$$P_{\bar{M}+B} = (\bar{F}\bar{p}\overline{V/P})/r + i/r = (\bar{F}\bar{p}\Sigma\bar{q}/\overline{M}) + i/r, \tag{18}$$

$$(\bar{F}\bar{p}\overline{V/P})/r = \bar{F}\bar{p}\Sigma\bar{q}/\overline{M})r = \text{constant} > 0, \tag{19}$$

$$P_{M+B} = i/r, \tag{20}$$

As he correctly visualizes, the purchasing power will increase to $2P_{\bar{M}+B}$. Velocity and the price level both fall by 50 per cent. He stops his analysis at this point. But, he had no right to do so. Now the interest income represents just one half of equilibrium interest income on the new price $2P_{\bar{M}+B}$. Correct this failure to honour the optimum money theorists' equation 20, and start to pay twice as many baskets. Purchasing power rises to $3P_{\bar{M}+B}$; and so on, *ad infinitum*. With this policy, it is the purchasing power of money that explodes. Suppose that we satisfy ourselves again with half of the loaf.

An exact equivalent of this policy would be a decision to mail to each holder of money (or, cars) as a gift a government bond of equal value, and require that this bond be permanently affixed to each unit of money (or, car). By doing so, we create a new asset: a money-bond (or, a car-bond). If we are willing to pervert well-understood terms, we may claim that the policy has increased wealth that the consumers are holding in the form of "money" (or, "cars"). Given this usage, the supporters of optimum money are entitled to claim that their policy has increased "real balances."

Those lucky enough to hold money when the policy is put into effect would receive a windfall (offset by the negative windfall imposed upon the taxpayers, whose fate Johnson fails to notice). All subsequent holders of the money-bond from then to eternity are unaffected in the accounting sense. With doubled purchasing power of money-bond, they must give up twice as many resources as before to obtain each unit. On each, they will receive twice as much income as before (half of it in kind on the money component, and half of it in money on the bond component). Of course, they have suffered a welfare loss: many of them may not want to invest at all, or may want to invest in some asset other than bonds.

The above two analyses reveal that these two policies of optimum money are in fact merely two policies that impose forced savings upon the public: whoever wants to escape barter must glue to his or her greenback a bond. The public is offered an apparently free lunch of interest payments, and it does not realize that this income will become capitalized into a bond. All subsequent purchasers of money will have to pay for it if they want to use money for transacting. This clearly results in a misallocation of resources. Unfortunately, any return to the *status quo ante* would be extremely difficult. Prohibition of interest payments would unjustly expropriate those who have purchased the bond component in good faith. The only solution would be to split the joint product in equation 18 into its two components, so as to enable everybody to hold of each as much as he or she may wish. Anybody who has ever tried to unscramble scrambled eggs will understand the difficulty of doing so.

It is peculiar that the proponents of the optimum money theory end their analyses with the conclusion that they have been able to secure for the money-holders equilibrium interest income. They have never bothered to analyze the costs of doing so, and have never compared the situations of the money-holders before and after. Had they done so they would have discovered—just as we have just now discovered—that there is no such thing as a free lunch. The government may give you a once-for-all windfall. But, in the long run, you only get what you pay for.

3. Deflation through money reductions

Because paying interest on currency is impossible, Friedman proposes as the best alternative a policy of deflation, at the rate equal to the equilibrium rate of interest (1969, pp. 34–5). He feels so strongly about the merits of this alternative that he ends his essay—viewed by him to be so important as to give title to a whole book of essays—with a "Final Schizophrenic Note" (pp. 47–8) in which he apologizes for his previously advocated policy of price stability.

How do we achieve the required deflation? By burning a proper amount of money in a furnace (p. 16). And, how do we obtain the furnace-fodder? By taxation. Of course, the holders of money would hardly wax euphoric if they would lose x per cent of their money and see the remainder rise by x per cent in value. So, Friedman proposes that we tax somebody else. To make sure that my gentle reader will not suspect me of slander, I shall quote verbatim:

It does not matter for our purposes what the tax is, as long as an individual cannot affect his tax by altering his cash balances. (p. 16)

A tax on widows would also fill this bill. Here we stumble over a milestone in the history of economics. A winner of a Nobel Prize—in economics—proposes (and no monetary theorist objects) that we benefit some, and do not care who will pay the bill because that "does not matter." With such a cost constraint, any number of optimum monetary and fiscal policies could be devised within minutes.

Another problem is that the policy is impossible to implement. It asks that the purchasing power of money at any time $t = 0, 1, 2, ...,\infty$ be

$$P_{M(t)} = (1 + d)P_{M(t-1)} \tag{21}$$

where $d > 0$ denotes the rate of deflation. If the policy is initiated in time $t = 0$, every money holder will be guaranteed by the optimum money theorists that in the future his or her dollar will yield not the former constant income $\bar{y} = \bar{F}\bar{p}\bar{V}/\bar{P}$ *per annum*, but

$$= \bar{y} + \frac{\bar{y}(1+d)}{(1+r)} + \frac{\bar{y}(1+d)^2}{(1+r)^2} + ... + \frac{\bar{y}(1+d)^\infty}{(1+r)^\infty} \tag{22}$$

Any accountant or price theorist will tell us that any belief in the possibility of coexistence of equations 21 and 22 is simply amazing. Keynes has described the problem most succinctly:

It is difficult to make sense of this [Irving Fisher's] theory as stated, because it is not clear whether the change in the value of money is or is not assumed to be foreseen. There is no escape from the dilemma that, if it is not foreseen, there will be no effect on current affairs, whilst, if it is foreseen, the prices of existing goods will be *forthwith* [emphasis mine] so adjusted that the advantages of holding money and goods are again equalized. (p. 142)

Instead of a steady rate of deflation described by equation 21, we shall get in period $t = 1$ a once-for-all jump in the purchasing power of money, which will be determined by the value of the sum of the infinite series in equation 22:

$$P_{M(t=1)} \to \infty \text{ as } d \to r \tag{23}$$

Of course, money is different from an investment asset that one can put aside in the expectation of a future capital gain. Thus, in the real world discounting to the present would not be perfect: with $d = r$, velocity and the price level would not instantly drop to zero because people would have to continue to buy necessities. However, with tens of trillion dollars tied up in contracts written in money terms, only an extremely courageous economist would want to find out to what an extent our textbooks' capitalization formula exaggerates reality.

Why do the optimum money theorists toy with deflation? All modern treatises and econometric models treat inflation and deflation in their equations as if they were the same phenomenon, merely with opposite signs: $\pm d$ (see e.g. Friedman, 1969, p. 17, Figure 6). In those works, a 10 per cent inflation and deflation are treated as equivalents. This would be true were we dealing not with inflation or deflation but only with unexpected once-for-all price changes. It is never taken into account that once they become repetitive and fully expected (in fact, guaranteed by the optimum money theorists), people will focus on their permanent incomes. The applicable capitalization formulas show that they are two *totally different phenomena*. Deflation promises in the very restrictive limit $(d = r)$ the paradise of an infinite gain. In contrast, inflation threatens in the very extreme limit $(d = -1)$ only the total loss of a relatively small fraction of the total asset portfolio.

As a result, even a triple digit inflation is a tolerated tax on the invaluable ability to trade.(Who would not ransom his or her current total money assets in exchange for a license to trade?) In contrast, as the rate of deflation grows from zero, the tax on investing—the disincentive to invest—grows. Even a very modest rate of deflation $(d = r)$ is a prohibitive tax on many types of transactions, which the policy of optimum money claims to foster. Why invest into any risky specialized assets when one may get the same or bigger yield from a general command over all goods in the form of money? Of course, the less is invested, the higher the rate of return on the remainder and the higher the rate of deflation needed for optimum money. While in the initially offered quotation Friedman and Schwartz expect in equation 10 $\partial T/\partial p_M < 0$, it will be—in fact—very strongly positive.

It is peculiar that our optimum money theorists have never related their policy to economic history, which confirms the above analysis. We have observed innumerable multiple-digit inflations and never (short-run and thus unexpected disturbances aside) multiple-digit deflations. And, even mild rates of deflation have usually been associated with economic distress. The proposal that we obtain optimum money (or, for that matter, neoclassical anti-Keynesian full employment equilibrium) through deflation is a R_X for an economic disaster.

9. OPTIMUM MONEY WASTES SHOE LEATHER

Paul Samuelson expects that optimum money will yield one additional benefit:

I can be more specific and talk in terms of real transaction costs that Professor Clower would like me to emphasize. Let me posit that the good ... comes from the fact that with twice the average real cash balances I have to use up only half the shoe leather in walking from my home to the bank during the week between getting paid. Who is worse off? There is as much land and capital as before, the same allocation of rents and wages among the factors of production. (Samuelson, p. 306)

Egalitarian Samuelson saves his own shoe leather; elitist Freidman fires his hired "errand boy" (1969, p. 17).

Let me apply to this claim—once again—what seems to be a specialty of my very own in monetary theory: the cost-benefit analysis. The above argument is based on Keynes's myopic model, in which the consumers' only alternative to money is bonds (p. 166). In fact, the consumers have innumerable choices, out of which my own myopia is able to focus on only four:

(1) Interest-bearing bonds;
(2) money;
(3) idle inventories;
(4) zero-cost debts (accounts payable).

Thus, some waste is inevitable. With barren money, the consumers waste resources by shifting between 1 and 2. When afflicted with optimum money, they will start wasting resources by shifting between 2 and 3 + 4. Which waste will be bigger? Given modern technology (*e.g.*, banking machines on streetcorners and in stores), the cost of shifting between 1 and 2 is negligible. How does it compare with the costs of shifts between 2 and 3 + 4?

Consider idle inventories. The consumer who used to buy cigarettes by the carton now buys them by the pack. That wastes errand boys or shoe leather. It also requires more cashiers. Second, output flows out of the factories in a steady stream, and there are significant economies of large-scale—and thus, infrequent—deliveries of it. Retailers and households must jointly hold a *fixed* stock of inventories. When household idle inventories stored at zero costs are reduced, business inventories stored, guarded and insured at substantial resource cost must increase.

Next, consider zero-cost debts or accounts payable. Financial pages confirm the experiences of our condominium. With barren—zero-yield—money[6], the consumers used to settle their bills (zero-cost debts) whenever convenient (e.g. every Saturday). Now, they make an effort to pay as close to the due date as possible. This wastes their resources. Second, it leads to external pecuniary diseconomies. Many small amounts may be less profitably invested than one big amount. Increases in the volume of zero-cost debts must increase condominium fees and retail prices by more than is the consumers' (illusory) gain of interest income.

It is peculiar that monetary theorists—mostly monetarists—have succumbed to the Keynesian aberration: to the notion that the only thing people do with money is to buy bonds. Once we grant that people also buy goods and pay off debts, a cost-benefit analysis strongly suggests that interest-bearing money leads to substantial pecuniary and resource costs.

10. GRESHAM'S LAW AND OPTIMUM MONEY

Just as interest payments on all money are expected to increase all transactions, interest payments on some money are expected to shift transacting towards this good money (Johnson, 1975, p. 284): to make the last derivative in equation 10 negative. Yet, history as told by Irving Fisher shows that exactly the opposite actually happens, and that this derivative becomes strongly positive:

... even what is made legal tender may, by general usage, be deprived of its practical character as money. During the Civil War the government has attempted to circulate fifty-dollar notes, bearing interest at 7.3 per cent, so that interest amounted to the very easily computed amount of one cent per day. The notes, however, failed to circulate. In spite of the attempt to make their exchanges easy, people preferred to keep them for the sake of interest. Money *never* [emphasis mine] bears interest except in the sense of creating convenience in the process of exchange. This convenience is the special service of money and offsets *the apparent loss* [emphasis mine] of interest involved in keeping it in one's pocket instead of investing. (p. 9)

One could hardly find a more concise way of rejecting the theory of optimum money, and of verbalizing the content of my analysis and of equations 15, 16, and 17. Negligible velocities of the American interest-bearing accounts provide a modern counterpart to the above historical experience. Surely, an economic historian would find many more. As way always the case, bad clipped coin—or bad barren money—must dominate the transacting activity.

It is peculiar that the proponents of optimum money have never felt any need to reconcile their theory with economic history as reported by Irving Fisher. Nor have they felt any need to face Sir Thomas Gresham (1519–79). If optimum money is such a boon (worth up to $1,842 billion), Gresham should have been shown to be dead wrong by bringing mere good money into such ill repute.

11. MACROECONOMIC BLIGHT OF OPTIMUM MONEY

Prior to American deregulation, the monetary policy-maker has faced two major groups of financial assets: (1) "Barren" currency plus demand deposits (in equation 15, the existence of the interest term was not permitted), and (2) time deposits (the existence of the first, transaction, term was not permitted). Our law used to insist on pure money or pure bonds, and has prohibited a joint product. We were able to quantify these two totally different assets: each with an opposite sign of its interest elasticity of demand. Whenever the public's decisions about spending have changed, it had to put the policy-maker on notice, by shifting between these two assets.

In accordance with the policy of optimum money, American policy-makers have permitted that these two totally different assets be scrambled into an interest-bearing joint product (money-bond) of equation 15. Now we face the hopeless task of making sense out of the aggregate. After trying a veritable kaleidoscope of various *ad hoc* measures of money, our central bank is now trying to apply equation 15 and split the money-bonds into their two components (the "Divisia Aggregate"): into the non-measurable FpV/P component, and the measurable i component. This is not promising. While equation 15 is analytically useful, empirically it is worthless. To treat FpV/P as a residual, we would have to know what is the current total yield (imputed plus explicit) on all assets. And, we would have to be sure that the differences among the observed explicit yields of different financial assets are due only to the differences among the invisible imputed yields. But, for all we know, some unknown parts of these differences in explicit yields are due to other factors: restrictions on spending and thus on FpV/P, resource costs associated with various assets, and demand and supply forces faced by different issuers. If we want to measure individually money on the one hand and various bonds on the other hand, there is no substitute for the above law that has been so carelessly abandoned.

Frank E. Morris, President of the Federal Reserve Bank of Boston wrote recently: "I have concluded, most reluctantly, that we can no longer measure the money supply with any degree of precision." (p. 6) By stating his case so mildly ("with any degree of precision") he reveals himself to be indeed a most reluctant witness. Faced with the lower limit to the stock of money-bonds of $676 billion $(M - 1)$ and with the upper limit of $3,967 billion (L) it seems more truthful to say that we are able to measure money with a zero degree of precision. As Harry Johnson put it: "Obviously, there is no point in monetary theory [and, I would add, to monetary policy] if we cannot define what it is that we are theorizing about". (1967, p. 95) How does one regulate intelligently what one admits to be unable even to measure?

NOTES

I am grateful for constructive criticism to my colleagues from Universite N.D. de la Paix (Namur), University of Vienna, Technical University of Wien, Institute for Advanced Studies in Vienna, and from the Universities of Florence, Giessen, Milan, Modena, and Venice. I am also grateful to my students in Milwaukee and Wien for their careful scrutiny of my analysis.

(*Postscript*: I have found it desirable to revise slightly the originally published version of this paper: not in the substance, but in the exposition.)

1. Notice one advantage of my joint-product analysis. Every equilibrium point shown in the figures in this paper lies on a demand function: demand for the factor, or demand for the factor-bond. In contrast, in the only extant geometrical exposition of the theory of optimum money the alleged equilibrium point floats in an empty space like a hot-air balloon (Johnson, p. 536).
2. The proponents of optimum money ignore two sources of misallocation of resources in their proposed solution:
   (a)   Some demanders located below the initial equilibrium point will not have the resources to buy the bonds which are now attached to the zero-cost factor.

The demand functions D_f^1 and D_f^2 will pivot towards the origin below the point L (or P), and thus full satiation with the factor will not be obtained.
(b) Should the factor be sold at a zero price, the resource investment into it would be zero. When it is sold along with a bond for a positive price, users of the factor must immobilize for this purpose resources for which they might have a better use.

3. With zero production costs, equilibrium will be reached only when the total output of the services of the factor implodes to zero, to the point E. Only a fixed positive price may prevent this. Of course, it is likely that the users of this factor will sooner or later comprehend the existence of external technical diseconomies, and will drop the factor in favour of the next best substitute.

4. Monetary theorists analyze demand for either "nominal" or "real" balances. They should then also speak about ounces of gold as "nominal gold" and about the market value of this gold as "real gold". Prices and quantities of "nominal" money or gold are related by the demand function $P = f(Q)$. Prices and market values of "real" money or gold are related by the total revenue function $P = g(QP)$. The two are subject to completely different rules of price theory. For instance, the latter may be positively sloping. Analytical confusion must result if both $P = f(Q)$ and $P = g(QP)$ are called "demand functions".

5. The imputed annual cost of using $247 billion of demand deposits in 1977 for transacting may be estimated to be $25 billion; check transactions have amounted to $37,331 billion (*Federal Reserve Bulletin*, Feb. 1978: A-13 and A-14).

6. The term "barren" money is a price-theoretic monstrosity. As Fisher's quotation (below) shows, no asset with a positive price can be "barren". That price is merely the discounted present value of the flow of income (imputed or explicit) that it yields. It is the firmly held belief that money is "barren" that leads directly to the idea that it is nonoptimal under *laissez faire*. (Samuelson, 1969, p. 303).

REFERENCES

Clower, Robert W. 1971. "What Traditional Theory Really Wasn't", *Canadian Journal of Economics*, May 1969, II-2, pp. 299–302.

Fisher, Irving 1971. *The Purchasing Power of Money*. New York: A.M. Kelly.

Friedman, David D. 1986. *Price Theory*. Cincinnati: South-Western Publishing Co.

Friedman, Milton 1969. *The Optimum Quantity of Money and Other Essays*. Chicago: Aldine Co.

———— 1976. *Price Theory*. Chicago: Aldine Co.

———— and Schwartz, Anna Jacobson 1970. *Monetary Statistics of the United States*. National Bureau of Economic Research. New York: Columbia University Press (distributed by).

Johnson, Harry G. 1969. "How Does Monetary Policy Affect the Economy?", *Journal of Money, Credit and Banking*. Feb. 1969, I-3, pp. 535–8.

———— 1975. "Is There an Optimal Money Supply", in Michael D. Intriligator (ed.), *Frontiers in Quantitative Economics*. Amsterdam: North Holland Co.

Keynes, John Maynard 1936. *The General Theory of Employment Interest and Money*. New York: Harcourt Brace Jovanovich Co.

Mansfield, Edwin 1970. *Microeconomics*. New York: W.W. Norton and Co.
Meltzer, Allan H. 1975. "Comments On the Two Above Papers", in Michael D. Intriligator (ed.), *Frontiers in Quantitative Economics*. Amsterdam: North Holland Co.
Morris, Frank E. 1982. "Do the Monetary Aggregates Have a Future as Targets of Federal Reserve Policy?", *New England Economic Review*, March/April 1982, pp. 5–14.
Patinkin, Don 1965. *Money, Interest, and Prices*. New York: Harper and Row.
Pesek, Boris P. and Saving, Thomas R. 1967. *Money, Wealth, and Economic Theory*. New York: MacMillan.
Samuelson, Paul A. 1969. "What Classical and Neoclassical Monetary Theory Really Was", *Canadian Journal of Economics*, March 1969, II-2, pp. 303–8.
Stein, Jerome 1970. "The Optimum Quantity of Money", *Journal of Money, Credit and Banking*, II-4, Nov. 1970, pp. 397–419.
Tsiang, C. S. 1969. "A Critical Note on the Optimum Supply of Money", *Journal of Money, Credit and Banking*, II-2, May 1969, pp. 266–80.

2   Microeconomics of Banking*

Credit could exist without money; money could exist without credit. Thus, each requires a separate analysis. In this century, we may find in texts three very different theories. All three agree with the effect that banks have on money: all banks expand money by the amount of deposits minus the reserves that they immobilize. However, with respect to credit there are sharp differences. Before 1921 all texts have claimed that each bank significantly expands credit, by borrowing only its reserves and lending a multiple of this amount, determined by the reserve ratio. Our modern theory claims, in contrast, that each bank contracts credit, by the difference between its total deposit liabilities and its loans; that is, by an amount given by its reserves.

Strangely enough, Chester Arthur Phillips's book *Bank Credit* has offered a synthesis of the pre-1921 thesis and of the modern antithesis. This book contains a theory, *supported by empirical evidence*, that each bank's effect on credit may be found somewhere in between these two extremes. Phillips's theory is currently honoured by words (as the cornerstone of our modern theory) but totally ignored by deeds.[1] Why and how it could have fallen into one of those rare black holes in academia is a question for the history of economic thought to answer.

In this paper I first present the three models. I then show by the use of empirical evidence supplied by Phillips that his theory is the only one applicable to modern banks. I also show that his theory is of major policy-making interest. Each bank's credit expansion multiplier (that co-determines the rate of interest and the level of investment activity) is shown to be a microeconomic issue. The individual credit multipliers are a function of secular changes in the number of banks, and of cyclical and seasonal changes in the structure of each bank's portfolio.

---

* From: Lectures at the Universities of Firenze, Giessen, Milano, Modena, Namur, Venezia, and Wien.

A major policy-making conclusion follows: banks' ability to "print" previously non-existent credit should be controlled no less than we control now the banks' ability to print previously non-existent money. And, an anti-merger policy is shown to be essential for the protection of competition.

1. PRE-1921 THEORY OF EVERY BANK

Before 1921 all money and banking texts (*e.g.*, Dunbar, White, Holdsworth, Scott, Moulton) have treated all banks as if each were—to use the term of modern theory—a monopoly (Phillips, pp. 34–8). In Table 2.1 each bank borrows $100 and creates a Primary Deposit. It sets aside this amount as reserves, and lends a multiple ($900) of its borrowing. Thus, it expands the supply of credit by $800. The bank is able to do so because of the (sometimes explicit, sometimes implicit) assumption that it experiences zero cash outflow as a result of its lending (Phillips, p. 33). Each bank lends more than it borrows and so does, by arithmetic necessity, their aggregate. Their net effect on credit is

$$dX = D_B(1 - r)/r - D_B \qquad (1\text{-A})$$

and

$$d\Sigma X = \Sigma D_B(1 - r)/r - \Sigma D_B \qquad (1\text{-B})$$

where r denotes the reserve ratio. Our modern theory declares this model to be applicable only to monopoly banks. But, it adds a major qualification, the effect of which is a rejection of the above equations. By declaring all deposits to be debts of any bank, the conclusion follows that even a monopoly bank and their aggregate contracts credit: bank Loans are claimed to be always smaller than borrowed bank Deposits.

2. MODERN THEORY: "ALL DEPOSITS ARE BANK DEBTS"

Uncashed loans are the cornerstone of Phillips's analysis of each bank's credit-expansion multiplier (equation 4-A). So, it is essential to consider the meaning of these loans right now, in the extreme and thus most illustrative case of a monopoly bank. A price-theoretic loan to (deposit with) the banker requires the depositor-lender to transfer an asset in his possession to the banker-debtor, as in Table 2.2. A negative entry on the asset side is essential for the proof that a banker's debt exists.

In contrast, in Tables 2.1 and 2.3 I have placed the second word in the term Derivative "Deposits" between quotation marks. That word is merely a trade name. "Uncashed Loans" would be a more descriptive term. In Table 2.3 a bank customer borrows, without handing over any

Table 2.1: Pre-1921 theory of all banks—modern monopoly

Assets		Debts and net worth
Reserves (R)	$100	$100 Primary Deposits ($D_B$)
Uncashed Loans (X)	$900	$900 Derivative "Deposits" (D_U)

asset of his to the banker. (Notice that placing a lien on some borrower's asset which secures repayment of the loan does not represent any loan (transfer) of assets to the banker). Modern theory is different: "Most people suppose that a bank lends the deposits to its customers. In fact, however, no bank ever lends its deposits." (Kamerschen, 8th Edition, p. 105). Every student in the class who has obtained a Student Loan and a chequebook from a banker knows better, but does not dare to say so.

In Table 2.3 the bank lends without borrowing, and to that extent is a producer of a previously non-existent credit rather than a mere intermediary of existing credit between lenders and borrowers. In fact, all borrowers in Table 2.3 could have entered the bank with pockets to let, with zero assets to transfer to the banker. In any case, the absence of any negative entry on the asset side of Table 2.3 *conclusively proves* that bank customers have not lent to the banker anything; have not "deposited" with the banker anything. Thus, the banker just could not have acquired a debt.

Modern texts verbally also describe the monopoly bank as borrowing $100 and lending $900 (e.g., Simpson, pp. 98–101). However, while in old texts Deposits $1,000 enter under the opaque—analytically inscrutable—catch-all single entry: "Liability and Net Worth" (e.g., Phillips, p. 17), modern texts and treatises place them under the specific "Liability" entry. Thereby, this monopoly bank becomes indistinguishable from a competitive one. Both are said to have debts equal to total deposits, to lend this amount minus reserves, and thus to contract rather

Table 2.2: Lender to the bank: primary depositor

Assets	$500	Liabilities
Depositor's-Lender's Cash	− $100	
Bank Primary Deposits (D_B)	+ $100	

Table 2.3: Borrowers from the bank: derivative "depositors"

Assets	$ 0	Liabilities	
Derivative "Deposits" D_U	+ $900	+ $900	Debt to banker

than expand credit. Microeconomic analysis of the presence or absence of competition in banking is thereby made to seem superfluous for a macroeconomic decision about the effects of banking on the supply of credit (explicitly stated in, *e.g.*, Simpson, p. 101).

How does the monopolist's borrowing of $100 become converted into his or her debt of $1,000 is—prudently—never explained on the spot. In general discussions of "deposits" elsewhere, most texts and advanced treatises take their character as liabilities to be self-evident; they don't offer any proof of this proposition. That is in any science always a dangerous decision to make. In the rare cases when an explicit justification is offered under pressure (see the quotation that follows), it ignores price theory. It rests entirely on the legal fact that all deposits make the banker "liable" to exchange them for cash on demand. Economists should be careful when they rest their theories on law: in their discipline, law—to use Charles Dickens's words—may prove to be an ass.

The legal term "liability" covers a broad spectrum of economic relationships; not just price-theoretic debts, but also all sorts of contracts unrelated to any borrowing. (Surgeons have liability insurance against the danger that they will borrow from their patients the wrong kidney.) As Table 2.3 proves, monetary theorists use not a price-theoretic meaning of a debt, but a legal meaning of a liability. Let me rent a hammer from a U-Rent outfit and get the right to exchange it for a saw on demand: a transaction identical in substance with that depicted in Table 2.3. The U-Rent outfit has a legal duty ("liability") to honour this contract; it has acquired no price-theoretic debt. Substitute bank "deposit" that I borrow in Table 2.3 for the hammer, and currency for the saw that I am entitled to demand in exchange, and banking theorists will find that the U-Rent outfit has borrowed from me the saw (has incurred a debt to me) when it has lent to me the hammer (neither of which I possess). They will find a price-theoretic debt:

Banks are engaged in financial intermediation when they issue promises to pay [cash] that are in excess of [cash] they hold in their vaults. These promises to pay are properly regarded as debts of the banks. (Friedman and Schwartz, p. 113)

A rebuttal to a serious challenge to the banking theory's fundamental doctrines that *all deposits* are banks' debts, and that banks are mere intermediaries, rests on these two flimsy—even frivolous—sentences.

The first sentence is non-discriminatory because it also describes most non-intermediating borrowers: most individuals and firms have debts in excess of their cash holdings. The debt-cash ratio is *totally irrelevant* for a decision as to whether banks merely intermediate credit or do more than that. The decisive issue here is each bank's loan-debt ratio. If it is smaller than unity, each bank contracts credit. If it is equal to unity, each bank allocates existing credit. In both cases each merely intermediates. If the loan-debt ratio is bigger than unity, each bank becomes a net supplier of credit; to that extent it isn't a mere intermediary. And, what is true about any bank is true about their aggregate: the banking industry.

The second sentence specifies a necessary but *not a sufficient condition* for a finding that a debt exists. In contrast with legal liabilities, price-theoretic debts must satisfy simultaneously two conditions:

•1. An initial transfer of some asset from Mr. Customer to Mrs. Banker for her use (the negative item in row 2 of Table 2.2).
•2. A promise by Mrs. Banker to return the asset or a promise to pay its cash value to Mr. Customer's assignee (the positive item in the left column).

Table 2.3 fails to meet the crucial first requirement. There, the banker does not acquire for her use any asset of the "depositor". In fact, the latter needs not own any assets at all. Without a proof that the bank customer has transferred some asset of his for the use of the banker (•1), the above promise (•2)—in isolation—signifies that the promisor is either a seller or the very opposite of a borrower, a lender:

(a) *Seller*: "I promise to pay back to you your money if you are not satisfied with the product we have sold": you may reverse the sale. The seller has a legal liability to pay, but no price-theoretic debt. (Should we treat such "promises to pay" as debts, we would have to conclude that Sears & Roebuck Co. has debts that greatly exceed its assets.)
(b) *Lender*: "I promise to return your debt certificate—or, I promise to pay you or to your assignee its cash equivalent—if you or your assignee are not satisfied with *my property*: with my bank money that I have lent to you. You may repay my loan."

Return of a debt certificate to every debtor is a standard practice ("Paid in Full"). The bank's alternative offer of the cash equivalent of this certificate, upon return of the asset lent by the bank (the "deposit" in Table 2.3) not just by the borrower but by anybody else is a refinement essential for the ability of the bank-owned money to circulate. The bank does not care which option is selected. It can replace the cash paid out to a third party by collecting on the debt certificate signed by the original borrower in Table 2.3—and lend the returned "deposit" to somebody else. That no debt exists is also made obvious by the direction of income flows. With zero-cost banking, the deposits in Table 2.2 *cost* the banker equilibrium interest income; the "deposits" in Table 2.3 *earn* equilibrium income for the banker. Were the latter debts, the second income flow (originating in Table 2.3) would be going the wrong way.

To use as a criterion "promises to pay" a fixed sum in the future is to look at *stocks*. Alternatively, one may look at *flows*. Don Patinkin follows this path and argues that in the case of resource-costly banking, the banks have obligated themselves to provide future flow of services to all "depositors" which proves that banks do have a debt (p. 1149). Given the fact that most of monetary and banking literature employs the "simplifying assumption" of zero-cost banking, Patinkin should feel obliged to agree that such banking has no debts. He certainly does not treat banks that way in any of his works. Besides, can any entrepreneur be found to have, or not have, debts to his or her customers depending on whether he or she does have, or doesn't have, factor costs? Patinkin's criterion is unable to distinguish between a debt and a service contract, and is therefore just as non-discriminatory as the Friedman-Schwartz criterion.

Even with full-cost banking, obligation to furnish services in the future does not prove that the bank has originally acquired a debt: That must be proven separately. Without a proof that some asset has been initially transferred for the use of the banker—absent from Table 2.3—we are simply facing a service contract: *e.g.*, my contract with Wisconsin Bell. Legally, there is a liability to deliver a service; price-theoretically, there is no initial transfer of assets for the use of Wisconsin Bell and thus no debt. In Table 2.3 the banker commits himself to supply an asset— "deposits" or (in the last century) National Bank Notes—that yields a flow of explicit or imputed services. She or he does this in exchange for a monthly fee yielded by the borrower's promissory note.

Banking theorists prefer to be para-lawyers to being price theorists. I say "para-lawyers", because no person admitted to the bar would confuse (a) a legal liability to do something in the future for a fee (as in Table 2.3) with (b) a price-theoretic debt resulting from a past transfer of resources (as in Table 2.2). In the former case, he may at times try to prove damages for the contracting party; in the latter case, he may frequently forcibly repossess the asset transferred to the borrower.

Once we get rid of the untenable notion that the bank in Table 2.1—that is explicitly described as borrowing $100—has somehow also acquired $1,000 of "Deposit" debts, it becomes obvious that a monopoly bank has a major impact on the supply of credit: it absorbs $100 of it and it supplies $900 of it. Microeconomic analysis of the extent to which each bank is competitive becomes imperative if we are to understand each bank's and the banking industry's effect on the supply of credit.

3. OUR MODERN THEORY

The pre-1921 model of every bank has been adopted by our modern theory as a model only of a monopoly bank (with the just discussed erroneous modification). And, a model of a perfectly competitive bank has been added. Each bank borrows $1,000, sets aside $100, and lends the rest. While in Table 2.1 the cash outflow is zero, here in Table 2.4 it is equal to loans made.[2] In Table 2.2, the two $100 entries now become replaced with two $1,000 entries. In Table 2.3 the $900 of "Deposits" becomes replaced with $900 worth of Assets, as the borrowers spend the proceeds of their borrowings. (The recipients of these proceeds have not lent anything to the banker either.) If we focus on each competitive bank's and the industry's *net supply of credit* we may write that

$$dX = - rD_B \qquad (2\text{-}A)$$

and

$$d\Sigma X = - r\Sigma D_B. \qquad (2\text{-}B)$$

Alternatively, we may focus on each bank's *net supply of money*. As our modern theory correctly perceives, there is in this case no difference between the monopoly bank in Table 2.1 and the competitive bank in Table 2.4 (or any other bank in between these two extremes). They and their industry reduce the stock of money by the holding of cash they have put aside as reserves and expand it by the bank money they have supplied:

$$dM = R(1 - r)/r \qquad (3\text{-}A)$$

and

$$d\Sigma M = \Sigma R(1 - r)/r. \qquad (3\text{-}B)$$

Table 2.4: Modern competitive bank

Assets		Debts	
Reserves (R)	$100	$1,000	Deposits (D_B)
Cashed-in Loans (X)	$900	$ 0	Net Worth

4. MODERN THEORY'S "FUNDAMENTAL PARADOX OF BANKING"

The three straightforward aggregations in equations 1, 2 and 3 are discouragingly humdrum. As in the case of any other industry, the whole is in all respects merely the sum of its parts. In contrast, there is magic in the famous "fundamental paradox of banking" (Campbell and Campbell, p. 171): each bank lends less while "The Banking System" lends more than it borrows (just as each firm pollutes while their sum—their industry—purifies). "The multiple expansion of bank credit" based on the summation of an infinite series of flows of money from bank to bank gives birth to one core chapter in every money and banking text.

We all have been brainwashed for too long by too many textbooks, and by decades of our classroom presentations, to see anything amiss. So let me try a parable: Boris borrows $1,000, lends to his friend $900, and puts $100 in a legally required escrow; thus he contracts credit. Milena borrows $900 from that friend, lends $810 to another friend, and puts $90 in an escrow; she also contracts credit. However, let's consider the two of us as a family unit. According to our orthodox theory, our family has "really" (whatever that means) borrowed from others only $190 placed in escrow, and has lent to others $1,710. While our two individual credit contraction multipliers are $900/1,000 = 810/900 = 0.9$, our family's single credit expansion multiplier—given that "really"—is $1,710/190 = 9$. I could now add, one by one, an infinite number of children, just as one core chapter in all our texts adds banks. But, what would be the purpose? I already know the two alleged credit multipliers 0.9 and 9. They will not change, regardless of how many links to the chain I add. To acquire knowledge of the sums of several infinite series, obtained in all texts, is totally superfluous for this purpose.

This parable and its textbook counterpart are, of course, total nonsense which we all should be ashamed to peddle to our students. There is no "fundamental paradox of banking." If we decide to measure the credit expansion multiplier by the relevant ratio (Lending)/(Total Deposit Borrowing) = 0.9, then each competitive bank and their industry contract credit (while a monopoly bank expands it). If we decide to measure the credit expansion multiplier by the irrelevant ratio that focuses only on a fraction of each bank's and the industry' borrowing (Lending/Reserves = 9), then each bank and The System expand credit. Paradoxical is merely our banking theorists' decision to apply the former yardstick to each bank and the latter yardstick to The System.

One is reminded of John Kenneth Galbraith's claim that "Much discussion of money involves a heavy overlay of priestly incantations ... This too is a well-established form of fraud." (pp. 4–5) I do hope that the next generation of banking theorists will put aside such priestly incantations and base its analyses on such simple aggregations as shown in equations 1, 2, and 3. By doing so, it will rejoin mainstream economics, where any industry is merely the sum of the firms belonging to it.

5. PRIMARY AND DERIVATIVE DEPOSITS

Before I proceed to Phillips's model, it is imperative for the sake of the reader's understanding to clear up a terminological mess: to describe the basic difference between the method that Phillips uses to classify deposits, and the completely different method employed by our modern theory. In Phillips's micro-analysis, (equation 4-A) the classification of deposits is based on measurable quantities in any single bank's T-account, without any information about any other bank (my Table 2.2 vs. 2.3; Table 2.5, col. 1 vs. col. 4; Table 2.7, col. 1 vs. col. 4):

(1) Primary deposits in each bank measure the amounts that the bank has borrowed from the outside (as in Table 2.2).

(2) Derivative "deposits" in the very same bank (repeat, in the very same bank) measure the amount of loans that have not been cashed in (are derived from its loans) and that therefore provide reserves enabling the bank to lend in excess of its borrowing (as in Table 2.3). Interbank flows, if any, are totally irrelevant for Phillips's classification.

Phillips has made this content of his terms seemingly foolproof verbally (pp. 40–5), by his key equation (4-A), and by his bar Diagram 3 (p. 61): there he shows even visually the relationship among the two types of deposits, reserves, and loans. There, one may even *see* each bank lending (bars $x_1,...,x_n$) more than it borrows (bars $c_1,...,c_n$). And he studied several dozen banks and has empirically measured the size of these two types of deposit. All in vain.

Our modern theory, despite its claim to Phillips's paternity, has completely changed the content of the two terms (e.g., Klein, p. 102):

(1) A primary deposit of $1,000 which reduces permanently the stock of currency in public hands enters Bank A. This bank lends $900 (Table 7-A, first row and column) and loses all of it. It has no derivative deposits.

(2) This amount flows to Bank B, which lends $810; to Bank C, which lends $729, etc. Deposits in these banks are derived from loans made by the first bank in the chain (Table 7-A, all but the first row in the first column). They have no primary deposits. The size of these deposits in any single bank cannot be measured, so that empirically the two are merely synonyms for aggregate reserves and aggregate loans.

The two modern concepts are totally irrelevant for any analytical or empirical purpose (except to provide a smokescreen behind which one hides the "paradox"). Besides, the imaginary scenario according to

which a loan by Bank A is totally deposited in Bank B, and so on
ad infinitum is too absurd for words. Suppose that somebody would
prove empirically an equally absurd scenario: on some Monday at 8 a.m.
all the banks have simultaneously opened for business, accepted deposits, made loans, and have never seen a penny of these loans return to the
lending bank or any other bank. According to our modern theory, there
would exist zero derivative deposits; according to modern empirical
practice, these would still equal aggregate reserves. Otherwise, absolutely
nothing in our existing banking theory would change. The two concepts
and the infinite series of inter-bank flows that they allegedly create are
totally worthless and superfluous ornaments, good only to give birth to
one core chapter in every text.

   However, that is no reason to object to our modern usage (except that
each text burdens our students in a core chapter with this excess
baggage). What is objectionable is that banking theory uses one pair of
terms for two pairs of completely different theoretical and empirical
concepts. This should be corrected. Our modern theory has acquired
squatter's rights to the terms "primary deposits" (a synonym for
aggregate reserves) and "derivative deposits" (a synonym for aggregate
loans). Those intent on discussing Phillips's theory should give them up
and start to use two new terms: Borrowed Deposits (D_B of Table 2.2) and
Unborrowed "Deposits" (D_U of Table 2.3); or, External Deposits and
Internal "Deposits"; the last could also be called Uncashed Loans.
Perhaps Bank-owned Money would be the best term for the latter,
because it describes the main reason why so many loans remain
uncashed.

   The reason for the ability of bank "deposits" in Table 2.3 to circulate
money is obvious: each bank guarantees the debts of its borrowers in
Table 2.3. It turns itself into a collection agency with respect to its
uncashed loans. According to the modern theory, banks "monetize their
total deposit debts." In fact, this is true only in the case of Table 2.2. In
the case of Table 2.3 the bank has no debts of its own to monetize.
Instead, it "monetizes its borrowers' debts."

6. PHILLIPS'S 1921 THEORY OF ALL BANKS

Modern theory analyzes two polar cases: competition and monopoly. It
offers no analysis of the intermediate cases. In 1921 Phillips offered to
us—in vain—a much richer theory that enabled him to place each specific
bank that we may desire to analyze with respect to credit (recall that his
book is entitled Bank Credit) anywhere between these two extremes. He

offers to us (p. 55) his bank credit equation (expressed here on a net basis):

$$dX = D_B(1 - r)/(kr + 1 - k) - D_B \qquad (4\text{-}A)$$

and

$$d\Sigma X = K\Sigma D_B \qquad (4\text{-}B)$$

In it, $1 - k$ measures the fraction of loans that result in a cash outflow from each bank. The factor k measures the fraction of loans X in each bank that do not become cashed in, and thus enable each bank to lend in excess of its borrowing. The sectoral net credit expansion multiplier K is simply a weighted average of all the individual multipliers, with banks' borrowing netted out. It is obtainable—in contrast with the modern credit multiplier—only after loans and borrowed deposits in every single bank have been measured. As must be always true, a sector is merely the sum of its parts. In economics, paradoxes need not apply.

The two types of banks on which modern texts exclusively focus are merely two polar cases: monopoly with $k = 1$ and competition with $k = 0$. Empirical research in 1921 has failed to find either (pp. 45–6), because they cannot exist. Even a monopoly bank would find some loans cashed in; even a perfectly competitive bank would find that some indolent customers do not cash in their loans the instant they are made. Our banking theorists should start to explain to our students banks that can and do exist. Of course, they know nothing about those.

7. OPERATION OF PHILLIPS'S BANK

Given the fact that all of us are conditioned by the hydraulics (*e.g.*, Simpson, pp. 98–101) of our modern theory, it may be useful to go briefly through the case of a bank that has a k that exceeds zero. Phillips's empirical research (p. 59) has caused him to believe that a median bank in 1921 was facing $k = 0.2$ and $r = 0.1$. In Table 2.5 an inexperienced banker borrows (as in Table 2.2) externally $820. The bank sets aside $82 as reserves and lends $738. (In the modern theory with its $k = 0$, all these loans leave the bank, so that this is the end of the matter. Column 4 and all the following rows remain empty.) Phillips's bank with $k = 0.2$ loses only 80 per cent of the amount lent; $147.60 remains uncashed and thereby becomes a Derivative "Deposit" or Internal "Deposit" (as in Table 2.3). It must be covered by reserves ($14.76) so that $132.84 is left in the form of excess reserves. In line 3 this amount is lent again, and the whole process repeats itself. The totals are shown in the last line. After borrowing $820 the bank lent $900.

Of course, this duplication of textbook hydraulics just doesn't make

Table 2.5: Inexperienced Phillips banker

Borrowing: External Deposits D_B	Loans	Cash Loss	Uncashed Loans: Internal "Deposits" D_U	Required Reserves	Excess Reserves
$820				$82	$738
	$738	$590	$148	$15	$133
	$133	$106	$ 27	$ 3	$ 24
	...	...	...	...	...
$820	$900	$720	$180	$100	

Table 2.6: Phillips's banker's T-account

Assets		Debts*	
Reserves	$ 82	$820 Deposits D_B Net worth*	
Reserves	$ 18	$180 Internal "Deposits" D_U	
Cashed-in loans	$720		
Uncashed loans	$180		

Note: * In Table 2.1 the subheadings have been left out so as not to anticipate my subsequent argument. Bank debts D_B are its income-costing assets (from Table 2.2). Banker's plus bank factor's net worth[3] is the bank's income-earning asset D_U (from Table 2.3).

sense (and Phillips has never suggested it). No experienced banker (or no experienced modern monopolist) would bear the heavy cost of making an infinite series of ever-decreasing loans on the basis of the delusion that each of his loans will be cashed in. He or she knows to what a cash loss each loan leads. After borrowing $820, she or he would lend in one swoop $900 to one or more borrowers. If we transfer the numbers in the last line of Table 2.5 into a T-account we obtain Table 2.6 (totals in which are identical with the T-account of a modern bank in Table 2.4).

8. THE BANKING SECTOR

Let me now compare the effects that the two theories have on "The Banking System" (I dislike this term, because it aims to separate us from the rest of economics where the terms "industry" or "sector" are always used: such separation seems to justify the "fundamental paradox"). I shall make the usual simplifying assumption that once reserves enter the industry, they stay there: no cash that enters row 1 leaks out. In Table 2.7-A I reproduce the modern case, as one finds it in every text. Bank A receives $820 of deposits D_B and lends its excess reserves of $738. This entire amount is withdrawn and is redeposited in Bank B, and the process repeats itself until no excess reserves are left. The industry then has a consolidated T-account containing the amounts shown in the last row of the table.

In the case of Phillips's model (Table 2.7-B) I start with the amounts shown in the last row of Table 2.5 (and, in the first row of modern Table 2.7-A). Bank A again borrows $820; but, it lends not $738 but $900. Instead of losing the entire amount lent, its excess reserves are reduced only by $720. This amount flows into Bank B, and the process repeats itself until no excess reserves are left. It should be noted that the number of banks needed to accomplish this will be smaller than in the modern case, because each bank in the chain holds on to more required reserves (and supplies more of deposit money).

Comparison of the two parts of Table 2.7 reveals several facts:

1. The consolidated T-accounts of the two models are identical.

Table 2.7-A: Modern banking industry

	Borrowing External Deposits D_B	Loans	Cash Loss	Uncashed Loans Internal "Deposits" D_U	Required Reserves
Bank A	$820	$738	$738	$0	$82
Bank B	$738	$664	$664	$0	$74
	...	...	...	...	...
Industry	$8,200	$7,380	$7,380	$0	$820

Table 2.7-B: Phillips's banking industry

	Borrowing External D_B	Loans	Cash Loss	Uncashed Loans Internal D_U	Required Reserves
Bank A	$820	$900	$720	$180	$100
Bank B	$720	$790	$632	$168	$ 89
	...	...	...	...	...
Industry	$6,725	$7,380	$5,905	$1,475	$820

2. With the same reserve inflow, both models supply the same amount of bank deposit money: $8,200 D_B in Part A, and $6,725 D_B plus $1,475 D_U equals $8,200 in Part B.

3. Both models supply the same amount of credit: $7,380. However, the modern model (with $k = 0$) must borrow $8,200: it contracts credit. Phillips' model (with $k = 0.2$) needs to borrow only $6,725: it expands credit.

Phillips has made one profound and one silly proposition: (1) Each bank contracts or expands net credit depending on the size of the factor k, that measures the fraction of loans that will not be cashed in. (2) Probably to differentiate himself from his predecessors who were assuming zero cash outflow, Phillips has invented a wholly incredible channel for his cash outflow: the total amount of cash loss by one bank (equal to or smaller than loans made) flows to bank B, Bank C, *etc.* until all additional reserves become converted into required reserves. One could just as well hypothesize that when I buy life insurance from Company A, a loan of that company will be fully spent on purchases of additional insurance in Company B, C, *etc.*, until my initial spending becomes embedded in the life insurance industry's cash reserves. Clearly, this second idea of Phillips is absurd, but harmless.

Our modern theory copies the latter and denies the former, on the basis of no empirical evidence that would contradict Phillips's evidence. As a result, all banks are classified as institutions which merely "intermediate" credit. This fiction, contrary to readily available empirical evidence (see section 10), has received a professional seal of approval by the heading "Intermediaries" found in the *Index of Economic Journals*, and in the index in each issue of the *Journal of Economic Literature* (both published by the American Economic Association). Empirically, this fiction found its way into all professional and government wealth accounts (see, *e.g.*, the T-accounts in the *Federal Reserve Bulletin*).

Besides teaching us a theoretical lesson, the two tables yield a major policy-making lesson. Start with Table 2.7-A and assume that the second one is empty, and that banks face constant costs. Now, let one half of the banks merge, so that one quarter of the initial number of banks moves into Table 2.7-B. With random deposits of loan proceeds flowing into all banks, the banks remaining in Table 2.7-A will soon vanish because of lack of reserves: compare reserves in- and outflow in the two tables. Permit another wave of bank mergers in the remaining Table 2.7-B: ultimately, we must end with a monopoly bank. Will relevant increasing internal resource costs prevent this from happening? Only if they were to rise at an incredibly fast clip, to offset ·irrelevant sharply decreasing external pecuniary costs: Bank A based on Tables 2 and 3 ($k = 0$) has, with its loans-debt ratio 9 : 1, a huge pecuniary cost advantage over a competitive Bank B based on Table 2 and Table 2.7-A ($k = 1$), with its loans-debts ratio 0.9 : 1. In banking, big fishes (even if grossly inefficient) eat small fishes (even if superlatively efficient).

This probably does explain why countries in Western Europe and Canada are each dominated by a handful of oligopolistic banks, with all (but one) surviving because of managements' vested interest and a fear of the public outcry. With our thirteen thousand banks, my country is the sole exception—no doubt, thanks to our robust anti-merger legislation and regulation. However, in the last ten years this protection has become very seriously eroded through quasi-legal and regulatory means. The consequences are as predicted above. In the words of James Tobin, "The system of depositories is drifting towards oligopoly of giant nationwide banks..." (p. 170). Let me add to the two previously discussed dogmas a third one: deregulation will foster efficiency and competition. In fact, it will do neither. It will merely cause us to join the rest of the Western world. We shall end up with a handful of banks, under no compulsion to be efficient.

9. EACH BANK'S EFFECT ON MONEY AND CREDIT

It may be interesting for the reader to inspect the effect that various other possible pairs of r and k have on the ability of each bank—and therefore, of the industry—to lend on the basis of borrowing of $1 (Table 2.8). Phillips's empirical research has revealed that each bank's niche changes secularly, cyclically, seasonally, and as a result of local competitive conditions. The numerous forces causing this are listed in section 10.

What effect do the various types of banks have on the macroeconomic variables such as the rate of interest and the volume of investments? We

Table 2.8: *Bank's and industry's net credit multipliers for various values of k, K and r*

k or K	$r = 0.1$	$r = 0.15$
0.0	− 0.10	− 0.15
0.2	+ 0.09	+ 0.02
0.4	+ 0.41	+ 0.29
0.6	+ 0.96	+ 0.73
0.8	+ 2.21	+ 1.59
1.0	+ 8.00	+ 4.67

need to consider two distinct forces:

1. Credit theorists know that an increase in demand for bonds—an increase in *the net supply of credit*—reduces the rate of interest and increases the volume of investments. To measure this effect, microeconomic analysis of banks and their factors k is imperative. The bigger the factor k, the less a bank needs to borrow per \$1 of loans: the bigger its expansion of the supply of loanable funds and the lower the rate of interest.

2. An increase in *the net supply of money* increases the demand for all assets. Some fraction of this additional spending (given the complexity of asset portfolios, probably a very small one) increases the demand for bonds, and thereby increases the loans available to investors. This reduces the rate of interest. Another fraction will be spent for consumption goods, and that may cause an increase in the demand for investment goods. Still another fraction will be spent as a down-payment on consumption and investment goods. The last two types of spending will increase the demand for loanable funds and thus push the interest rate up. The net effect of an increase in the supply of money on the interest rate seems unpredictable.[4] It is predictable only in naive Keynesian models in which people spend money only on bonds.

An expansion of the banking industry causes both money and credit to change simultaneously. However, it is possible to separate and quantify the two conceptually (just as one does with the income and substitution effects):

1. In the first step, assume that some law denies to bank deposits the characteristics of money (transferability, liquidity, *etc.*). For instance, banks must borrow only foreign money from domestic lenders and must issue perpetuities that may be sold only once, by the initial borrower. Table 2.9 shows the size of the Credit Effect, associated with a competitive bank, Phillips's median 1921 bank, and a monopoly bank. Each modern bank occupies its own niche in between the two extremes.

2. In the next step, introduce the Money Effect. Assume that banks borrow domestic money and convert the perpetuities into marketable bank money. All banks expand the stock of money by the same amount: by the volume of their deposits minus reserves.

The policy-making importance of Phillips's analysis is made obvious by Table 2.9. Suppose that the policy-maker decides on macroeconomic grounds to maintain the existing equilibrium values of all variables and freezes bank reserves. And, in a seemingly unrelated decision, she or he also decides to foster microeconomic efficiency and to permit bank

Table 2.9: Effect of various banks on net credit and money

	CREDIT EFFECT		MONEY EFFECT	
	Funds Borrowed	Funds Lent	Cash Absorbed	Bank Money
Competitive Bank	− $1,000	+ $900	− $100	+ $1,000
Phillips's Bank	− $ 820	+ $900	− $100	+ $1,000
Monopoly Bank	− $ 100	+ $900	− $100	+ $1,000

mergers. The fewer the banks, the bigger the likelihood that some loans will remain uncashed: in Table 2.9 many banks move closer to the bottom row. As they do, the credit multiplier grows rapidly. With all banks homogeneous with respect to the Money Effect, the consequences for the measured stock of money are nil. But, with all banks dishomogeneous with respect to the Credit Effect, the absorption by banks of credit per dollar of loans is reduced (the money stock being kept fixed), and these now flow to direct finance or to other types of intermediaries. The supply of credit increases: the rate of interest and the volume of investments are affected. Neglect of the Credit Effect causes the policy-maker to fail to meet the stated objective. A permissive credit policy requires a restrictive monetary policy.

Let me, however, point out a much more fundamental consequence of Phillips's discovery. Currently, we see an explosion of credit. For instance, E. Gerald Corrigan (President of the Federal Reserve Bank of New York) said recently: "Since the last quarter of 1983 ... corporate debt has increased by a staggering $600 billion." One may add that consumer credit has experienced a similar rate of growth. As long as we believe that all financial institutions are mere intermediaries, we are unable to make a principled case—a case based on price theory—for curbing such excesses. Once we recognize that the flow of credit to the banks from the private sector bears no relationship to the return flow of credit from the banks to the private sector, we may—nay, must—get rid of our unfounded scruples against "interferences with the free market" in this area.

Just as we have long recognized the necessity to control banks' ability to print previously non-existent money, so we must also recognize the necessity to control banks' ability to "print" previously non-existent credit. As seems to be the rule in economics, this may impose upon us conflicting goals. Some compromise, based on the discovery of the relative empirical strengths of the Credit and Money Effects may be the best that we can do.

10. DETERMINANTS OF PHILLIPS'S FACTOR k

Let me now share with the reader Phillips's careful and unfortunately unique empirical research. He has analyzed data and has interviewed bankers in twenty-six big and small cities (pp. 45–6). This has enabled him to discover some of the innumerable forces that determine k and thus the ability of each bank to lend more than it borrows:

1. "A certain proportion of checks drawn by borrowers will be in favor of depositors of the drawers' bank, and, to that extent, *cause no loss of cash by that bank*" [Phillips's emphasis] (p. 57). It should be noted that Phillips is right only if we assume that the cheques move only within Tables 2.2 and 2.3; that there is no flow between these tables.

(The *Federal Reserve Bulletin* (p. 179) puts this proportion at 51 per cent of all cheques written. If we assume that the number of cheques also measures their dollar value, and if we ignore that some cheques are written by the depositors to obtain cash—one big and one small "if"—this alone would enable banks to lend $1.56 per each $1 borrowed.)

2. "Overflow cash [cash outflow] ... particularly in a country having few banks, and especially in one-bank towns, would be reduced..." (p. 57). (The drastic drop in the number of banks since 1921 should be remembered.)

3. "Any given bank A ... which has extended its loans on the basis of new reserves may become depository of overflow cash lost by other banks ... that they have themselves loaned on the basis of ... loans made by Bank A." (p. 57). Phillips is dead wrong here. Cash lost to other banks from Table 2.3 may return, but it must return to Table 2.2 and represents each bank's borrowing D_B. Interbank flows must not be netted out.

4. "Indeed, borrowers are required by many city banks to maintain an average balance equal to a definite percentage, usually 20 per cent ..." (p. 42). (Note that modern theory views these "deposits" D_U not as a major tool affecting the crucial factor k (that is unknown to it), but merely as a tool for disguising interest rates).

5. A borrower does not withdraw his loan immediately, and accumulates balances before repayment (*cf.* Graph 1, p. 43). With many loans due every day, this creates a revolving fund of uncashed loans D_U (Diagram 2, p. 53) and increases k.

6. Among the forces that adversely affect k Phillips lists "...bank advances [in] the form of paper bought from paper dealers—notes from distant borrowers..." (p. 48).

7. Mortgages and loans against a collateral are usually associated with $k = 0$. (p. 49).

8. Short term loans are associated with a bigger k than long term loans. (p. 49).

9. Loans below \$5,000 are said to be associated with $k = 0.4$, while large loans are said to be associated with $k = 0.1$ (p. 49).

10. In booms, banks are claimed to force borrowers to withdraw a smaller fraction of their loans (by increasing or enforcing more rigorously compensatory balances). (p. 51) (Several studies show that this remains true today.)

11. High interest rates cause loans to be spent the day they are obtained, and very little is deposited against them before the maturity date. (p. 47)

12. Renewable loans do not result in increased balances prior to the maturity date. (p. 49)

13. Small borrowers fear to withdraw the entire loan, while major borrowers do not. (p. 50)

What a sophisticated understanding of each banker's decision-making process! And what an excellent explanation of the modern banker's meticulous attention to every detail of their "cash flows"! Every loan that the banker makes determines the constantly shifting position of the bank between the two extremes: $k = 0$ (in modern terms, not a very profitable competitive bank) and $k = 1$ (in modern terms, a most profitable monopolistic bank). Each banker constantly strives to maximize profits by increasing the supply of net credit.

Phillips's empirical work makes it obvious that commercial banks' resource costs of some \$100 billion—totally ignored by all money and banking texts and advanced treatises dealing with banking—must be given careful consideration.[5] Bank factor costs co-determine the structure of the bank portfolio—and thus the factor k and bank credit multiplier K—because each type of loan makes a different demand on bank factors. And, must one really believe—as our modern theory demands—that the size of the banking industry and the stock of bank money would remain unaffected should bank resource costs—say—double or triple, and absorb not some 5 per cent but 10 or 15 per cent of our GNP?

11. CONCLUSION

The issues discussed here are important for monetary and banking theory. Phillips had shown in 1921 empirically what T. R. Saving and I deduced in 1967 theoretically: that banks are not merely intermediaries which lend less than they borrow but are also net suppliers of credit. Theoretical treatment of such two-headed hydras is bound to be much more complex. And, it will not be much help unless empirical research enables us to decide which of the two parts of the analysis applies to which part of the current meaningless aggregate called Bank Deposits. However, scoring theoretical debating point would be—especially at my age—a trivial pursuit. We all should try to earn our keep: it is the policy-making that is of supreme importance.

In modern analysis, all banks are claimed to be homogeneous both with respect to their fortunate ability to expand money (all Deposits less Reserves) and their unfortunate necessity to contract credit (Loans less all Deposits). (The influence of "the Paradox" causes an intuitive feeling that this sentence is wrong: but, take a cool look at the T-accounts and ignore the verbal pyrotechnics.) Thus, microeconomic analysis of banks seems superfluous. Phillips's overwhelming empirical evidence shows this to be false. Each bank's contribution to credit is determined by microeconomic variables, which should henceforth be measured. Secular changes have reduced very drastically the number of banks and thus must have increased substantially the credit-expansion multiplier K (see item 2). Cyclical changes in the bank portfolios (*e.g.*, changes in the Investments-Loans ratio) introduce cyclical instability in the multiplier K (see Items 4, 5, 7, 10). Seasonal changes (see construction loans in Item 10) are also important. Finally, the recent wave of bank mergers and the legal and extralegal expansion of banks' territorial boundaries must have increased significantly the factor k (see Items 1 and 2) and thus the aggregate credit multiplier K.

Without microeconomic analysis of the banking firms, of the changing interest and factor costs, and of interest incomes associated with various loans, our understanding of macroeconomic forces that determine the supply of credit, interest rates, investments, and inflationary pressures is bound to be grossly deficient. It is a pity that Phillips's theory has been ignored for such a long time. Now we don't know how his credit-expansion multiplier co-determined our economic history in the past sixty-five years. Without understanding the past we are ill prepared to guide the future.

At the present time, in most macro models credit ("the bond market") is simply dismissed on the basis of Walras's Law, and on the basis of the claim that direct or intermediated bond-debts offset bond-assets. Once we learn Chester Arthur Phillips's lesson contained in his pioneering *Bank Credit*, this will cease to be a tenable position. Just as we know now that money cannot be made subject to *laissez faire*, so we should recognize that the same is true about credit. Macroeconomics, monetary theory, and banking theory—containing bank-money theory and a reborn bank-credit theory—should all be applied to guide our economy to stability and prosperity.

NOTES

I am most grateful to Professor Richard Timberlake, Jr. who has greatly helped me to understand Phillips's work. I am also grateful to my colleagues from the Universite N.D. de la Paix (Namur), University of Wien, Technical University of Wien, Institute for Advanced Studies in Wien, and from universities of Florence, Giessen, Milan, Modena, and Venice. Finally, I am grateful to my students in Milwaukee and Wien for their careful scrutiny of my analysis.

1. My former student David Kamerschen wrote the only modern text that spends two pages (pp. 116–7) on Phillips's analysis, and shows that banks may lend "... somewhat more ..." than they borrow. In the rest of the book, however, he offers only the orthodox theory of banks as intermediaries. Clearly, he does not care to or—given my experience—dare to mention that the above two pages show this theory to be slightly pregnant.

   Similarly, Jürg Niehans in his treatise points out that under certain conditions a bank may lend more than it borrows (p. 194). He clearly does not recognize that this statement fundamentally affects the two key dogmas of monetary and banking theory: (1) that all banks are mere intermediaries, and (2) that all bank money is bank debt.

2. Our law permits banks (and no other financial institution) to place in their T-accounts face values of assets and liabilities. (That came to be called recently "creative accounting", without which several giant American banks would be in a receivership.) Not to burden this paper with extraneous issues, I follow here the banking theorists' preference for law over price theory. I realize, of course, that face values are price-theoretically wrong, and empirically irrelevant: no bank stockholder would and no bank examiner should be guided by them. But, wrong as they are, they do not affect the argument offered in this paper.

   However, a word of explanation may be useful. In Table 2.4, Loans and Deposits should show the discounted present values of banker's interest income i and interest costs c: i/r and c/r. The difference between the two values must cover the cost of holding reserves and of bank factors. The latter measures the positive Net Worth, even of a perfectly competitive banking sector.

3. Friedman and Schwartz realize (p. 113) that a monopolist (as in Table 2.1) does derive his or her Net Worth from banking. But, to satisfy the dogma that all deposits are debts, they reform that table. They change the sign attached to the income stream yielded by uncashed loans (Table 2.3) from a positive to a negative one: they place the interest-earning (rather than interest-costing) "Deposits" of Table 2.3 into the Liability column of Table 2.1. (My notion of Paradise is to be satiated with such income-earning "Liabilities".) This leaves the lucky monopolist who borrows $100 and lends $900 no better off than is a competitor in Table 2.4, who borrows $1,000 and lends $900.

   This problem they take care of in a frivolous way. On the Asset side they add to "Loans" another asset: monopoly "Charter". Of course, the banker has just one income stream, the discounted present value of which may be given one of the above two names. I could just as well ascribe my single flow of royalties to (1) this Book and also to (2) my monopoly Copyright protecting its sales. After listing each as my Assets, I would be forced to invent some imaginary Liability of mine to offset this double-counting. However, that would not be accounting but finger-painting.

4. Numerous empirical studies that do show a strong relationship between money and interest rates do not persuade me. They are all misspecified, because they do not include the Credit Effect.

5. Just as in every other branch of economics resource costs are given careful consideration. Can one imagine, say, transportation economists making our orthodox "simplifying assumption"—found in all banking texts and all advanced monetary theory treatises? Can one imagine them assuming "for simplicity" that freight levitates by itself, and daring to make policy recommendations on this basis?

REFERENCES

Campbell, Colin D. and Campbell, Rosemary 1981. *Money and Banking*. Hillsdale, Ill.: Dryden Press.

Corrigan, E. Gerald 1987. "Remarks Before the Canadian Club of Toronto, Canada, November 16, 1987", (Unpublished lecture).

Federal Reserve Bulletin, March 1982.

Friedman, Milton and Schwartz, Anna Jacobson 1970. *Monetary Statistics of the United States*. National Bureau of Economic Research. New York: Columbia University Press (distributed by).

Galbraith, John Kenneth 1975. *Money*. Boston: Houghton Mifflin Co.

Kamerschen, David R. 1984. *Money and Banking*. Eight Edition. Cincinnati: South-Western Co.

Klein, John J. 1982. *Money and the Economy*. New York: Harcourt Brace Jovanovich Co.

Niehans, Jürg 1981. *The Theory of Money*. Baltimore: Johns Hopkins University Press.

Patinkin, Don 1969. "Money and Wealth: A Review Article," *Journal of Economic Literature*, Dec. 1969, VII, pp. 1140–60.

Phillips, Chester Arthur 1921. *Bank Credit*. New York: MacMillan Co.

Simpson, Thomas D. 1981. *Money, Banking, and Economic Analysis*. Englewood Cliffs: Prentice-Hall.

Tobin, James 1987. *Restructuring the Financial System*. Federal Reserve Bank of Kansas City.

3 Fiat and Bank Money as Wealth

FIAT MONEY AS PART OF NET WEALTH[*]

Money, as we have seen earlier, is a part of the net wealth of the community because it yields services to the owner while it yields no negative service to the non-owner. The service yielded is based on the role of money as a medium of exchange or store of value; for the performance of these roles the physical substance of a unit of money is of no consequence whatever. But then fiat money is just as much a part of the net wealth of the community as is commodity money. This is most easily shown by pointing out that it could not make any difference if someone would replace, overnight, commodity money with fiat money that would serve the citizens equally well in all respects. Similarly, it would not make any difference in our conclusions if the barter economy skipped the step represented by competitively produced commodity money and shifted directly to a monopolistically produced commodity money or to fiat money. In any case, money—*simply money*—would yield the services that we discussed in detail in connection with commodity money, and would be a part of the total net wealth of the community. It should be pointed out that net wealth surely cannot decrease if fiat money rather than commodity money is used to provide the services that (any) money yields. On the contrary, net wealth will increase. Monopoly production of money will utilize fewer resources than would be utilized under competitive conditions. Thus the community has more resources available for the production of non-money capital goods; so it will have, under conditions of monopoly production of money, a greater flow of non-money services. Since the flow of money services is independent of the stock of units of money in existence, it will also have the same quantity of money services. Therefore, the wealth of the community is

---

[*] From: *Money, Wealth, and Economic Theory*. Coauthor: Thomas R. Saving

greater when the production of money is undertaken by a monopolist. Parenthetically, we might mention that it obviously makes no difference whether this monopolistic producer of money is a private firm or the government—though the second is, of course, more likely. Moreover, monopoly production gives us the additional advantage of choosing a commodity that has a lower value and lower production costs than one produced by a competitive money industry. This leaves more resources available for other uses and hence further increases the wealth of the community over what it would have been with competitive production of the money commodity.[1]

Therefore, we have shown that the introduction of monopoly-produced fiat money has increased the wealth of the community. But has this assumption affected our previous conclusion that money is an asset not offset by a corresponding debt? A little reflection on our argument of the previous section will lead to the conclusion that the method of production of money does not affect this important conclusion. For the monopolist producer of money has all the same choices open to him as any commodity producer. If the producer of money desires to increase his consumption of services, he may borrow capital goods from others and thus incur a debt (whether or not the lender requires him to pay interest) or he may produce and sell additional fiat money, which is—as we have just shown—not a debt. We conclude again, therefore, that money, whether fiat or commodity money, is not a debt of the issuer of it, but is an asset to the holders. In other words, money yields a positive flow of services to the holders of it, and does not yield an offsetting negative flow of services to either the non-holders or to the producer and seller of it.

Objection: fiat money is not net wealth

In the literature the conclusion that fiat money is net wealth and therefore not a debt is being vigorously denied. James Tobin summarized the two main arguments that are being used in support of this position as follows:

The community's wealth now has two components: the real goods accumulated through past real investment and fiduciary or paper "goods" manufactured by the government from thin air. Of course, the non-human wealth of such a nation "really" consists only of its tangible capital. But, as viewed by the inhabitants of the nation individually, wealth exceeds the tangible capital stock by the size of what we might term the fiduciary issue. This is an illusion, but only one of the many fallacies of composition which are basic to any economy or any society. The illusion can be maintained unimpaired so long as the society does not actually try to convert all of its paper wealth into goods.[2]

Let us consider these two arguments: First, goods are being placed in quotation marks and denied existence if they are manufactured "from thin air"; if their market value exceeds their resource cost. Market valuation of goods is being rejected on the basis of a subjective decision that these goods are "really" worthless! Are we to deny that opera singers add to national income, and the capitalized value of this income is net wealth, since the product they produce is manufactured out of thin air? If so, a great deal of non-monetary wealth must be removed from our accounts. Are we to deny that monopolistically produced goods, the resource cost of which is smaller than their market price, are not wealth to the extent of the difference? Then much of the tangible non-human wealth must be removed from our accounts; the fate of all art treasures becomes extremely doubtful. Second, the assertion is made that a good, the value of which depends on the continuing demand for it, is merely an "illusion." If so, then each and every single item of wealth is an illusion because its value, to use Tobin's words, "continues unimpaired so long as the society does not actually try to convert all of" it into other goods. The total wealth of the society is, if we accept this economic analysis, zero by definition. Clearly, neither argument could stand scrutiny if applied to anything else but money. Indeed, it is inconceivable that either argument would be used in support of a decision to remove some part of the non-monetary ("tangible") capital from the measure of wealth. But then, why should either argument be more persuasive when we undertake economic analysis into the nature of money?

However, as the reader is surely well aware, there are numerous other arguments denying that fiat money is net wealth and asserting that it is merely a debt. Orderly presentation of our own economic analysis of commodity money, fiat money, and bank money prevents consideration of all of them at this point, especially since many cover simultaneously fiat money and bank money; the economic analysis of the latter we have not yet had a chance to present. At this point, all we can do is to ask the reader's forbearance and offer him assurance that the other arguments denying fiat money the character of net wealth will prove no less hollow that the two basic ones just discussed.

Effects of changes in the relative price of fiat money
Since we have concluded that fiat money is no different from competitively produced commodity money in its characteristics, we should expect that the analysis used in the previous section would apply without change here. And this is, indeed, the case. Consider, say, an increase in the value of our fiat money in terms of the non-money goods of the community. Such an increase makes the holders of the fiat money better off because the exchange value of their holdings of fiat money has

increased or, put in income terms, the flow of services of their money holdings has increased because each unit of money now supports more transactions than before the increase in value. However, the non-holders of fiat money are no worse off, since every combination of goods available to them before the change in the price of money is available to them now. This result stems from the fact that for the non-holders of money, prices have not changed, because the increase in the value of a unit of money has simply resulted in a proportional increase in the volume of services yielded by a unit of money, leaving the price of a unit of the services of money unchanged. Here we have a wealth effect stemming from the change in the value of money affecting the holders but not the non-holders of money.

Conclusion
The use of fiat money does raise problems that do not exist in the case of a competitive production of commodity money. First, a monopolistic producer of (fiat) money is able to become such only if the community is willing to give him the powers he needs to enforce his monopoly. Second, we have seen that there are significant savings of resources to be realized from a monopolistic production of money; these savings, of course, at least partly enrich the monopolist himself. It appears inevitable that the monopolist will get from the community the powers needed to enforce his monopoly only if he will place the control over the income derived from his monopolistic power in the hands of the community. Finally, there are numerous alternatives open to the monopolist for placing the money he produces into use. He may sell the money and refund the purchase price to the buyer: we shall call this a gift of money. He may sell the money and use the proceeds for his own purposes. Or he may sell the money and distribute the proceeds to the individual members of the community: we may call this payment a subsidy, or a decrease in taxes, or a transfer payment. The truly important issue discussed in this chapter is that money is in one respect identical with and in another respect completely different from all other commodities. It is different from all other commodities in that it has a technical property of yielding its owner real income that depends completely on the price ratio between other real goods and money. It is identical with all other commodities in that it is a claim of the owner on the resources of others, but it is not a debt of others to the owner. The difference between a claim based on ownership of any real resource and a claim based on a debt of someone else is that the first merely enables the owner to attempt to induce owners of any other good to trade at the basis of the current market prices, whereas the second enables the owner to insist on the repayment of a contractually stipulated type and quantity of some other commodity.[3] The "producer"

of a debt is a debtor because he has acquired resources through no effort of his own; they were simply transferred to him by the creditor. The producer of a money commodity is not a debtor because he sacrificed his effort or other resources to produce commodity money. Were he, in a legal or economic sense, to become a debtor, the monetary commodity would not exist at all, since he would never produce it; he would be sacrificing his real resources to produce it and, after production and sale, he would then be in no better position than someone who merely induced others to transfer resources to him.

We have also shown that fiat money is a mere substitute for commodity money. A substitute that is made possible by the exercise of monopolistic powers by the producer of money; monopolistic powers that—in the case of money—enhance rather than diminish efficient use of resources. Even though no (or almost no) resources are sacrificed in the production of fiat money, this money is nevertheless a substitute for commodity money. The reason is the special technical property of money that makes the real output yielded by it independent of the physical substance of it. For this reason, all the conclusions reached with respect to commodity money must hold with respect to fiat money. The two most important are (1) that fiat money is a genuine part of the net wealth of the community, not offset by any corresponding debt, and (2) that changes in the price of the fiat money will change the wealth of society.

BANK MONEY AS WEALTH

We are now prepared to turn our attention to the case of bank-created money. This case is, unfortunately, a complex one. As a result of this complexity, the basic similarity between the operations of the banking system and the production and sale of commodity and fiat money has had a tendency to become lost. The so called *Old View* that perceived this similarity is nowadays in general retreat, and a *New View* dominates monetary theory. James Tobin, who coined the terms we just used, expressed the currently dominant opinion most succinctly when he wrote:

Unlike governments, bankers cannot create means of payment to finance their own purchases of goods and services. Bank-created "money" is a liability, which must be matched on the other side of the balance sheet.[4]

In this chapter we intend to show that the *Old View* still holds and that commercial banks are producers and sellers of money called demand deposits and that this money is part of the net wealth of the community.

Our analysis will contain three main parts. First, we discuss a general and abstract type of "private money producer," who is in the business of producing and selling private money. Initially, we impose on him no restriction other than a limit on the quantity of his output; next, we subject him to the rule that his output must be convertible into "the coin of the Realm." Second, we show that commercial banks insofar as they are producing demand deposits are as such private money producers and that all the conclusions reached earlier apply to them. Specifically, we show that their output is a part of the net wealth of the community. Third, in a separate chapter, we show that certain changes in the restraints under which private money producers operate can reduce them to mere financial intermediaries.

Private money: The general case
For simplicity we assume that the only money in use in the economy is fiat money (in the following discussion we refer to this primary money as the "dominant money") produced by a monopolist—the government, if you like. Suppose that the government allows certain firms to enter into the production and sale of a substitute for dominant money, provided that convertibility into dominant money on the demand of a private money holder is guaranteed at fixed exchange rate—presumably, since most conveniently, at a one-to-one rate.[5] Thus each unit of private money sold must contain an instant repurchase clause; this clause guarantees that the producer of private money will repurchase his product, on demand of the buyer or of any subsequent holder, at its original sale price. Assume, finally, that the private money producers are prohibited by the government from stimulating demand by bribing their customers; they are forbidden to pay interest to the holders of bank money. This last assumption is made merely for the sake of an orderly presentation and will be dropped in due course.

Benchmark: Unrestricted private money producer
As a benchmark for the consideration of the private money producer, let us establish the addition to net wealth resulting from the introduction of a private money with no strings attached, i.e., all sales final. In this case, private money producers are in the same position as is the fiat money producer of the previous chapter. Hence, so long as some limit is imposed on the output of their money, the change in net wealth is simply the total sales of private money, i.e.,

$$\Delta w = \frac{M_p}{P} \qquad (3.1)$$

where (w) is the level of the community's net wealth and (M_p) is the nominal amount of private money sold. This result follows from the same analysis applicable to the fiat money producer. In other words, the sale of money can only take place if the purchasers value the money at least as highly as the goods transferred to the private money producer. But since, for the private money producer all sales are final, the money sold cannot be a debt of his and therefore the money must be net wealth. To the extent that the production of private money (or dominant money for that matter) uses up resources that would have been used to increase the stock of other capital goods, the *net* change (net of reduction in other items of net wealth) *in net* wealth will be smaller. However, this simply means that the community prefers to hold its net wealth in the form of money rather than in the form of these other capital goods, and does not imply that money is not wealth.

While a positive resource cost of production of private money will affect the net change in the community's net wealth, it will not affect our decision concerning the classification of private money as net wealth. Thus, we can simplify our analysis without losing any generality if we assume that the resource cost of producing the physical units of private money is zero; that the cost of producing paper notes or accounting entries that make up the private money stock is zero.[6] Given this assumption, the increase in the producers' net wealth that results from the outright sale of private money (all sales final) is precisely equal—as in the case of the production and sale of fiat money—to the change in the community's net wealth. We may, therefore, rewrite equation 3.1 as follows:

$$\Delta w = \frac{M_p}{P} - \Delta \frac{y}{r} + \Delta \frac{y}{r} = \frac{M_p}{P} \qquad (3.2)$$

where $(\Delta \frac{y}{r})$ represents the value of the capital goods transferred by the purchasers of money to the private money producers and is of course equal to M_p.

Private money producer, restricted by the instant repurchase clause
We have now laid the groundwork for consideration of the economic effects of the instant repurchase clause through which privately produced money becomes convertible, on demand, into the coin of the Realm—into dominant money. This clause requires the producer of private money to repurchase his product on demand of the holder of it at a fixed price. This repurchase clause, as we shall show, (1) helps to determine the equilibrium level of output that the private money producer will be able to produce and sell, and (2) changes the contribution of this producer to the net wealth of society.

Determination of equilibrium output of private money

To insure that in equilibrium both private and dominant money exist, assume that these two types of money are not perfect substitutes for each other in all uses. In other words, both monies are media of exchange, but there are some exchanges that are more convenient to undertake by the use of one type rather than the other.[7] Thus, given (1) the repurchase clause requiring a one-to-one exchange ratio (or, more generally, any other fixed ratio), and (2) the prohibition of interest payments to the purchasers of private money, there will exist some proportion between dominant and private money that will make them perfect substitutes on the margin; there will exist a proportion of dominant money to private money that makes consumers indifferent between a unit of private money and a unit of dominant money. Hence, even if the private money producers did not hold any dominant money inventories as a reserve against unexpected runs of repurchases, a limit to the sale of private money would still exist. Given the two restraints specified above, this limit depends on the nominal stock of dominant money and the proportion of dominant money to private money at which the consumers are indifferent between the two types of money. In such a case the equilibrium stock of private money is

$$M_p = \frac{M_d}{\gamma} \qquad (3.3)$$

where (M_d) is the nominal stock of dominant money and (γ) is the ratio of dominant money to private money desired by consumers. If the existence of the instant repurchase clause causes the private money producers to hold some dominant money reserves, equation 3.3 overstates the equilibrium stock of private money. This overstatement results from the removal of some dominant money from the community's use whenever the private money producers sell their own product. In this case the equilibrium stock of private money is given by

$$M_p = \frac{M_d}{(\gamma + \rho)} \qquad (3.4)$$

where (ρ) is the ratio of dominant money reserves to private money sales desired by the private money producers.[8]

The effect of the repurchase clause on net wealth produced

Given the instant repurchase clause, the private money producer can no longer sell his money outright, but now has a restriction placed on his actions. Whereas before he had, of course, the option to repurchase his money when he so desired, now he must repurchase his money whenever the holder of it so desires. This restriction, at best, will leave the wealth of the private money producers unaffected and, at the worst, will wipe out the entire gain from the sales of private money. Hence, 3.2 above represents the upper bound to the change in the net wealth of the private money producers. Since a zero change in wealth represents the worst the private money producer can do—if he were to do worse he would not enter into the production and sale of private money—the following bounds are established for the change in wealth of the private money producers:

$$0 \leqslant \Delta w \leqslant \frac{M_p}{P}. \tag{3.5}$$

Since the change in the wealth of the private money producers is equal to the change in the community's net wealth, we need a more exact statement if we are to succeed in determining the extent that private money represents net wealth. Careful consideration of the nature of the instant repurchase clause will enable us to measure the change in wealth more precisely. This clause forces the private money producers to be ready at all times to redeem their money with dominant money. If the goods purchased by them cannot be exchanged for dominant money instantly and at no cost, the private money producers will have to hold some inventories of dominant money.[9] These inventories serve as buffers against unexpected exercises of the instant repurchase clause. The bigger these inventories, the smaller the quantity of nonmonetary goods the private money producer is able to acquire for his use by selling his product because his budget constraint is:

$$\frac{M_p}{P} - \Delta \frac{M_d}{P} = \Delta \frac{y}{r} \tag{3.6}$$

where (ΔM_d) is the nominal quantity of dominant money held as inventory.

Let us now make allowance for the acquisition of some dominant money for use as a reserve against the possibility of runs of repurchases by the holders of private money. A simple noting of the wealth transfers shows that (1) the purchasers of privately produced money gained privately produced money and paid for it partly with dominant money and partly with real wealth (the first term in equation 3.7 below), whereas (2) the producers of private money lost nothing while gaining the above mentioned dominant money and real wealth (the second term in 3.7 below):

$$\Delta w = \left(\frac{M_p}{P} - \Delta \frac{M_d}{P} - \Delta \frac{y}{r} \right) + \left(\Delta \frac{M_d}{P} + \Delta \frac{y}{r} \right) = \frac{M_p}{P} \tag{3.7}$$

where

$$\Delta \frac{M_d}{P} = \rho \frac{M_p}{P} \tag{3.8}$$

and

$$\frac{M_p}{P} = \Delta \frac{y}{r} + \Delta \frac{M_d}{P}. \tag{3.9}$$

Acceptance of equation 3.7 as the final result would lead to the conclusion that the change in wealth in this case is identical with the one that occurs in the case of a sale of fiat money or the one that results from the sale of private money not subject to the repurchase clause (equation 3.2): this clause would have to be considered costless to the producers of private money. However, this is not the case. Looking at these inventories with the eyes of the producers,[10] we find the cost of holding them is simply the cost of being in this particular business: the producers are forced by the instant repurchase clause to forego income yielded by real assets they would have purchased in the absence of this clause. Thus the capital cost of the instant repurchase clause to the money producers is the capitalized value of the income foregone; it is equal to the value of the capital goods that could have been held if they did not have to hold dominant money reserves. Therefore, the change in net wealth is not as expressed in 3.7 but instead is

$$\Delta w = \left\{ \frac{M_p}{P} - \Delta \frac{M_d}{P} - \Delta \frac{y}{r} \right\} + \left\{ \Delta \frac{y}{r} + \left(\Delta \frac{M_d}{P} - \frac{Y_f}{Pr} \right) \right\} \tag{3.10}$$

where (Y_f) is the money income foregone by the private money producers. We put the last two terms in this equation in parentheses as a reminder that these two terms precisely offset each other, since the capitalized value of income foregone as a result of holding dominant money inventories is precisely equal to the value of these inventories.[11] It might be illuminating now and it shall prove most helpful in our subsequent discussion to present the content of equation 3.10 in terms of accounting identities so familiar to all economists as shown in Table 3.1.

Although equation 3.10 is useful because it shows all the changes in income flows and in the capitalized value of these flows that occur as a result of the production and sale of private money, many terms within this equation offset each other and hence the equation may be more simply stated as follows:

$$\Delta w = \frac{M_p}{P} - \frac{M_d}{P}. \tag{3.11}$$

The change in the stock of money and hence, in the net wealth of the

Table 3.1 Changes in balance sheets: Equation 3.10

Rest of the economy		Private money producer	
Assets	Liabilities	Assets	Liabilities
$-\Delta\dfrac{M_d}{P}$	(no change)	$+\Delta\dfrac{M_d}{P}$	$+\dfrac{Y_f}{rP}$
$-\Delta\dfrac{y^*}{r}$		$+\Delta\dfrac{y}{r}$	
$+\dfrac{M_p}{P}$	Net Worth (no change)		Net Worth $+\Delta w$

* Note that if the real assets the community pays to the private money producer are transferred to him physically, there is a negative change on the asset side of the Rest's T-account. Should the banker be satisfied with a promise to receive the real income that these real assets yield while leaving the physical possession of them undisturbed, this item would shift to the liability side of the Rest's T-account and change sign. In equation 3.10 the third term would not then read $(-\Delta\frac{y}{r})$; it would read $+(-\Delta\frac{y}{r})$.

community is precisely equal to the total sales of private money minus the decrease in the stock of the dominant money outstanding. Most important, we conclude that the change in the net wealth of the community is precisely equal to the value of sales of private money minus the resource cost of producing this money: that private money is an asset that is not offset by a debt. If commercial banking as the creator of demand deposits were subject to no other restrictions than the one represented by the instant repurchase clause that we imposed on the private money producers in this section of the chapter, we could rest our argument. However, the operations of banks are more complex, and in the next section this complexity will be given attention. It will be discovered that it has no effect whatever on the conclusions reached here for the general type of "private money producer".

Effect of changes in the relative price of private money

Up to this point all our discussions of effects of changes in the relative price of money have been concerned with only one type of money at a time. However, we are now considering a system containing both a dominant (fiat) money and a general type of private money. Will this change in the composition of the money supply affect the conclusions reached earlier? Specifically, will the existence of the repurchase clause cause the private money producers to be affected by changes in the value of money in a way that offsets the wealth effect of changes in the price of money? Consider an increase in the price of money.[12] Such a change will make the holders of all money, dominant or private, better off because it increases the exchange value of their holdings of money. But, the non-holders of money are no worse off because all the prices they face (including the price of the service yielded by money), and the stocks of assets they hold, remain the same. Thus, as far as the non-holders are concerned, everything remains the same. We believe we have proven this earlier; however, merely as an aid to memory let us remind ourselves that a non-holder and a potential purchaser of money is indifferent to the change in the price of money in terms of other commodities because the power of money to purchase other commodities in turn changes *pari passu*. Thus, as far as the non-holders are concerned, all opportunities that were available to them before the price change are still available; however, the holders of money now have a larger set of opportunities available. Therefore, neglecting any possible effect on the private money producers, the community's net wealth has increased. How will the increase in the value of money affect the private money producer? For simplicity let us assume that the private money producers as producers are non-holders of money except, of course, for the dominant money reserves. They can be affected only if the change in the price of money changes the quantity of inventories of dominant money that must be held against possible runs of repurchases. But, since we are assuming provisionally (*cf.* note 12) that a change in the price of all money does not change the relative usefulness of private and dominant money, the level of inventories of dominant money that must be held remains unchanged; therefore, the producers of private money will be unaffected by a change in the price of money. Therefore, we conclude that the fact that private money must be sold with a repurchase clause in no way affects the conclusion reached (in our book) that changes in the price of money—now including the privately produced money—result in proportionate changes in the monetary wealth and in less than proportionate changes in the total wealth of the community.

Bank money

The concept of the private money producer was used as an expository device so that we could abstract from many of the complex modes of operation of commercial banking, and demonstrate that privately produced money is a part of the net wealth of the community. As is true of every simplification, the concept of the private money producer is not fully adequate. To make him viable in the face of changes in the price of money, we must introduce refinements into his mode of operation. We shall discover that these refinements are precisely those that are employed by the commercial banking system. After we have finished, it will be obvious that by describing a viable private money producer we are, simultaneously, describing commercial banks. We shall also show that the refinements introduced do not affect in any manner the basic conclusions reached in the preceding section: in particular, that privately produced money is a part of the net wealth of the community and that changes in the price of this money change the net wealth of the community.

In what follows we shall first discuss the operating refinements that must be introduced to make private money producers viable and that, simultaneously, make their behaviour indistinguishable from that of commercial banks. Second, we shall discuss the reasons that lead commercial banks to differentiate their product from a competing product, from fiat money, and cause them to give it the form of demand deposits. Finally, we show that some additional restraints that the government imposes on commercial banks do not affect the conclusions reached previously; that their sole effect is to circumscribe more restrictively than would otherwise be the case the size of the output of the commercial banks and to force them to sell their product only to customers who meet government approval.

OPERATING REFINEMENTS NECESSARY TO PROTECT PRIVATE MONEY PRODUCERS FROM BANKRUPTCY

Solvency requirement
We have already seen that the instant repurchase clause requires the producers of private money to hold inventories of dominant money. However, the repurchase clause—regardless of whether it must be satisfied instantly or whether the producer is given time to convert some of his income-earning assets into dominant money to satisfy it—has another consequence that we have ignored until now. In a world in which there is not perfect certainty there is always a possibility, however remote, that *all* customers of the private money producer will exercise the repurchase clause. The only defence the private money producer or a commercial bank has against such a possibility is to remain solvent at all times. Thus the solvency requirement under which commercial banks operate is not an independent restriction, additional to the repurchase clause, but merely one implication of it. The question then arises: Does the existence of the solvency requirement affect our measure of the change in wealth resulting from the production of bank money? If a private money producer, a commercial banker, wishers to consume more than the income yielded by the wealth he purchased by selling his output of private money (Δ_r^y in equation 3.7 and following), he may not do

so by selling these assets if such a sale would result in insolvency.[13] On the surface, a requirement that prevents the money producers from disposing of the wealth obtained from the sale of money would seem to be a burdensome one. However, as long as the money producers have access to the capital market they can, if they desire, consume or invest the capitalized value of the income streams they purchased simply by selling their titles to these income streams.[14] Whereas an unrestricted private producer of money could sell the capital goods he owns and dispose of the proceeds as he sees fit, the commercial banker subject to the solvency requirement may simply sell his titles to the incomes yielded by these goods and thus may also dispose of the proceeds as he may see fit. Hence, the solvency restriction cannot affect our conclusion that commercial banks, as private money producers, contribute to the wealth of the community by the amount specified in equation 3.11.[15]

Bank money must be sold for financial assets
As we have seen, the repurchase clause contains in itself the implication of the solvency requirement; the solvency requirement, in turn, contains in itself the need for the banks to purchase not real but financial assets. That this is the case can be most easily shown by considering the effect of a price change on the solvency of the private money producer discussed in the previous section who, by virtue of our provisional assumption, was said to buy real wealth (Δ_r^y in equations 3.2 and 3.10). Suppose that the price of money increases. Such an increase will cause the value of the dominant money reserves, plus the non-monetary wealth held, to become smaller than the value of the stock of private money outstanding. Thus, a change in the price of money will cause the private money producer to become insolvent (in the technical meaning of the word specified above). The only way of escaping this risk is to sell private money not for titles to income fixed in real terms but for titles to income fixed in money terms: to sell private money for *financial assets*. This is precisely the manner in which the actual private money producers, commercial banks, conduct their business. They sell their product, bank money, either "for cash" or "on an instalment plan"; they sell it either for dominant money or for a bond executed by the purchaser and promising to the bank a stream of income fixed in money terms. Once the private money producers, commercial banks, proceed in this manner, the threat to their solvency inherent in the risk of a change in the price of money (change in the general price level) is overcome. The market value of these financial assets changes proportionately with, and therefore remains equal to, the market value of the private money produced and sold. But then equation 3.10 does not express the behaviour of a private money producer who is viable in the face of price changes; it must be

replaced with its modified version that reads

$$\Delta \frac{W}{P} = \left\{\frac{M_p}{P} - \Delta \frac{M_d}{P} - \Delta \frac{Y}{rP}\right\} + \left\{\Delta \frac{Y}{rP} + \left(\Delta \frac{M_d}{P} - \frac{Y_f}{rP}\right)\right\} = \frac{M_p}{P} - \Delta \frac{M_d}{P}$$

$$(3.12)$$

where all the variables are the same as in equation 3.10, except that capital letters now denote variables that are fixed in money terms.

It might again prove illuminating to present the revised equation 3.12 in terms of the accounting identities with which economists are so familiar as is done in Table 3.2.

What are the economic consequences of this necessity to purchase financial assets? In the preceding section dealing with the private money producer, we—arbitrarily and for simplicity—limited ourselves to the simplifying assumption that he buys only streams of income fixed in real terms. But surely our conclusions would not change if, after the sale of his money for real wealth, the private money producer decided to rearrange his portfolio and exchanged some of it for financial assets. But the our conclusions would also not change if the private money producer sold his money for financial assets in the first place. Therefore, the only difference that might affect the conclusions reached earlier may be found in the fact that a commercial bank has to do what the private money producer was assumed to be free to do. Does *this* difference affect our conclusions? As long as the commercial banker has access to the capital market, he may hold exclusively financial assets in order to remain solvent and then may enter the capital market and sell the titles to the income streams yielded by these assets for sources of income streams

Table 3.2 *Changes in balance sheets: Equation 3.12*

Rest of the economy		Bankers	
Assets	Liabilities	Assets	Liabilities
$-\Delta \dfrac{M_d}{P}$		$+\Delta \dfrac{M_d}{P}$	$+\dfrac{Y_f}{rP}$
	$+\Delta \dfrac{Y^*}{rP}$	$+\Delta \dfrac{Y}{rP}$	
	Net Worth		Net Worth
$+\dfrac{M_p}{P}$	(no change)		$+\Delta \dfrac{W}{P}$

Note: * For the position of this item, c.f. the note to Table 3.1.

requirement has not changed the relative prices of assets, every opportunity that was available to the banker is still available to him. Therefore,
this second consequence of the solvency requirement will also not affect
the change in wealth that occurs when we introduce private money; the
change in the community's net wealth will still be measured by the sales
of private money minus the private money producers' holdings of
dominant money reserves.

Sale of money for financial assets redistributes the price risk
We have seen that the repurchase clause forces the banks to satisfy the
solvency requirement; the solvency requirement forces the banks to sell
their product for financial assets; finally, the necessity to purchase
financial assets results, in turn, in a redistribution of the risk inherent in
the possibility of a change in the price of money. The shift from equation
3.10 to equation 3.12 has no immediate economic consequences whatever; the change in wealth that either one of these equations will show as
a result of private money production will be identical. The sole difference
between these two equations is to be found in the manner in which they
allocate susceptibility to some future possible price change among the
various sectors of the economy: [16]

1. A money producer sells his product (commodity money or fiat money)
for real wealth. There is, subsequently, a decline in the price of money:
   a. the current owner of money is made worse off;
   b. the rest of the community (including the producer of money) is,
   unaffected.
2. A private money producer sells his product for financial assets. There
is, subsequently, a decline in the price of money:
   a. the current owner of privately produced money is, again, worse off;
   b. the rest of the community as a whole is, again, unaffected.
   However, the sale of money for financial assets has the consequences
   that there are now additional contracts specified in money terms:
   (1) the original purchaser of private money is committed to pay to
   the banker a stream of income fixed in money terms; the fall in the
   price of money makes him better off;
   (2) the private money producer, who is receiving this income flow in
   money terms is, of course, worse off.

The two redistributive effects described in 2b(1) and 2b(2) will manifest
themselves in offsetting changes in the new wealth (accounting term, net
worth) of the non-banking sector and the banking sector, the former
gaining precisely what the latter is losing. However, the non-banking
sector also contains the current owners of the product of the banking

sector, bank money, and on this wealth it suffers a loss described above by the 2a effect, identical to that described by 1a effect. Since the value of private money is bigger than the value of financial liabilities, the non-banking sector is a net loser; its net wealth (net worth) falls. Since the net wealth of both the banking sector and the non-banking sector falls, obviously the total wealth of the community falls. The net amount of the loss is measured, since the 2b(1) and the 2b(2) effects offset each other, by the 2a effect. Note that this result conforms fully with the conclusions reached in our book (in the section "Effect of Changes in Relative Prices of Money on Wealth") and demonstrates again that the operating refinements introduced into the behaviour of the private money producer do not affect the main analysis of his effect on the net wealth of the community.[17]

The two refinements just discussed, the solvency requirement and the sale for financial assets requirement, leave completely unaffected our analytical conclusion that privately produced money net of reserves is, like fiat and commodity money, net wealth of the community. At the same time, the introduction of these two requirements makes the private producer fully viable in the sense that there is now no microeconomic or macroeconomic mechanism that would prevent his *continuous* economic existence.[18] Also, the introduction of the two requirements so modifies the mode of operation of the private money producer that it makes him indistinguishable from a commercial banker. Thus all the conclusions reached about commodity money production, fiat money production, and private money production also apply to the production of bank money. This money may be—and sometimes is—physically indistinguishable from fiat money; it may be bank notes. However, like many other producers, banks find it profitable to differentiate their product from the competing product.

Product differentiation: demand deposits

In our discussion of the determinants of the equilibrium stock of private money, we simply assumed that the two types of money, dominant money and privately produced money, are not perfect substitutes for each other. Although both are media of exchange we assumed that some exchanges can be more conveniently undertaken by the use of one or the other. Given this, and given the requirements that both be convertible at par, the conclusion followed that there is some proportion of both upon the attainment of which the community will be indifferent (on the margin, of course) between the holding of either. We have also seen that this proportion determines the capacity of the private money producers to produce and sell private money (equation 3.4); hence, it also determines the size of the income streams that the producers of private money will be able to exchange for their output of this money. However, none of the discussion or of the conclusions reached depends on the *form* of private money. Hence, the more attractive the private money producers make their own product, the bigger will be the sales of it (the smaller will be the (γ) in equation 3.4) and the bigger the gain of the producers. Suppose that to make their product more attractive, these private money producers introduce a number of innovations:

(1) Their product is insured against loss or theft *from the current owner* until he decides to use it and signifies so by signing it.

(2) Their product is made in one single all-comprehensive denomination in that the current owner determines the denomination at the time of use simply by writing out any amount he chooses.

(3) Their product is insured against loss or theft *from the purchaser* in that it is made property only of the buyer whose name is written on the note itself.

(4) Their product is such that it, automatically, gives to the current owner of it evidence that he has paid his bills and thus protection against a dishonest purchaser of private money (and seller of some other wealth).

(5) Their product depends for its existence on record-keeping by the private money producer, which may be made available to the purchaser free of charge or for, a nominal charge.

All these items will make the product of private money producers distinctly superior to the dominant money, at least in some uses. Thus, such extra features tend to increase the equilibrium stock of private money by decreasing the proportion of their money holdings consumers desire to hold as dominant money; they increase the demand for the banker's product.

Clearly, none of these extra features of private money affects our measure of the change in wealth resulting from the introduction of this money, even though it may affect—indeed, is designed to affect—the absolute magnitude of the change. The change in net wealth of the community will still be the value of sales of private money minus the holdings of the dominant money reserves. But surely the reader must have noticed that when we were describing the extra features designed to increase the attractiveness of private money, we were simply describing the characteristics of demand deposits. Thus, whatever we have said in the preceding sections about private money also applies to the special type of money that becomes divorced from any physical substance and becomes a mere accounting entry—a demand deposit.

Public control of the banking industry

We have shown in the fiat money section that, because of the fact that the real income yielded by money is independent of the stuff money is made of, this income is independent of the value of resources utilized to produce money. This makes production of substitutes for commodity money advantageous. We have also shown that competitive production of resource-cheap substitutes for commodity money is impossible because competitive producers, by equating marginal costs to marginal revenue, would so increase the output of the substitute as to reduce its value close to zero and convert the substitute into commodity money. By doing this, they would destroy the ability of the money substitute to serve as money because, with value so low, huge quantities would be required to facilitate an average-valued transaction. By destroying the usefulness of money substitutes the producers would, of course, simultaneously destroy themselves. A competitive zero-cost money industry is suicidal. If commercial banking producing demand deposits is a competitive private money industry, it is also suicidal[19] and public control of it is essential if a decision is made to permit its existence and utilize it as a tool of producing money other than fiat money. However, this point is a complex one and is left for further discussion.

Public control of the private money industry takes numerous forms: restrictions on entry into the industry; prohibition of interest payments to the customers of this industry; requirement that a part of the proceeds of the sale of private money be lent interest-free to the central bank (reserve requirements on demand deposits); requirement that a part of the funds borrowed by the private money producers be lent interest-free to the central bank (reserve requirements on time deposits); and, finally, a myriad of rules that specify (a) to whom the private money producer may sell his product on credit (from whom he may purchase financial assets), and (b) the conditions of the credit extended, especially the duration of it; these rules are usually summarized in the "short-term, *bona fide*, commercial paper" principle.

The sole issue that we are interested in here is whether privately produced money is net wealth and whether our measure of the contribution of this money to net wealth is the correct one. It is obvious that these tools of public control of the private money industry do not affect this issue any more than do the rules restricting the output and sale of, say, weapons, affect the decision that weapons are net wealth. In its end effect, public control of the private money industry restricts the output of this industry and could—in this purely analytical context—as well be replaced by a simple statement of the quantity of output of the private money industry that the producer of the dominant money will permit—a statement such as the one we applied to our otherwise unrestricted private money producer discussed in connection with equation 3.1. The sole exception is the reserve requirement that, instead of producing a specific limit on output, makes this limit a function of the amount of the dominant money that the private producers are able to attract. In equation 3.4 we have seen that the size of the output of the private money producer depends on the size of the reserves that he has to hold to make himself able to satisfy the instant repurchase clause. The minimum reserve requirement simply augments the ratio ρ used in that equation. While the absolute amount of wealth the private money producer is able to produce becomes smaller, the economic analysis of private money presented in this chapter remains completely unaffected.

CONCLUSION

In the first section of this chapter we have shown that private money producers are indistinguishable from the producers of fiat money discussed earlier; they add in precisely the same way to the net wealth of the community. The imposition of the repurchase clause and the prohibition of interest payments do furnish an automatic economic mechanism restricting the output of these private money producers that is not imposed on the fiat money producer. Yet, as far as the changes in wealth are concerned, the imposition of the repurchase clause does not affect qualitatively the conclusions reached. As in the case of the commodity money producer (but to a smaller extent), this clause makes the net addition to net wealth supplied by the private money producers smaller because it forces an expenditure of resources in the production of money. The commodity money producer has to withdraw from other uses the resources necessary to produce the money commodity; the private producer of money has to withdraw from other uses the dominant money inventories. The key question as to whether private money net of reserves of dominant money is a part of net wealth, is possible to answer in the affirmative.

In the next section we supplemented the result obtained by imposing on the private money producer all the additional restraints, and modes of operation resulting from these restraints, that govern the behaviour of private commercial banks producing demand deposits: the minimum reserve requirement, the solvency requirement, and the necessity of selling bank money for financial assets. We have shown that none of these affects the conclusion reached in the preceding section that covered private money producers. But then the conclusion is inescapable that commercial banks, insofar as they are producing a medium of exchange called demand deposits, *are* private money producers. Thus, all the conclusions that we reached are applicable not only to the abstraction, called by us "private money producers," but also to the phenomenon very much in evidence in the world around us, the producers[20] of demand deposits called commercial banks. These banks sell their product, demand deposits, to their customers for financial assets, for titles to streams of incomes that, conceptually, may be permanent but that, in reality, happen to be finite. If they do so, these sales of their product on an instalment plan give rise to what is in the literature called "derivative deposits." Of course, all buyers of these demand deposits have a choice of buying them for the present capitalized value of such streams of future incomes; they have a choice of buying them for cash. If they do so, these sales give rise to what is in the literature called "primary deposits." In both cases, the repurchase clause and its logical consequence, the solvency requirement, create the purely superficial impression that we are facing a loan of resources and a debt rather than an exchange of two pieces of wealth accompanied by special contractual arrangements— arrangements, we might add, that are not typical in the case of transactions involving non-monetary wealth but not unheard of either. A repurchase clause is, occasionally, attached to contracts involving a sale of non-monetary wealth.

NOTES

1. The same point may be made in a somewhat different way. We have seen that commodity money is a part of wealth, regardless of whether it has or does not have some other non-monetary use. Suppose that it has no non-monetary use. Why should the wealth of society change if someone would, overnight, replace this commodity money with fiat money? Wealth would *not* change. Suppose that the money commodity has some other use and that someone, again, replaces this commodity money with fiat money. As far as the services of money are concerned, the community is getting no less income than before, and it is now able to rechannel the money commodity that has some other use to this use: it must be better off.
2. James Tobin, "Money and Economic Growth," *Econometrica*, 33 (October, 1965), p. 676.
3. At times, the fiat money producer gives the holders of fiat money the right to demand a specific quantity of another commodity; e.g., gold. A slight modification of the results obtained in this chapter is then needed. The nature of these modifications will become obvious in the next chapter [of our book].
4. James Tobin, "Commercial Banks as Creators of 'Money'," in Dean Carson (ed.), *Banking and Monetary Studies* (Homewood, Ill.: Irwin, 1963), p. 415.
5. Since our problem is purely analytical, we need not inquire why the monopolistic producer of fiat money should be willing to share his monopoly. The reasons are complex. Partly they are historical: actually, the banks existed before the appearance of the fiat money producers who found it convenient to make use of them, perhaps to hide their innovation from the

public eye. Also, the monopolists—as we have seen—must determine the quantity of money, and these private money producers may be a very convenient tool for changing this quantity rapidly.

6. We stress the resource cost of production of physical units of private money because, as we shall see in the discussion of the effect of the repurchase clause, it is possible for the community to impose a resource cost on the private money producer that is not connected with the production of physical units of private money.

7. We shall discuss the reasons for this later in the chapter.

8. For a thorough discussion of the determinants of the equilibrium stock of a reserve money, see Milton Friedman and Anna Jackson Schwartz, *A Monetary History of the United States, 1867–1960* (Princeton, NJ: Princeton University Press, 1964), pp. 784–789.

9. The amount of reserves held may be chosen so that expected returns from the capital held are maximized subject to the repurchase clause. This would require some idea of the distribution of repurchases and knowledge of the cost of having to convert assets into dominant money on short notice.

10. Looking at these inventories with the eyes of the community as a whole, we find that the income the community would receive from the use of these inventories if they served as money is lost; either way, the existence of the repurchase clause introduces an additional cost of production and sale of private money. A third way of stating the *same thing* is directly related to the measurement of wealth. The producers acquire $\Delta y/r$; in the absence of the repurchase clause, they could use this wealth with the same efficiency as the original owners. With the repurchase clause, they have a choice either of using this wealth less efficiently by having it all the time in their physical possession and in instantly usable form or of holding inventories of dominant money. In the first case, the repurchase clause would make *all* of the wealth purchased by the private money producers less productive; in the second case, a part of the total is devoted to the purchases of inventories and the remainder to purchases of real wealth that can then be used at full efficiency. On the margin, these two alternative ways of accomplishing the same purpose, the satisfaction of the repurchase clause, should be equally costly; either measures the economic cost of the repurchase clause and the determination of total wealth that results from its existence.

11. The reader may wonder whether we are saying that all inventories of all wealth should be removed from the wealth equation. We are not. All that we are doing is to guard against double counting. Given the repurchase clause and the necessity to hold inventories resulting from it, the community has now two alternatives: either it can gain the use of the privately produced money and lose the use of the dominant money, or it can give up the use of the privately produced money and gain the use of the dominant money inventories. It cannot do both.

12. We now assume, provisionally, that the change does not change public demand for private money; we are assuming the quantity demanded to be constant. In the next section of this chapter we shall amend the private producer's mode of operation by making him buy not real but financial assets. Only then shall we dare to remove the constant demand assumption. However, the present discussion is still useful, since its conclusions will be shown to remain unaffected by any subsequent complications.

13. This last qualifying phrase has been added to make the statement accurate

even in cases in which the private money producer allowed the income (y) to accumulate as an increment to his initial holdings of $\Delta(y/r)$. A sale of this accumulation—precisely as a continuous consumption of it—cannot affect the solvency of the firm producing private money.

14. Economically, this means that they can divest themselves, to any desired extent, of the business of the production of private money and use the proceeds to enter into the production of anything else or consume the proceeds.

15. The reader may wonder whether instead of disposing of the economic relevance of the solvency restriction, we did not merely dispose of the restriction by selling it to somebody else. This is not the case. The statement that an owner must remain solvent is another way of saying that he cannot consume his principal without selling it. But most—perhaps all—nonmonetary wealth today is of such a nature. The owners of this wealth cannot consume the principal directly; they also *must* sell first to somebody who wants to hold the wealth only for the income it yields, and *then* they may consume the proceeds. A prime exception to this rule would be the Knightian perennial "that grows at a constant (geometric) rate, except as [its] tissue is cut away for consumption." (Frank H. Knight, "Diminishing Returns from Investment," *Journal of Political Economy*, LII (March, 1944), p. 30.) (The original word in brackets is "new." However, since Knight explicitly permits disinvestment to occur, this must be a slip of the tongue.)

16. We say deliberately "among sectors," since the necessity to engage in this hedging operation is not likely to affect the distribution of risk among persons. The price risk preferrers will simply move now into the sectors that assume the price risks; the price risk averters will move out of it.

17. We might point out that if we forget the 2a effect and concentrate only on the two offsetting 2b(1) and 2b(2) effects, or if we—as is more frequent—forget the 2b(2) effect and concentrate on the partly offsetting 2a effect and 2b(1) effect, we are likely to conclude that we have found support for the hypothesis that money is but an asset of some and a liability of others and that the absolute amount of them cannot affect the wealth of the community. Both conclusions are the essence of the *New View* to which we referred at the beginning of this chapter. Cf., e.g., Joseph W. Conrad, "The Causes and Consequences of Inflation," Commission on Money and Credit, *Inflation, Growth and Employment* (Englewood Cliffs, N.J.: Prentice Hall, 1964), p. 135; George L. Bach and Albert K. Ando, "The Redistributional Effects of Inflation," *Review of Economics and Statistics*, XXXIX (February, 1957), pp. 1–13; Don Patinkin, *Money, Interest and Prices*, 2nd ed. (New York: Harper & Row, 1965), pp. 296–7; finally, as a demonstration of strict justice, Boris P. Pesek, "A Comparison of the Distributional Effects of Inflation and Taxation," *American Economic Review*, L (March, 1960), pp. 147–53.

18. We stress the word "continuous." Certain short-run problems that can be surmounted by purchases of financial assets of suitable maturities are discussed further in our book.

19. Lest the impression is gain that this terse summary conflicts with equation 3.4 that yields an *equilibrium* output of private money other than zero, let us point out that even that equation was arrived at on the basis of the stated assumption that the private money producer is prohibited from payment of interest to the purchasers of private money.

20. We use persistently the terms "to produce money" and "producers of money"; we avoid studiously the terms "to create money" and "creators of money." "The producer" is a *terminus technicus* of value theory; "the creator" has become the weasel term of monetary theory. There it is used both by those who believe that banks produce money and by those who assert that banks are merely intermediaries incapable of producing net wealth.

4 Modern Bank Deposits and the Theory of Optimum Undefined Money*

Monetary theory is in a crisis which, given vested interests in accumulated research, probably only fresh blood drawn from other branches of economics can cure by returning it to the mainstream of economics. Does this sound melodramatic? Let me offer a few examples:

(1) Demand and supply analysis is the cornerstone of theoretical and empirical work in economics. Monetary theorists merely pretend its use. Numerous studies offered by prominent monetary theorists (see lists of "Representative Demand Equations" in Havrilensky and Boorman (1978: pp. 186 and 190) and Patinkin (1965: pp. 656–7)) claim to yield one single demand for money function for periods as long as 1892–1960, 1900–1958, ... Would any other branch of economics entertain for a second the notion that in the case of any other asset, tastes, preferences, technology and economic organization have remained constant during such long periods to enable it to obtain *one* demand function? In fact, all known "demands" for money functions are merely connections—trend lines, if you please—of intersections of innumerable demand and supply functions that have existed during the periods covered.

This is reinforced by the fact that according to well-established econometric theory, demand and supply functions may only be obtained simultaneously, after careful handling of the identification problem (Tintner 1962: Chapter 6). Yet, none of the "demand" for money functions has been obtained by the use of the supply function which only now the *New View* has started to develop, theoretically.

(2) Before the work on the demand and supply functions may even start, the product which they cover must be specified. Monetary theorists consider as co-equal the concepts of money M_1–M_5 (*Federal Reserve Bulletin*, Feb. 1978: A-14). The two products entering M_1 (currency and

---

* From: Maurice B. Ballabon (ed.) *Economic Perspectives*.

demand deposits) have one key theoretically predicted and empirically confirmed characteristic: negative interest elasticities of demand. In M_2-M_5 more and more products are added (various time deposits) with the opposite key characteristic.

Thus, the functions dealing with M_2-M_5 yield "elasticities" of demand—so hotly debated because so crucial for policy-making—that are nothing more than *haphazard* averages of two elasticities with opposite signs, determined by rapidly changing weights attached to them: e.g., only from 1950 to 1977 the ratio of assets with positive (time deposits, in M_2) and negative elasticities has exploded from \$59/\$117 to \$542/\$344 (*Federal Reserve Bulletin*, July 1956: p. 722 and Feb. 1978: A-14).

Can one visualize any other branch of economics that would calculate and base its policy recommendations on a demand elasticity of a product that is, in fact, a mix containing explosively changing proportions of one normal and one inferior good?

(3) Even the very empirical "evidence" used to calculate elasticity of demand is of most dubious value, e.g., the sound economic principle that money printed but not issued or retired by the monetary authority is not money has been converted by modern monetary theory into the strange proposition that the Federal Government—an economic giant now completely out of the money-production business—is the only economic organization known to man able to hold no working money balances (*Federal Reserve Bulletin*, April 1978: A-14, footnote 1). Every dollar it receives is, consequently, subtracted from the measured stock of money M_1-M_5.

Suppose that Washington would tomorrow reverse the historical trend (strongly affecting measured "demand") and get rid of its huge defence and welfare budgets by farming them out to the General Motors and to state and local governments, and by transferring to them the taxes and working balances needed for the performances of these tasks. The measured stock of money would increase sharply, start to fluctuate differently, and so affect all the above "demand" functions. Or, suppose that all businesses would get nationalized. Measured business working balances would drop to zero, the measured stock of M_1 would drop by two-thirds.

How is such utter confusion possible? All other branches of economics are fortunate in having countervailing constituencies (labour, management, consumers) which make a *total* divorce from reality impossible. Monetary theory is deprived of this. The consuming public is overawed by the carefully cultivated *mystique* of banking, and the bankers are ineffective because they are offering two sharply different products and thus have conflicting interests.

In this chapter I shall focus on one of the above major problems: the specification of the product which is the subject of monetary theory, money. As a vehicle for my analysis I shall take "the theory of optimum money" because it lends itself best for what I want to show, and also because it is extremely relevant. It is now being converted into reality by all bank regulatory bodies that are permitting more and more of effortless (electronic) transfers from one type of deposit to another. I shall show that the theory of optimum money is wrong and will cause substantial harm.

OPTIMUM MONEY

Monetary theorists unanimously agree that money that is produced at zero cost should be subjected to the familiar competitive solution of price theory: if it costs nothing to produce, it should cost nothing to hold. In the words of Don Patinkin (1972: p. 227) " ... the Golden Rule in the case of money states that ... the optimum real quantity of money is that which renders its marginal utility equal to zero—which, under the present assumptions, is also the marginal costs to society of producing real outside-money balances. This satiety level of balances can be assumed to be achieved when the alternative cost of holding money, as measured by the money rate of interest, i, is also zero."

Here, the competitive rule $MC = MR = P$ is handled as if it were price theory's Ten Commandments rolled into one, and "satiation" its Golden Fleece. Price theory is more complex than that. Any student of public utilities with $MC < AC$ (shared by some monies) will set aside the former rule and reach for a different one. And, any student of assets with $MC = 0$ (shared by some monies) that perform a service *only* when held short of satiation (nobility titles, Nobel Prizes, gems) will set aside both rules: "When everyone is somebody, nobody is anybody." Similarly, ancient wisdom warns that when everyone is satiated with money, nobody holds any. Can we escape this fate by applying the above rules indirectly (get zero cost of holding money) while we still don't dare to apply them directly (get zero cost of acquiring money)? With interest rate $i > 0$, can we achieve holding cost $Pi = 0$ and purchasing power $P > 0$?

ANALYTICAL FRAMEWORK FOR THE MEASUREMENT OF MONIES

Irving Fisher (1911: p. 53) has measured "the moneyness" of monies by *the average quantity* V of the transaction service that each unit renders:

$$M_1 V_1 + M_2 V_2 + ... + M_n V_n = P(T_1 + T_2 + ... + T_n). \qquad (1)$$

Let me rewrite this equation. If we multiply the left side of this equation by V_i/V_i (the selection of *numeraire* such as M_i for the purposes of aggregation is always arbitrary) we get

$$V_i(M_1 V_1/V_i + \ldots + M_i + \ldots + M_n V_n/V_i) = PT \qquad (2)$$

where the velocity ratios represent the quantity-of-transaction-services weights. Equation 1 may be restated as

$$(V_i) (\sum_1^n M_F) = PT, \qquad (3)$$

where $\sum_1^n M_F$ equals the sum in the parentheses of equation 2.

This summation[1] represents the stock of money as measured according to the gospel of Fisher's Quantity Theory of Money.

In the book that I published with Thomas R. Saving (1967: p. 289) "the moneyness" of money is measured *by the market value* of the transaction service that each unit renders. Write

$$r_i + m_i + i_i \equiv y_e, \qquad (4)$$

where r_i denotes all real incomes that an asset also serving as money may yield (such as ornamental value of silver), m_i the value of the transaction service, i_i the explicit interest income, and y_e the equilibrium level of income yield by each unit of assets A_i ($i = 1, 2, \ldots, n$) that has a real market value equal to that of one unit of nominal money. The real value of the transaction service m_i is, of course, simply the product of the quantity of this real service per unit of money (equation 1) and of the price p_i that the market attaches to a unit of this service:

$$(T_i/M_i)p_i \equiv (V_i/P)p_i \equiv m_i. \qquad (5)$$

The discounted present values of the income streams r_i and m_i measure the values of the final or intermediate services, and the contribution of these assets (or, tautologically, of the factors of production supplying these assets) to the net (aggregate) wealth of the society by use (or, tautologically, by origin).[2]

The stock of money wealth—according to the gospel of A. C. Pigou's Cambridge version of the Quantity Theory of Money or of the consumption-wealth theorists—is measured by

$$\sum_1^n M_{PS}/P = \sum_1^n A_i(m_i/r_e) \qquad (6)$$

(where r_e is the equilibrium interest rate that evaluates the present value of the real income stream m_i). Here, Fisher's quantity-of-service weights are replaced by *the value-of-the-service weights* (or, monetary wealth weights) m_i/r_e.

In contrast, the measure of money exclusively used by current monetary theory is based on a selection of some collection of assets A^* and a measurement of the total market value of these assets:

$$\Sigma M_C/P = \Sigma A^*(r_i + m_i + i_i)/r_e. \tag{7}$$

In all the other branches of economics, measurements of a resource either by the quantity of a service rendered (e.g., hours worked) or by the value of this service (e.g., wages received) are old hat. Incredibly, in monetary theory these two standard measurement tools are unknown. Money is measured only by the value of the sum of all incomes that it yields, regardless of their source. This is like measuring labour only one way, and a most quaint way at that: by the value of the sum of all incomes a person—perhaps unemployed—may be receiving including, say, interest income i. Why is this? Mysteriously and inexplicably Fisher's easily measurable quantity-of-transaction-service weights V's have never been recognized for what they are. Even the most recent literature rejects the medium of exchange criterion as merely verbal, non-operational (Friedman and Schwartz 1970: p. 105). Consequently, the value-of-the-transaction-service weights could not become understood either.

VALUE WEIGHTS AND THE TOTAL PRODUCT OF MONEY

These weights have been rejected because they allegedly yield incommensurate money wealth and become unstable over time. This is said to happen when the imputed income stream m in the form of transaction services of money is being replaced with explicit asset transfers $\pm i$. (Since current monies yield no real service such as ornamentation, r may be ignored.) By arithmetic necessity, when

$$i = y_e \tag{8}$$

then

$$(V/P)p = m = 0. \tag{9}$$

In the above mentioned book we have hardly more than asserted that equation 9 holds because

$$V = 0.^3 \tag{10}$$

Transaction services of money disappear, and money wealth falls to zero: value weights are useful. In a paper that I published subsequently (1973: pp. 647–60) this proposition has been supported by a theoretical analysis based on Gresham's Law. Though that paper remains uncontradicted, continuing advocacy of optimum money has shown—through neglect[4]—that my paper has failed to persuade. What must have proven persuasive is the counter-assertion (Friedman and Schwartz 1970: p. 114) that equation 9 holds because

$$p = 0. \tag{11}$$

If deposits transferable by cheque pay interest equal to the market rate of interest (cf. equation 8) people will indeed be induced to hold an amount such that, at the margin, an additional dollar will render no additional services in facilitating transactions. *The transaction services rendered by demand deposits have become a free good* [emphasis mine], available with cost (cf. equation 11) to the holders of demand deposits.

Money wealth when measured (as all wealth must be measured) in constant initial prices such as p increases rather than decreases as "optimum" money wealth is reached. Thus, ΣM_{PS} is not a useful way of measuring money wealth.

The core of the conflict is depicted in Figure 4.1. There I show money M produced at zero cost (SS), and the demand for it (MM).[5] The quantity is exogenously fixed at M_1. This simultaneously fixes the purchasing power of money at $1/P_1 = m/r_e$; $m = y_e$.

(1) Elimination of the constraint results in a quantity given by the point C and in a price or purchasing power of money $1/P_2 = m/r_e = 0$; in a destruction of money. In the left quadrant we move along the total product (total transaction services) function AC. This is non-controversial.

(2) Simultaneous imposition of interest payments endows M with a price support which, if correctly determined, fixes $1/P_1$ along MD. When the quantity given by the point C is reached, $m = 0$. The equilibrium interest rate is paid on money: $i = y_e$. Again, this is non-controversial. *But now*:

(a) In my analysis, Gresham's Law is unleashed. The total product of M falls along a function similar to but not necessarily identical with AC, except for the terminal point C. There money is—as before—destroyed ($V = 0$). It has been converted into a pure bond which the price support has endowed with a price, or purchasing power, equal to that of the destroyed money: $1/P_1 = i/r_e$ (which is offset by $-i/r_e$).

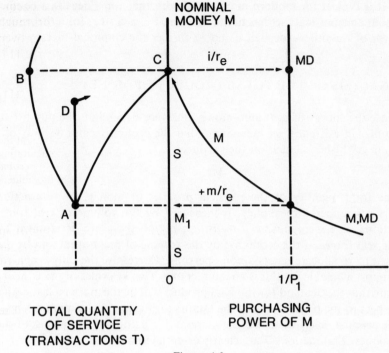

Figure 4.1

(b) In the dominant Friedman-Schwartz type of analysis, the total product of money increases along the curve AB, only *partly* because of some unknown Anti-Gresham's Law (at the expense of currency) (1970: p. 114). I say partly because in an analysis in which Friedman assumes (a quotation documenting this follows) only one money, he again postulates the AB function. When the services of money reach their peak at B, they become a free good ($p = 0$). Thus money becomes "optimum money"; a free good held to satiation, but without a zero price, thanks to the bond component of it.

Clearly, the dominant claim (e.g., Friedman and Schwartz (1970: p. 114), that the difference $p = 0$ vs. $V = 0$ is due to my remarkable *theoretical* confusion and to my failure to distinguish prices and quantities, and marginal (zero) and average (positive) product at the point B is not correct. I never get to B. I get to C. The true source of the conflict is our assertions about an *empirical* fact, about the shape of the total product curve of money: AB vs. AC.

It is typical for modern monetary theory that for a decade a conflict about an empirical fact has been mistaken, by each side, for a theoretical error of the other side. Let us now consider the empirical fact.

ANALYSIS OF THE TOTAL PRODUCT OF MONEY

Since the theory of optimum money does not depend on the number of monies in existence, let me assume that the economy employs only one money.[6] Fisher's equation then reduces to

$$MV = PT \tag{12}$$

The total quantity of the physical product of money, of transaction services rendered by money, is measured by the volume of real transactions T. Except during *a transition period* these are determined by the real forces of the economy: by the volume of real output and by the need to re-allocate assets among persons. Currently, the only empirical support available for this is an indirect one. Two key rules of price theory state that the demand for the final product will be the more inelastic with respect to the price of one of the factors producing it, the more essential the product, and the smaller the share of the factor in the total cost of the product. Transactions T are clearly essential in a market economy. And, the costs undertaking them are numerous: not just the cost of holding money, but also the cost of time and transportation spent on shopping, wages of purchasing and selling agents, legal and tax advice as to whether, how, and when to buy. In all these costs, the cost of using money is amazingly microscopic: $0.0006 per $1 of T.[7] Reduction of this cost to zero—planned by optimum money theorists—cannot be expected to stimulate any desire to increase the quantity of real exchange of goods and assets T. Thus, the total quantity TQ of the product of money in the form of transaction services (depicted by the line AD in Figure 4.1), the average product AQ and the marginal product MQ are:

$$TQ = T = constant, \tag{13}$$

$$AQ = T/M = V/P, \tag{14}$$

$$MQ = \partial T/\partial M = 0. \tag{15}$$

(Of course, no individual perceives this; each *thinks* that his share of the last equation is positive and is given by his AQ. Such dichotomies are well-known in price theory: e.g., each competitive firm thinks that it is facing a horizontal demand (AR) while the industry is not).

Friedman in his *Price Theory* (1976: p. 284) agrees—strangely enough—with the empirical expectation expressed by equation 13:

The stock of money differs from the two other categories [i.e., material wealth and human wealth] because *the production services rendered by money do not depend on the number of physical units there are, but primarily on the mere existence of a stock* [emphasis mine]. Consider two societies that are alike except that in one there are twice as many pieces of paper, each labelled one dollar, as in the other. The only effect will be that nominal prices will be twice as high in the first as in the second society. *The total stream of services from the stock of money is the same in the two societies* [emphasis mine].

This last conclusion surely holds in a third society where the stock of money is also doubled, but an interest income subsidy is used to induce the consumers not to spend the increment (to reduce V); spending would destroy it. Equation 15 disposes of one of the two pillars on which the theory of optimum money stands, described (Friedman 1969: p. 18) as follows: "It is natural to assume diminishing marginal return [called in the preceding sentence more accurately 'the marginal product of money'] throughout." There is nothing natural about this. Price theory discusses a bell-shaped total product curve (such as AB in Figure 4.1) so as to exhaust all empirical possibilities, but does not claim that each individual resource possesses it in its entirety. Chemical catalysts, critical masses in atomic reactions, heat needed to convert solids into liquids come readily to mind as resources with truncated total product curves. And, the above quoted empirical assertion (not theoretical assumption) is most unnatural in the case of money which Friedman—in his *Price Theory*—has declared basically different from typical human and material wealth exactly in this respect. With the total quantity of the transaction service of money constant, the total real value TV that the market attaches to this quantity must remain constant as well:

$$TV = Mm = Tp = constant, \tag{16}$$

from which and equation 13 it follows that

$$p = constant; \tag{17}$$

p does *not* fall to zero when $m = 0$ and $i = y_e$. The average value AV is then a rectangular hyperbola asymptotic to the axes AV and M in Figure 4.2 and the value of the marginal product MV is zero:

$$AV = m = (T/M)p = (V/P)p \tag{18}$$

and

$$MV = \partial(Tp)/\partial M = 0. \tag{19}$$

Equation 19 disposes of the second and remaining pillar of the optimum quantity of money specified as follows (Friedman 1969: p. 18): "Let us suppose that we can express the marginal value of these [i.e., transaction] services in money equivalent, as cents per year per dollar of balances ... And, again, it is natural to assume diminishing marginal returns."

It is rare in the history of science to find a theory, such as the theory of optimum money (giving title to a major book, stimulating a number of major articles, and influencing major public policy), which rests on nothing more than an empirical assertion. Can one imagine any other branch of economics simply asserting as "natural" an empirical fact (e.g., the constancy of the marginal product of labour) and then shaping labour legislation on this basis?

My paper could stop right here. With the existing quantity of money facilitating all the economic exchanges that people want to undertake, increases up to "the optimum quantity" on money are just as worthless as increases in the quantity of a catalyst which already is sufficient to bring about the desired chemical reaction. However, so powerful is the sway of the theory of optimum money over modern monetary theorists that, for them, elaboration of the implications of my analysis is imperative. The *general reader* will, however, be well-advised to pass directly to the next section dealing with the macroeconomic costs of Optimum Money.

FIAT MONEY BECOMING "OPTIMUM MONEY"

Simple increase in fiat money

For comparative purposes, let me first double the quantity of fiat money in Figure 4.2 from M_1 to M_2. The initial value m of the transaction services per unit of money, and thus the equilibrium real income yielded by one unit of money, drops by one-half. From $Tp/M_1 = Vp/P_1$ the economy moves to $Tp/2M_1 = Vp/2P_1$.

Below equilibrium interest income: price level constant

Interest payments i start to be used that provide price support for M at the level $(m + i) \equiv y_e = constant$. What will be the new equilibrium? Some of the holders of pure debt certificates will so much value being freed from shifting out of them into M and back again that they will be willing to accept some cut in the equilibrium interest income; others will not. The demand function MD will be positively sloping. Assume, for expositional simplicity *only*, that it intersects the $y_e y_e$ function at $M_2 = 2M_1$. From $Tp/M_1 = Vp/P_1$ the economy moves to $Tp/2M_1 = 0.5 Vp/P_1$: people hold twice as much of purchasing power, and use it half as much.

Cui bono? The *consumers* have sacrificed some additional assets (say, US bonds) to obtain additional fiat money from the government, and start to receive the explicit yield of these resources on their holdings of all units of money. An identical result would be accomplished by a law requiring each holder of currency to affix to it a US bond before being permitted to spend it.

In this and all the following cases, "the optimum money" is an exercise in taxonomy. Assets formerly called by two names (currency and bonds, demand and time deposits) are welded together and when the new total is called "money," money increases up to an optimum; should someone decide to call the new total "bonds," money would disappear. A non-arbitrary taxonomy depicted by Figures 4.1 and 4.2 will call the new total a *joint product* (a money-bond or a money-debt MD) with shares of the two determined by the ratios m/y_e and i/y_e.

The sole gain here—and in *all* the following cases—is the famous saving of shoe-leather. Some consumers who are not strong savers (who are willing to accept $0.5y_e$ as the explicit income i on their investment) stop wasting time on conversions of the zero-yield money into positive-yield bonds. An unbiased observer will keep looking and also discover a waste of shoe-leather that, given the relative sizes of financial and real assets, will *much* more than offset this gain. The consumers start wasting time by more frequent but smaller conversions of the positive-yield money into zero-yield (idle) inventories of real assets. The number of shopping trips increases and the average size of a purchase decreases, as the consumers attempt to hold on to their "good" money as long as possible.[8]

Can one argue that the consumers should be free to accept or reject the joint product? They will always accept it because they suffer from the false notion of *ceteris paribus*. In the initial equilibrium, they will want to do individually what they cannot do collectively: hold the same real quantity of money, use it with unchanging intensity, *and* start collecting an extra income. Also, they are aware of the time they are currently wasting on conversions of money into bonds, and are unaware of the time they will start wasting instead on conversions of money into real goods.

Money stock constant, profits exhausted

Suppose that the government holds the quantity of money constant, and initiates interest income that fully exhausts initial monopoly profits $M_1 \times y_e$. Money starts to earn $2y_e$. Doubling of the real income yielded by each M must result in capitalization of this income by those who happen to be the present owners: in the doubling of the purchasing power of each M. We move from $Tp/M_1 = Vp/P_1$ to $Tp/M_1 = 0.5Vp/0.5P_1$. Of course, demand for the joint product (pure money and pure bonds) may not double. In such a case, P and V will be multiplied

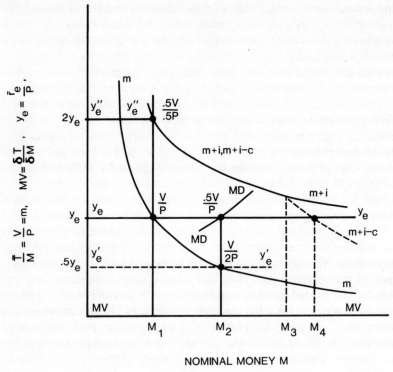

NOMINAL MONEY M

Figure 4.2

by a different factor and the initial holders' windfall will be smaller or bigger.

Since payment of interest income to the holders of currency is technically impossible, income yielded by steady deflation has been proposed (Friedman 1969: p. 34 and Patinkin 1972: p. 227) as a substitute. It is and it will suffer the same fate.[9] Any additional income that any asset starts to yield will be capitalized into a windfall benefiting only the existing holders.

Cui bono? In the new equilibrium demanders pay twice as much for each *M* but are indifferent to this because they are fully compensated with interest or deflation income on their extra outlay. Instead of satiation with money, "the advantages of holding money and holding goods are again equalized." (This hastily added quotation reveals my belated discovery that Keynes (1936: p. 142) has used, in three brilliant sentences, the same capitalization argument to dispose—*he, ex ante*—of optimum money.)

But, shall we merely get nowhere? Monetary theory's optimum money and macro-theory's real balance effect share between them a credit effect. Halving of prices doubles by many trillion dollars the burden of all borrowers; this causes mass bankruptcies and thus mass transfers of ownerships of real assets; it doubles national debt and the burden of foreign debt. We face a transition not to a new equilibrium of optimum money or full employment but to a total economic and political collapse.

Zero government profits; variable quantity of M
Until now I have assumed either a fixed price or a fixed quantity, and I let the interest income adjust itself to them. Let me reverse the procedure: let me fix the income that the government will pay. (1) Assume that the government pays out to the holders of any quantity of M_n its non-competitive profits nM_1/M_n (where $0 < n < y_e$), and (2) pays out the yield $i = y_e$ obtained by selling money M_1M_n for financial assets, such as US bonds. With OM_1 yielding $m = y_e$ per unit, and with M_1M_n yielding $i = y_e$ per unit, scrambling of these two assets into OM_n will result in the income $m + i = y_e$ per unit. The addition of nM_1/M_n to this income endows money with an above-equilibrium income; an explosion of the real income yielded by money y_e (implosion of the price level P) follows. However, a desire for a balanced portfolio will yield an equilibrium. As the nominal quantity of money increases and the purchasing power increases, the consumers' portfolios get disturbed: they are holding more and more of money and less and less of other assets.

Cui bono? Equilibrium is reached when the above-the-equilibrium yield of M is just high enough to cover the negative imputed income resulting from a sub-optimal portfolio. Profits on the production of money have been dissipated on compensations for unnecessary suffering.

BANK MONEY BECOMING "OPTIMUM MONEY"

Competitive banking
An industry with over 14,000 firms must be assumed to be fully competitive even though government regulations—as in the case of many other industries—distort the outcome. Thus, assume provisionally that the quantity of pure non-interest bearing money M_1 in Figure 4.2 is competitively produced. And, assume also that the government restricts banking with respect to the type of product that may be offered. By prohibiting interest payments on chequable deposits and chequability of others, it forces banking to offer either pure money OM_1, or pure debt certificate M_1M_3, but not a joint product. Let us consider the currently well-advanced destruction of these rules through an administrative fiat by the Federal Reserve Board, the Comptroller of Currency, and other

banking authorities. While they maintain—as they must—the legal fiction of distinct demand and time deposits, they are destroying its substance by permitting costless telephonic, electronic and automatic shifts between the two (see the NOW accounts). What are the consequences?

Supply forces. Banks used to have non-interest-bearing (demand) and interest-bearing (time) deposits. If we make the simplifying and not unreasonable assumption that it does not matter to them (given modern computers) whether the expense of handling cheque transactions is concentrated on demand deposits or diluted to all deposits, the banks' supply function of chequeable deposits is horizontal and coincides with the line $y_e y_e$ in Figure 4.2 until the quantity of the chequable deposits reaches the quantity of total bank deposits M_3. Thereafter, the supply function becomes negatively sloping; the price of earning assets increases with the volume of bank business, and this reduces the ability of banks to pay interest.

Demand forces.   The demand for chequable deposits MD in Figure 4.2 must be positively sloping, and intersects the supply function before this function becomes negatively sloping.

The new equilibrium quantity of deposits which are chequable and pay interest is established where the supply function intersects the demand function. For simplicity of geometry only, assume that this happens where previously we have found an equilibrium with a pure money injection: where the new quantity of money is $M_2 = 2M_1$. From the value of transaction services of money given by $(Tp)/M_1$ or $(Vp)/P$ the economy moves to a level given by $(Tp)/2M_1$ or $(0.5 Vp)/P$. Chequable deposits have doubled, and they move half as fast.

Cui bono? Previously, the consumers have been receiving on each unit of demand deposits a pure transaction services income $m = y_e$, and on each unit of time deposits a pure explicit interest income $i = y_e$. Now these two assets have become scrambled together and each consumer starts getting $0.5 y_e = m$ plus $0.5 y_e = i$. Nobody is better or worse off than before.

Non-competitive banking
However, the literature dealing with optimum money rests on the (empirically totally unsupported) hypothesis that the cost c of producing bank money is either zero or negligible. If so, any specific quantity of money starts by earning an imputed income $m > 0$. After the reform, each unit starts to earn its share of non-competitive profits $i - c$. And,

every additional unit of money M is obtained by the consumers through a sacrifice of resources that yields y_e per unit of M which income the banker will refund. Thus, the total income depicting the yield of money to the consumers is given by the curve $m + i - c$ that approaches the line $y_e y_e$ asymptotically from above. An explosion follows.

Once we take into account desires for balanced portfolios, equilibrium will be reached. As the bankers acquire more earning assets they have to start paying a premium for them. In other words, the yield of these assets to the banker falls.[10] This is bound to happen when the volume of income earning assets starts to exceed the original level. The holders of M will be charged for an ever-increasing cost of intermediation c. Equilibrium is reached, say, at M_4 where the costs of excess bank intermediation c have fully exhausted the income m.

Cui bono? Monopoly profits have been dissipated on subsidies needed to reallocate the intermediation function away from other intermediaries to the banks.

THE MACROECONOMIC COSTS OF "OPTIMUM MONEY"

Microeconomically, the optimum money yields no benefits and does cost extra shoe-leather. There are also *major* macroeconomic costs:

Measurement of money and credit

Under the *former* prohibition of interest income on a pure medium of exchange such as demand deposits, and prohibition of circulation of pure debt certificates such as time deposits, the measurement of the part of the net aggregate wealth in the form of *money*, $+\Sigma A_i(m_i/r_e)$, was easy, and so was the measurement of offsetting *credit*, $\Sigma A_i(\pm i_i/r_e)$: until recently, the former was M_1 and the latter $M_n - M_1$. Unscrambling of the new joint product given now by the Federal Reserve System the label M_1+ becomes, indeed, well-nigh impossible because r_e and the share of the imputed income m_i are hard to quantify (Friedman and Schwartz 1970: p. 152). It becomes impossible to distinguish changes in aggregate wealth consisting of the value of the transaction services of money from changes in the volume of credit (efficient allocation) of money. This is equivalent to reporting not the number of cars in existence and the number of cars being leased but only the sum of the two, which is meaningless. Congress (and the Federal Reserve System, to which it has delegated some of it powers) has been deprived—*via facti*—of its ability to perform its constitutional duty to regulate money, and of its legal right to regulate credit. Henceforth, empirical fog will force it to regulate only the meaningless sum of the two.

Inefficiency caused by Gresham's Law

The corpus of modern monetary theory focuses on money as an asset held in equilibrium. This is shown by the fact that the stock of money is always explained by the usual stock equilibrium conditions specifying *the equilibrium* portfolio *held*: MU \$1 $M_i = MU$ \$1 $A_1 = \cdots = MU$ \$1 A_n (where MU stands for "marginal utility"). The trouble is that every act of trading is a conclusive proof that equilibrium does not exist. The asset sold must have a below-equilibrium MU, the asset purchased an above-equilibrium MU, with the difference being equal to the MU of the resources spent on trading. But, if trading is a disequilibrium phenomenon, then money that facilitates it is a disequilibrium phenomenon.[11] To perform its task it is absolutely essential that money be purchased (goods sold) and sold (goods purchased). This is the same thing as saying that money's MU must *pulsate* around the equilibrium MU of all other assets. To analyze the stock of money by focusing on the fleeting and incidental moment when it has the equilibrium MU is like trying to analyze artillery shells by observing them when they are momentarily stationary in their apogees.

The indispensable pulse-wave of the MU generated by monies provides another way of explaining Gresham's Law in *this* case. As long as the pulse-waves of the *imputed* incomes m_i and m_j are unhampered, M_i and M_j compete on an equal footing. Once M_i starts to earn i_i, the situation changes. The *paid* income stream i_i represents a generalized command over goods and its MU must be constant, just as the MU of any paid income is constant. Thus i_i creates a floor below which the pulse-wave of the MU of $m_i + i_i$ yielded by bank deposit money cannot fall. In a one-money economy, the higher the floor the higher must become the MU of any real asset before it becomes eligible for purchase: efficiency of allocation of resources among persons is diminished. In a two-money economy bad money M_j—such as currency with its pulse-wave of the MU unchanged—will fill the gap, though certainly not fully. It will start to be used in transactions in which it is still technically inefficient, but now economically preferable. The higher the floor to the pulse-wave of the MU of $p_i + i_i$ provided by i_i, the more sizable will become both these inefficiencies.[12]

Destabilizing effect of optimum money and of low transaction costs

For the sake of stability of the real sector the wave-length of the MU of money should be short, which is another way of saying that the velocity of money should be high, which in turn is another way of saying that the quantity of money—given income—should be small. For those who focus on comparative statics the absolute level of velocity makes no difference: doubling of velocity of *any* size will double prices. However, from the standpoint of the size of transitional shocks to the real sector that result from either permanent and—especially—haphazard and passing changes, the absolute level of velocity does make a huge difference. When people hold 1/100th of their income in the form of money, a fleeting desire to double this amount will cause 1/100th of the annual output—which cannot be adjusted readily—to pile as unwanted inventories. The theory of optimum money aims to and will increase this ratio. When people start to hold (e.g.) 10/100th of their income as money, the same erratic doubling of demand increases the inventory shock to 10/100th of the annual output. Worse still, the longer the wave-length of the *MU* and thus the lower the velocity, the bigger is likely to be the percentage size of the shock. People paid daily (with high velocity) can afford capricious changes in their spending patterns much less than people paid monthly or annually, with low velocity.

Until the modern comparative statics macro-model swept the field, economists knew about and carefully studied the business cycle. Keynes himself devotes four separate chapters to "Expectations" (1936: pp. 46–51, 107–12, 147–64, 194–209) and returns to this topic repeatedly. Our world, as Keynes still knew it, faces in the short run erratic, playful, hysterical, speculating human beings kept—imperfectly—to the straight and narrow also by transaction costs. It is much cheaper and thus much more likely to become hysterical about one's common stock than about one's house. In physics, it has been long recognized that friction, burdensome as it may be in some cases, is an indispensable stability condition in a non-static world. Who would advocate an ice cover for "optimum" highways? Modern monetary theory focuses solely on static equilibria, and thus views an equivalent stabilizing force, transaction costs, as an evil to be eliminated through "optimum money."

In contrast, any responsible policy-maker, staggering from one disequilibrium to the next, would surely not wish to see (e.g.) all US bonds becoming equally acceptable, having the same low transaction costs, as currency. Nor should responsible policy-makers be so eager (as they are today) to change the quantity of the most volatile overhang over the real sector of chequeable bank deposits, from the current level of $344 billion by an increase up to $1,400 billion predicted by the proponents of optimum money (Friedman 1969: p. 44). Certainly not Keynes, who advocated the very opposite of optimum money: tax-costing rather than income-earning money (1936: p. 234).

THE KEY SOURCE OF TROUBLE: NO DEFINITION OF MONEY

There are several sources of the fallacy of the optimum money. A fundamental one is the lack of an operational specification of money, which results in two definitions being used simultaneously:

(1) When economic changes happen one at a time, the definition of money that I favour is generally used: m/r_e in equation 6. For instance, when Confederate dollars have ceased to circulate ($m = 0$), they are agreed to have ceased to be money. This conclusion would surely remain unchanged should, *subsequently*, these dollars become a favourite type of wall-paper (start earning r) or should they become cheap papers on which to write loan agreements (start earning i). *Nobody* would say that Confederate dollars have become resurrected as money, and that in the latter case they have even become "optimum money." Circulation here is deemed crucial, and thus money here is mortal.

(2) When the economic changes occur *simultaneously*, a different definition of money is used: $(r + m + i)/r_e$ in equation 7. The same changes described above become invisible. Circulation here (and thus the size of m) is deemed irrelevant, and money is immortal. Of course, since $r + m + i$ is defined as encompassing *all* the various types of incomes existing in the economy, money by this definition may be absolutely anything, including wall-paper.

This simultaneous use of two sharply different specifications of what is "money" leads to the conclusion that identical policies will have totally different outcomes according to whether applied consecutively or simultaneously. Money is said to be destroyed when m/r_e is first driven to zero and then replaced with i/r_e; money is said to be unaffected and, indeed, optimized, when both changes happen simultaneously. Which of the two definitions is a tenable one?

Generalists in economics specify, *a priori* and verbally, physical characteristics of some broad categories of resources: e.g., we have seen in one quotation the use of the concepts of human and material wealth, in which a verbal *a priori* criterion (animate-inanimate) surely dominates. Specialists then provide a more detailed verbal and *a priori* specification of their subject matter. Transportation economists specify what segments of material and human wealth they will study (those engaged in physically definable transportation of goods); labour economists specify the physical characteristics of "labour," etc. Monetary theorists are the *sole* exception. They declare that money has no physical characteristic that may be specified *a priori*, and verbally (see the quotation below). *If true, this ipso factor means that monetary theory cannot exist*—just as labour theory could not exist if labour theorists would declare themselves unable to specify what labour is, and is not (e.g. bridges). Even the most obvious characteristic of money (used in dictionaries that reflect the wisdom of centuries)—the medium of exchange characteristic as measured by Fisher's V's—has been rejected. Without realization of what is happening, an unnoticed specific, measurable, and operational criterion has been replaced not with a better one but none at all: this is called "the empirical approach" to the definition of money.

The only *a priori* statement that monetary theorists are willing to make—and explicitly only tentatively—is that money is something in between M_1 and M_5, \$360 billion $< M <$ \$1,500 billion: something more narrow (on totally unstated grounds) than the grand total $(r + m + i)/r_e$ but much broader than m/r_e. How do we then select *the* stock of money from this huge range? In other words, how do we select from all assets A_i in existence the group of assets A^* for equation 7? The generally accepted recipe is the following (Friedman and Schwartz 1965: p. 650):

Just where the line should be drawn between assets regarded as money and those regarded as near-moneys or simply as "other assets" is not something that can or should be decided either once for all or on the basis of verbal considerations. It must depend on the purpose and on the empirical relevance of a particular distinction for that purpose under specific circumstances, which is to say, on the empirical stability and regularity of relationships between the chosen total and other variables.

What does this[13] mean? Monetary theorists theorize that a cause (M) leads to an effect (e.g., GNP). First, they measure precisely the effect, correlate it on all sorts of numbers N_1, N_2,....,N_n lying within the above range, and then select that N yielding the best fit, which becomes defined as $N \equiv M$. Given the powers of modern computers and the fact that practically all variables in the economy move together, and given the succour offered by dummies, lagged terms, first differences, arithmetic and logarithmic functions, etc., the chances of not finding a convenient cause N (or, several equally good N's) are nil. Modern monetary theory cannot be contradicted by empirical facts. Well, not quite. If "the empirical definition of money" is a valid one, a critic should have equal rights to it. He should be entitled to find any N' yielding the worst correlation possible, define $N' \equiv M$, and conclude that he has rejected the theory.

DIVORCE OF MONETARY THEORY FROM EMPIRICAL RESEARCH

Such *ex post*—allegedly "empirical"—measures of the subject of monetary theory have caused a *complete divorce* of monetarists' theorizing from empiricizing:

(1) *All* existing microeconomic theories of money derive negative interest elasticity of demand. The empirical concepts of money M_2-M_5 contain assets with positive elasticities which in the case of M_2 probably and in the case of M_3-M_5 certainly dominate the aggregate. Either all these theories are wrong, or these assets are not money: *tercium non datur*.

(2) *All* existing macro- and monetary theories deduce—because of the above micro-theory—a positively sloping *LM* function. If M_2-M_5 are equally eligible as "money," all texts must be rewritten, declare the above a mere special case, and in alternative chapters discuss equally eligible negatively sloping *LM*. In the latter case, doubling of "money" will reduce the price level, and thus become a novel tool for fighting inflation.

(3) Monetary theory postulates a relationship between wealth and consumption, while empirical works "test" this proposition by using M_2 in the value of which offsetting asset-debts (time deposits) dominate (Patinkin 1965: pp. 656–7).

Monetary theorists should in the future specify—not necessarily exactly at first—the empirical counterpart of the theoretical concept "money": something that is today lacking in all the most influential treatises. *Pragmatists* may at some time become tempted to offer a new economic theory that would causally explain the unquestionably good performance that they obtain by the use of the empirical quantification of N through correlation analysis (which never shows causality, and fails to disprove but never proves anything). Of course, the item N should be more accurately given a different name from "money" because it does not fit any currently known theoretical specification of the properties of money. Perhaps, as in the above quotation, the item N might be called "the chosen total" instead. Either (or both) groups may then make a contribution to the development of the theories of money *and* credit, and to policy-making.

ECONOMIC PERSPECTIVES

To monetary theory *especially* applies the presidential address by E. H.

Phelps-Brown: "On the view I have advanced our own science has hardly yet reached the 17th Century" (1972: p. 10). And, in the words of Richard Kahn, "Monetary economics is in a state of shameful confusion," (1978: p. 545). And so it is. Phelps-Brown sees a cure in the reversal of our priorities: towards "the hewers of wood and drawers of water" and away from those "able to soar into the empyrean of abstractions" (1972: p. 9). In the case of monetary theory, simple and elementary decisions such as what is money, what are its basic technical properties such as the total product curve, how to measure money to get at these properties, what are the shapes of the supply functions of the producers and of the demand functions of the consumers, should get priority over the most intricate theories of optimum (undefined) money and of the Golden Rule of Growth of (undefined) money. Until then, much of monetary theory will be either irrelevant because lacking an empirical counterpart or even—as the theory of optimum money and many related reform proposals show—will be harmful. One cannot regulate what one cannot, with a reasonably small margin of uncertainty, define.

ACKNOWLEDGMENT

I am grateful for critical comments by J. Walter Elliott and Thomas Mayer.

NOTES

1. Of course, like all weights Fisher's are usable only if stable over time. One of the advantages of his approach is that aggregation is not necessary.
2. Monetary theorists agree (quotations follow) that money fields a flow of a valuable *service*: $m_i > 0$.
   They also agree (though never on the same page) that money is not a productive resource or wealth ($m_i/r_e = 0$) because a key monetary dogma has it that money is an asset of the holder fully offset by a liability of the issuer. Here, money is indistinguishable from a personal loan to a friend yielding interest transfers $\pm i_i$ and thus adding to wealth $\Sigma \pm i_i/r_e = 0$.
   Clearly, both claims cannot be right. Here I opt for the former.
3. In the real world equation 10 cannot be satisfied because almost all assets have a positive velocity: ratio of trades to stock. An insignificant velocity must be enough to confirm equation 10—such as the velocity 1.7 of time deposits (*Federal Reserve Bulletin*, Feb. 1978: A-13).
4. The response to *any* criticism of optimum money seems to be silence. Equally unanswered remains J. Stein's conclusion that "If anticipated

deflation [another form of i_i] exceeds the rate of return on capital [y_e] ... investment is not profitable ... the instability of Friedman's proposal is apparent," (1970: p. 417). The same is true about C. S. Tsiang's conclusion that "... for the sake of stability and efficiency of financial markets we should keep the yield differential [$y_e - i_i$] sufficiently high," (1969: p. 279).

(Note that in the three analyses $y_e = i_i$ is the borderline between a monetary world and an abyss: a line that a wobbly world had better avoid. However, the Stein-Tsiang world seems flat (AD?), while mine has a curvature AC in Figure 4.1. Here, *natura non facit saltum*.)

5. Theoretical rigour would require MM to be a rectangular hyperbola. However, that would force me to waste space by replacing the opposing claims $V = 0$ and $p = 0$ with verbiage describing approaches to these values. Besides, "theoretical rigour" here is empirical sloppiness. Are people really indifferent between $M = \$100$ billion (and the price of a hamburger $1) and $M = \$100,000$ billion (and a price of $1,000)? The cost of accounting (e.g., computer print-outs) has quadrupled.

6. Friedman uses the same simplification (1969: p. 13).

7. The imputed cost of holding $247 billion of demand deposits in 1977 may be estimated to be $24 billion; cheque transactions have amounted to $37,331 billion (*Federal Reserve Bulletin*, Feb. 1978: A-13 and A-14). Note that this empirically supports Sir John Hicks's theorizing that transaction money is "... impervious to direct economic incentives," (1967: p. 15): like salt in food, money is essential for transactions and its share in total costs of them is negligible. But, it contradicts the orthodox "inventory-theoretic approach" to transaction money which yields an interest elasticity of demand that is independent of these two orthodox factors.

8. Note that inventories do not fall. Given *major* economies of large scale deliveries of inventories, factories will not start shipping daily to match consumers' purchases. Consumer inventories fall and expensive retail inventories rise. (My student Jeffrey Pantages deserves credit here.)

9. Exogenous deflation proposed by some is worthless: Who would benefit if taxed $-Mr_e$ and recoups through $-Pr_e$? And, endogenous deflation $-Pr_e$ proposed by others would be a miracle because output and the demand for money grow at unpredictable and unsteady rates, unrelated to r_e. So, the capitalization argument kills a still-born child.

10. The argument is frequently made that m_i represents interest income in kind, and thus is indistinguishable from explicit interest income i_i. This fails to perceive the crucial difference between *production* of m_i and mere *transfers* of old assets M from the debtors to the creditors.

11. Sir John Hicks tried to bring this to the attention of monetary theorists eleven years ago (1967: pp. 14–15).

12. Gresham's Law changes the total product function AD in Figure 4.1 into the function AC. This will be true even in a one-money society because if bad money does not exist, it will be invented. Bad money always exists, only sometimes its quantity happens to be positive and at other times, zero.

13. The terms "once for all" and "verbal" are merely an attempt to make the opposing view look silly, since *doctrinaire* in a changing world. We *do* have a once-for-all verbal definition of (e.g.) the transportation industry, which *does* permit empirical elimination of horses and inclusion of airplanes, in accordance with services rendered.

REFERENCES

Federal Reserve Bulletin.

Fisher, I. 1911. *The Purchasing Power of Money.* Reprints of Economic Classics. New York: Kelly [1971].

Friedman, M. 1969. *The Optimum Quantity of Money and Other Essays.* Chicago: Aldine.

────── 1976. *Price Theory.* Chicago: Aldine.

────── and Schwartz, A. J. 1967. *A Monetary History of the United States 1867–1960.* New York: National Bureau of Economic Research, distributed by Princeton University Press, Princeton.

────── 1970. *Monetary Statistics of the United States.* New York: National Bureau of Economic Research, distributed by Columbia University Press.

Havrilensky, T. M. and Boorman, J. T. 1978. *Monetary Macroeconomics.* Arlington Heights, Ill.: AHM Corp.

Hicks, Sir. J. 1967. *Critical Essays in Monetary Theory.* Oxford: Clarendon Press.

Kahn, Richard 1978. "Some Aspects of the Development of Keynes' Thought," *Journal of Economic Literature,* XVI, 2, June 1978.

Keynes, J. M. 1936. *The General Theory of Employment, Interest and Money.* New York: Harcourt Brace Jovanovich Co.

Patinkin, D. 1965. *Money, Interest and Prices.* Second Edition. New York: Harper and Row.

────── 1972. *Studies in Monetary Economics.* New York: Harper and Row.

Pesek, B. P. and Saving, T. R. 1967. *Money, Wealth, and Economic Theory.* New York: Macmillan.

────── 1973. "Equilibrium Level of Transaction Services of Money," *Journal of Finance,* XXVIII, 8, June 1973.

Phelps-Brown, E. H. 1972. "The Underdevelopment of Economics," *The Economic Journal,* 82, March 1972.

Stein, J. 1970. "The Optimum Quantity of Money," *Journal of Money, Credit and Banking,* II, Nov. 1970.

Tintner, G. 1962. *Econometrics.* New York: John Wiley.

Tsiang, C. S. 1969. "A Critical Note on the Optimum Supply of Money," *Journal of Money, Credit and Banking,* II, May 1969.

5 Equilibrium Level of Transaction Services of Money*

When price theory deals with goods and services other than money, the flow of output of any good or service X per unit of time is explained by the demand for and supply of it:

$$d(X) = s(X). \tag{1}$$

The stock of some resource R_x^n that, in cooperation with other resources R_x^1, R_x^2, ..., R_x^m, yields this flow is then explained by the demand for and supply of this resource for this and, perhaps, other uses:

$$d(R_x^n) = s(R_x^n). \tag{2}$$

The equilibrium average flow of output X per unit of the input R_x^n is a very complex outcome of forces that price theory as yet has not tried to approach directly. It analyzes, say, the volume of freight transported by trucks, and the quantity of trucks, and the quality of truckdrivers but not the average load per truck or per truckdriver. One of the reasons for this is that the flow adjustments are typically faster than stock adjustments so that observed values will be equilibrium values more rarely in the case of R_x^n than in the case of X; and, in the case of X/R_x^n, only if there happens to be a double coincidence of equilibrium values of X and R_x^n. Thus, the ratio X/R_x^n will reflect non-equilibrium values most of the time and thus be much harder to explain analytically than either X or R_x^n.

In Fisher's analysis of transactions and money we find the variables T_M and $T_{M'}$, which represent the total flow of transaction services per unit of time (in Fisher's terms, "total exchange work done"[1]) yielded by the two monies M and M'. Fisher's velocities V and V' are then merely the ratio of this *flow* of transaction services to the *stock* of one of the resources (M or M') which, in cooperation with other resources, yields this flow. In equilibrium,

---

* From: *The Journal of Finance*. June, 1973.

$$V = \frac{d(T_M) = s(T_M)}{d(M) = s(M)},$$ (3)

$$V' = \frac{d(T_{M'}) = s(T_{M'})}{d(M') = s(M')}.$$ (4)

For a price theorist, velocities V and V' are therefore indistinguishable from the ratio of equations 1 and 2. Fisher makes use of equations 3 and 4 to explain the general price level P, which is the reciprocal of the price of the resources M and M' in terms of real goods. He writes

$$MV + M'V' = Pt$$ (5)

where M and M' denote currency and deposits respectively, and t the sum of the trades measured in real terms. By substituting 3 and 4 into 5 we obtain

$$T_M + T_{M'} = Pt.$$ (6)

In this formulation, the real value of money is said to be determined by the total quantity of transaction services yielded annually by the two monies. This, theoretically, is akin to a statement that the real market price of trucks is explained by the quantity of freight, measured in real terms, that trucks annually transport; given the value of this service, by the discounted stream of expected real returns yielded by trucks.

Post-Fisherian quantity theorists have attempted to short-circuit the painstaking procedure of price theory that analyzes flows and stocks but not the ratio of a flow to the stock of one of the many resources yielding it; that analyzes X, R_x^n, but not X/R_x^n. They have attempted to analyze not T_M and M separately but $T_M/M = V$ and not $T_{M'}$ and M' separately but $T_{M'}/M' = V'$. Such analysis is extremely ambitious and empirically hard to test since—for reasons stated in connection with the ratio X/R_x^n—the observed values of V and V' will be non-equilibrium values most of the time and thus hard to interpret.

In this chapter I shall try to lower my sights, follow price theory, and analyze only the *flow* of the transaction services yielded by M and M'. I hope to persuade the reader that such adherence to well-established methods of price theory will yield significant analytical dividends.

1. TRANSACTION SERVICES MARKET EQUILIBRIUM

The transaction services market may be approached by the use of our established apparatus of indifference curves and production function. Given the economic organization of the society, we may assume along with Fisher that the consumers want to undertake each year a given quantity of real trades t or, tautologically, a given sum of real transactions $T_M/P + T_{M'}/P$. Were we dealing with some "real" good or service X and Y, the consumers' ability to obtain any given sum $X + Y$ would depend on the endowment of the society with the resource producing these two flows. In the case of transaction services T_M/P and $T_{M'}/P$ the problem is simpler. As long as:

(1) either type of transaction requires zero quantities of resources co-operating with M and M' in the production of T_M/P and $T_{M'}/P$ (to be relaxed next),

(2) M and M' are freely convertible so that the consumers may obtain any M/M' ratio and thus enable themselves to produce any ratio of T_M/P to $T_{M'}/P$,

(3) the price level P is flexible so as to enable any "nominal" quantity of $(M + M')$ to produce any desired "real" quantity of $(T_M + T_{M'})/P$,

the production function relating T_M/P to $T_{M'}/P$ will be straight line with the slope of minus one (AB in Figure 5.1), with its position determined by the consumers' preferences alone.

However, with positive resource costs this will be merely a macroeconomic transaction isoquant function, while the production function facing the consumers will be a different one. When undertaking T_M/P, the consumers will have to hand over a part of the proceeds to, say, a bodyguard who protected them when they carried M to the market. The cost of this bodyguard represents the difference between (macroeconomically relevant) gross transactions and (microeconomically relevant) net transactions T_M/P. Similarly, when undertaking $T_{M'}/P$, the consumers will have to hand over part of the proceeds to the bankers who must clear the cheques. If we assume S-shaped total cost functions facing those who desire to undertake T_M/P and $T_{M'}/P$ transactions, and if we subtract these costs from the gross production function AB, we obtain the net production function $A'B'$ that shows the net gain that the consumer will obtain from his transacting activity.

Of course, the assumption that the consumers will want to engage in a constant total quantity of real trades is not the only possible one. For instance, we could assume that as the total cost of the transacting activity increases because society's technology requires increased specialization in either type of transacting activity, the consumers will prefer to reduce the total quantity of trades that they will want to engage in. In such a case, the function AB would also be concave to the origin. Conversely, we could assume that the consumers will insist on a specific quantity of resources to be obtained through trading, regardless of costs (i.e., have perfectly inelastic demand for them). In that case, the function $A'B'$

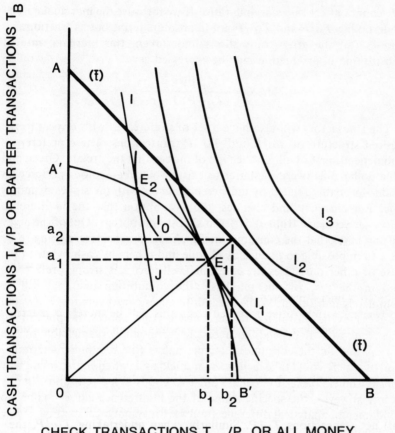

CASH TRANSACTIONS T_M/P OR BARTER TRANSACTIONS T_B

CHECK TRANSACTIONS $T_{M'}/P$ OR ALL MONEY

TRANSACTIONS $T_{M+M'}/P$

Figure 5.1

would have the slope of minus one and the gross production function AB would be concave from above. However, the basic conclusions that we shall reach below will remain unaffected as a result of any of these assumptions and thus I shall limit myself to the exploration of what I view to be "the Fisherian case" of a constant quantity of trades gross of costs.

The slope of the net production function $A'B'$ at any point will measure the marginal rate of substitution in production of T_M/P and $T_{M'}/P$ facing the society's transactors. Notice that given convertibility at par of M and M', the production costs of obtaining ("earning") M and

M' cannot affect this marginal ratio. If we measure the marginal cost of undertaking T_M/P and $T_{M'}/P$ not in absolute terms but as fractions c_M and $c_{M'}$ of the gross transactions undertaken, this marginal rate of substitution in production may be expressed as

$$MRS_P = \frac{(T_M/P)(1 - c_M)}{(T_{M'}/P)(1 - c_{M'})}. \tag{7}$$

The transactors will also have a set of preferences with respect to the desired structure of T_M/P and $T_{M'}/P$ transactions. These preferences will depend, first of all, on the type of money that they relate. Green and blue dollar bills (were the latter to exist) would be—colour preferences aside—probably related by indifference curves with the slopes of minus one. For currency and cheques, the assumption that the indifference curves are concave from above seems most appropriate. Out of the array of purchases that the consumer makes, some purchases are going to be next to impossible to finance by cheque and others by cash, while in the case of other purchases the consumer will have less strong preferences and in the case of one purchase (the equilibrium one), he will be completely indifferent. While the indifferences curves relating T_M/P and $T_{M'}/P$ may be postulated to be concave from above, the position of these curves will depend both on the economic organization of the society and on the consumers' buying habits (the economic determination of which would take us just as far afield as an attempt to explain why the consumers prefer to demand any two goods in a given ratio). In any event, however, the specific shape of the indifference curves makes no fundamental analytical difference; our existing analytical method is able to handle all of them. Whatever the shape of the indifference curves, their slope at any given point is the marginal rate of substitution in consumption between the rates of the flow of transactions T_M/P and $T_{M'}/P$. If we denote marginal utilities of these transactions by MU_T and $MU_{T'}$ and the marginal rate of substitution by MRS_C, we have, by definition,

$$MRS_C = \frac{MU_T}{MU_{T'}}. \tag{8}$$

Equilibrium requires that the marginal rate of substitution in production and the marginal rate of substitution in consumption be equal to each other, which in Figure 5.1 happens at the point E_1. The consumers will annually purchase for themselves Oa_1 quantity of resources by the use to T_M/P at the resource cost a_1a_2; they will purchase for themselves Ob_1 quantity of resources by the use of $T_{M'}/P$ at the resource cost b_1b_2. For the sake of simplicity I am assuming here that factors necessary to produce T_M/P transaction services get paid by currency and that factors necessary to produce $T_{M'}/P$ services get paid by cheque. An opposite or more complex assumption would complicate the analysis without adding anything substantive to the conclusions reached.

2. EXCISE TAXES AND SUBSIDIES ON TRANSACTION SERVICES

Suppose the government imposes excise taxes t_M and $t_{M'}$ or subsidies s_M and $s_{M'}$, stated in real terms and as fractions of transactions. As shown by Friedman, such taxes and subsidies will not affect the production possibilities of the *society*.[2] Distribution effects aside, the total volume of trades that the consumers will want to engage in and be able to engage in will remain unaffected, since for every subsidy receiver there is going to be a tax payer. However, the slopes of the price lines that face each transactor will be affected. To each transactor individually it would now seem—incorrectly from the standpoint of the society as a whole—that the relative cost of engaging in T_M/P and in $T_{M'}/P$ transactions has changed. The subjective marginal rate of substitution mrs_p will now replace MRS_P as the variable that determines each consumer's decisions:

$$mrs_p = \frac{(T_M/P)(1 - c_M - t_M + s_M)}{(T_{M'}/P)(1 - c_{M'} - t_{M'} + s_{M'})}. \tag{9}$$

The transactors will now find an equilibrium where $mrs_p = MRS_C$ at a point consistent with the society's production possibilities; that is, on the $A'B'$ function. If mrs_p is given by the slope of the line IJ in Figure 5.1, we shall obtain the equilibrium point E_2 which will replace the point E_1. Equation 9 makes it obvious that there is no upper limit upon subsidies since they may have to overcome perhaps sharply increasing costlines of the transactions that they are supposed to foster. In contrast, the limit to transaction taxes t_M and $t_{M'}$ is unity. Even if marginal costs of T_M/P or $T_{M'}/P$ transactions should be zero, a one hundred per cent tax on the proceeds of the transactions will clearly make the slope of the price line facing the transactors horizontal and vertical, respectively, and make either transaction prohibitively expensive. Of course, with positive marginal costs the limit to t_M or $t_{M'}$ will be smaller than unity. Finally, it will be even smaller than that if indifference curves happen to intersect the relevant axis; in that case, we shall obtain corner solutions.

The discrepancy between the economy's true production possibilities given by the slope of the net production function $A'B'$ (by MRS_P and the individuals' production possibilities as they appear to each consumer as a result of excise taxes or subsidies (depicted by mrs_p) indicates that the consumers are misinformed and as a result are wasting society's resources. Note that it makes no difference as to who misinforms the consumers. It may be the government, but it also may be the fractional reserve bankers. Suppose that the latter are able to produce the asset M' at zero resource cost so that with zero cheques to clear they would be able to pay to the holders of M' the explicit rate $r_x = r_e - r_e r_b$, where the subscripts e, b, and x distinguish the equilibrium rate on capital, the reserve ratio, and the explicit rate paid on M'. The more cheques are written, the higher the costs of clearing them, and the lower will be the rate r_x that the consumers will get: r_x is a subsidy on non-use of M' in $T_{M'}/P$ transactions or, to look at the opposite side of the coin, it is a tax (similar to $t_{M'}$) on use of M' in $T_{M'}/P$ transactions. (It may also be noticed that with a uniform r_x the non-transacting or seldom transacting holders of M' will be forced to help to foot the resource-cost bill imposed by the transacting holders of M'.)

In contrast, if competitive bankers are prohibited from paying the explicit rate directly, they will simply reduce or give up service charges that they would have to charge to $T_{M'}/P$ transactors to cover the cost of producing this service. Such waiver of service charges will be, from the viewpoint of the transactors, indistinguishable from a subsidy $s_{M'}$, that may reward transacting by cheque. As equation 9 indicates, this will induce the consumers to consume a bigger quantity of $T_{M'}/P$ transactions than they would otherwise consume, were they not misinformed by mrs_p about the social costs of paying by cheque.[3]

Clearly, the distorting interest-payment subsidy on non-use of M' in $T_{M'}/P$ transactions *and* the distorting service-charges-waiver subsidy on use of M' in $T_{M'}/P$ transactions would both become impossible with a hundred per cent reserve requirements or with prohibition of interest payments accompanied by the requirement that banks charge for cheque-clearing services. Either would assure allocative efficiency; distributive justice in the second case would have to be provided through taxation of non-competitive profits that previously were dissipated through r_x or through the waiver of service charges.

3. SUBSIDIES ON THE RESOURCES PRODUCING TRANSACTION SERVICES

As we have just seen, competitive bankers could (if permitted to do so) pay to the holders of M' the interest income $r_x M'$ provided that the factor of production M' remain idle; that it not be employed in facilitating $T_{M'}/P$ transactions. This is analytically indistinguishable from a decision by the government to pay welfare income to the owners of another factor of production necessary for the flow of service $T_{M'}/P$, such as bank employees. It is demonstrable that the use of a factor (M' or bank employees) in the production of T_M'/P must cease entirely—and that therefore the flow of the service $T_{M'} P$ must cease entirely—when a subsidy on non-use (of M' or bank employees) reaches the equilibrium return obtainable by these two resources through use: if r_x equals the market rate r_e, or if welfare payments equal the equilibrium wage rate. However, it will be useful to analyze not just this limiting case, but also the path towards this final disappearance of $T_{M'}/P$ transactions. Space limitations suggest that we limit ourselves to the frequently suggested subsidy r_x on the factor M' and leave the parallel case of subsidies to other factors which cooperate with it in the production of the service $T_{M'}/P$ to the reader's diligence.

As in the case of subsidies and excises on $T_{M'}/P$, so in the case of subsidy on holding M', for every receiver there must be a payer, so that the quantity of transactions that the transactors will want to undertake will remain unaffected and, therefore, the gross and net production function AB and $A'B'$ will remain unaffected. However, the relative cost facing each individual consumer who wants to engage in T_M/P or $T_{M'}/P$ transactions will change:

(1)   As before, the transactor may give up \$1 of M/P to engage in \$1 of T_M/P transaction and obtain the net benefit of (\$1 $T_M/P)(1 - c_M)$ of resources gained as a result of his transacting activity.

(2)   As before, the transactor may give up \$1 of M'/P to engage in \$1 of $T_{M'}/P$ transactions and will obtain again the benefit of (\$1 $T_{M'}/P)(1 - c_{M'})$ of resources gained. However, by giving up \$1 of M'/P he *now* also sacrifices the income flow of (\$1$M'/P) \times (r_x)$ per annum, the present worth of which is (\$1$r_x)/(r_eP)$. After setting aside the necessary quantity of the resources gained to replace this loss, his net benefit is *now* reduced to (\$1 $T_{M'}/P)(1 - c_{M'} - r_x/r_e)$.

As in the case of subsidies or taxes on $T_{M'}$ so in the case of a subsidy on M' the social costs of producing T_M/P and $T_{M'}/P$ transactions (MRS_P) remain unaffected (for any given ratio of quantities of the two). And, as in the case of subsidies or taxes on $T_{M'}/P$, so in the case of a subsidy on M' the slope of the price line facing each consumer will be affected:

$$mrs_p = \frac{(T_M/P)(1 - c_M - t_M + s_M)}{(T_{M'}/P)(1 - c_{M'} - t_{M'} - r_x/r_e + s_{M'})}. \tag{10}$$

In accordance with commonly held beliefs, direct and indirect interest payments benefit the holders of M'. But, as equation 10 shows, direct interest payments r_x/r_e (rewarding the holding of M') increase the cost of giving up M' in the course of the production of the $T_{M'}/P$ service while indirect interest payments (akin to $s_{M'}$) reduce the cost of this service. The same difference would exist between welfare payments to unemployed bank employees and free lunches given to those employees for a specific quantity of cheques cleared. While either will benefit bank employees, the former must increase and the latter reduce the cost of inducing these employees to give up their (labour) resource in the course of producing $T_{M'}/P$. Or, looking at it with the eyes of the transactors, the former must increase and the latter reduce the cost of paying by cheque.

Equation 10 makes it obvious that the same conclusion that we reached earlier with respect to transaction taxes $t_{M'}$ burdening $T_{M'}/P$ will hold with respect to the reward r_x/r_e for holding M'. Transaction services $T_{M'}/P$ will become more expensive as r_x/r_e increases and will become prohibitively expensive (even in the favourable case in which marginal resource costs $c_{M'}$ fall to zero as $T_{M'}/P$ transactions are reduced) once r_x/r_e starts to equal unity.[4] And, as previously in the case of taxes $t_{M'}$, the transaction costs r_x/r_e will become prohibitive even sooner if resource marginal costs remain positive or if indifference curves intersect the vertical axis.

To Sir Thomas Gresham this conclusion would not be at all surprising since interest payments on M' represent merely one of the many possible ways in which this money may become "good" money: the income, flow r_x on M' is conceptually no different from an imputed income flow due, say, to increased numismatic value of M. While increases in quantity of the money that has become "good" may drive to zero the marginal utility of a specific (imputed) income flow and restore thus the money in question to circulation, no increase in quantity may drive to zero the marginal utility of a general (paid) income r_x in a society with unchanged production possibilities and thereby restore that money to circulation.

4. MONETARY ECONOMY, BARTER ECONOMY, AND SELF-SUFFICIENCY

We have seen that the consumer qua holder of M' benefits from r_x (while the payer of r_x suffers) and that all consumers qua transactors suffer because r_x makes $T_{M'}/P$ transactions appear to be relatively more expensive than T_M/P transactions and thus induces the transactors to economize needlessly with the apparently more expensive transactions. Suppose, however, that the consumers qua money holders convert, upon initiation of r_x, every M into M' so that the alternative T_M/P transactions become completely unavailable to the consumers qua transactors. Or, suppose that r_x comes to be paid on both M and M' by the government and by the bankers. Will the above conclusions be affected?

Until now we have ignored the fact that currency and cheque transactions are not the only two choices open to the transactor: he may also engage in barter transactions or shift to no transactions or shift to self-sufficiency. To analyze these cases, all we need to do is to replace in Figure 5.1 cash transactions T_M/P with barter transactions $T_{M+M'}/P$ (where M may or may not be zero). Needless to say, the slopes of the production functions and of the indifference curves will be different, since the two goods on the axes are now different. However, specific shapes of these functions have no basic analytical consequences and thus, for simplicity, the same figure shall be used.

If we denote the marginal costs of barter transactions by c_B (and drop as uninteresting the possibility of excise taxes and subsidies on transactions), the marginal rate of substitution in production of barter and money transactions as it will appear to each transactor becomes:

$$mrs_p^* = \frac{(T_B)(1 - c_B)}{(T_{M+M'}/P)\,(1 - c_{M+M'} - r_x/r_e)}. \tag{11}$$

This rate becomes prohibitive when $r_x/r_e = 1$. And, should the resulting increase in barter transactions cause the marginal resource costs c_B to keep increasing, barter will keep being replaced with self-sufficiency. Needless to say, in the real world we would not expect the society to put up with either outcome and, instead, preserve the monetary economy by making $r_x = r_e$ impossible.

The reason for the just deduced decrease in money transactions is easy to understand. In the case of *all* tradings the consumer sacrifices from his portfolio—at the time of trading—an asset that *to him* yields a below-the-equilibrium level of income and purchases an asset that *to him* yields an above-the-equilibrium level of income. The time of trading occurs when the difference between the present value of the two income flows is high enough to finance transaction costs. Thus, for money to circulate (be merely a temporary abode of purchasing power) it is absolutely essential for it (a) to have low transaction costs *and* (b) to yield income that in the case of each consumer oscillates sharply over short periods of time, exceeding the equilibrium level one moment and falling below it shortly thereafter. With money yielding merely an *imputed* income, oscillations are possible and the high velocities of currency and of demand deposits attest that they actually do occur. Once money starts to yield *paid* (general) income, a floor is put to these oscillations: the marginal utility of paid income worth \$1 on the market cannot become lower than its marginal utility on income in kind worth \$1 on the market that is yielded by an asset most enjoyed by the consumer himself. And, if the paid income becomes the equilibrium level of income (if $r_x = r_e$), the floor to oscillations becomes so high that for every consumer, at any time, it must be true that he (1) either has equilibrium holdings of money or (2) has excess demand for money. No consumer whose money rests on this floor can ever have an excess supply of money, without which purchases of goods for money cannot happen. The sole exception is to be found in the case of those consumers who (e.g., in preparation for dying) may be liquidating their entire economic substance.

5. DEFLATIONARY SUBSIDY ON HOLDING MONEY $M + M'$

It is sometimes suggested that, in lieu of r_x paid on M by the government and on M' by the bankers, we select a deflationary rate r_d of equal size. Though the way of doing so is typically left unspecified, there are two possibilities:

(1) A tax on money assets may cause a constant decrease in $M + M'$ at the rate $-r_d$ and thus bring about a constant rate of deflation that increases the purchasing power of the remaining nominal balances at the rate $+r_d$. It seems obvious that such deflation will leave everybody in the society unaffected. The money holders will face every evening a tax $-r_d$ on their existing money balances only to wake up the next morning and discover a price change that has added an offsetting capital gain $+r_d$ to their remaining balances. The transactors will be unaffected as well. By transacting now rather than tomorrow, they avoid this evening's tax on money not spent but forgo tomorrow's offsetting capital gain on the remaining unspent money.

(2) Growth in the economy may cause the quantity of real goods and services in the economy to increase and thus, presumably, the quantity of the total trades that the society will want to or will have to engage in to increase. Thus, the functions AB and $A'B'$ will be shifting upwards and prices will be decreasing at (perhaps) the constant rate $+r_d$. Money holders will benefit and transactors suffer. For the transactors, it cannot make the slightest difference whether, when contemplating money transactions $T_{M+M'}/P$ in the course of which they will sacrifice the resource $M + M'$, they give up the annual paid income $r_x(M + M')$ or the annual capital gain $r_d (M + M')$. Thus, all we need to do to account for deflation's effects on the slope of the price lines facing the transactors is to replace in equation 11 the term r_x/r_e with r_d/r_e. Notice that the path to the limiting case will be different from the path (E_1, E_2, A') obtained previously because of the above discussed shifts of the production functions AB and $A'B'$. However, the slopes of the price lines will dominate the final outcome in both cases; when the slope of the price line

indicates that the cost of engaging in $T_{M'}/P$ or in $T_M/P + T_{M'}/P$ transactions has become prohibitive as a result of $r_x = r_e$ or $r_d = r_e$, respectively, the positions of the functions AB and $A'B'$ in Figure 5.1 are of no consequence.

6. DEFLATION AND INFLATION

While equation 11 indicates that a permanent rate of deflation smaller than the rate of return on capital would be resource-wasting by inducing the consumers to hold onto their monies more and to engage in barter more than previously and that a (fully expected) rate of deflation equal to the market rate would destroy our monetary economy, it should be noted that (fully expected) inflation of any size is possible. The reason for this is that inflation and deflation are opposites more thoroughly than is frequently realized:

(1) The rates r_d and r_i ($= -r_d$) of deflation and inflation reduce and increase, respectively, the cost of holding money. Thus they, *pari passu*, increase and reduce the cost of giving up money in the course of the transacting activity: they make circulation of money more and less expensive, respectively.

(2) However, the size of these costs depends on the expected duration of these costs. Until now, I assumed for simplicity that r_x, r_d, and r_i are expected to be received permanently, in which case the discounting formula used in the previous equations reduces to the factor $1/r_e$. However, less than infinite expected duration n changes this factor to $[1 - (1 + r_e)^{-n}]/r_e$. It is obvious that $dn/dr_d > 0$ and that $dn/dr_i < 0$: the higher the rate of deflation, the longer will each consumer try to benefit from it by holding on to his money, and the higher the rate of inflation, the shorter time will the consumer try to suffer it by spending his money.[5]

Taking bequests into account, the limit to personal duration n of deflation rewarding each transactor's existing money holdings is infinity, the above factor reduces to $1/r_e$, and thus the limit to a fully expected deflation r_d in equation 11 is given by r_e. When fully expected r_d starts to equal r_e, money transactions become prohibitively costly (even if their marginal resource cost is zero), money as a medium of exchange disappears, and therefore a fully expected deflation rate r_d that is higher than the market rate r_e becomes a contradiction in terms: it would imply increases in the purchasing power of a non-existent ("non-purchasing") money. In contrast, the limit to personal duration n of inflation that penalizes each transactor's existing money holdings is zero, since the consumer may spend his money immediately upon receipt. With zero n, the factor $[1 - (1 + r_e)^{-n}]/r_e$ equals zero, so that the limit to a fully expected inflation r_i in equation 11 is infinity.

Economic forces cause each price level to come equipped with its own nearby floor and no ceiling (except for unexpected and thus short run changes). This may provide a more satisfying explanation of world-wide and millenia-long inflationary bias than assertions that *all* rulers have propensity to debase currency, while *all* subjects have a propensity to conspire against wage reductions. And, the latter assumption is then not needed to uphold the Keynesian less-than-full-employment equilibrium since the real balance effect caused by endogenous deflation will restore full employment in an economy that remains a monetary economy only if this deflation is sudden, once-for-all, and thus unexpected: an unlikely eventuality. Otherwise, the cure will be worse than the sickness.

7. EMPIRICAL AND THEORETICAL SUPPORTING EVIDENCE

The next to unanimous support given during the Sixties to the "Golden Rules" of monetary policy—to explicit interest payments or to a deflationary rate—indicates the massive intuitive appeal of these ideas, despite empirical and theoretical evidence that contradicts them:

1. It is striking that, during the Sixties, the Golden Rules have driven Gresham's Law out of circulation (and thereby, have confirmed F. H. Knight's dictum that bad talk drives out good talk.) The currently dominant theory has never attempted to reconcile the notion that $r_x = r_e$ or $r_d = r_e$ will make "optimum" money out of the money subjected to this measure with Gresham's principle that bad money will drive good money (not to speak about optimum money) out of circulation $T_M/P + T_{M'}/P$.

2. It is striking that no account has been offered for empirical evidence that confirms the validity of Gresham's Law even in cases in which the source of "goodness" (nay, of optimality) are precisely interest payments. As Fisher recounts:

During the Civil War the government attempted to circulate fifty-dollar notes, bearing the interest of 7.3 per cent, so that the interest amounted to the very easily computed amount of a cent a day.

"Easily computed amount" implies that these notes were next to perfect substitutes for other $50 notes in production of transactions (had negligibly higher marginal cost c_M). And, they were clearly perfect substitutes in consumption for other $50 notes and next to perfect substitutes for at least the nearest higher denomination. Thus, if the Golden Rules are really golden, this money should have driven out of circulation all other $50 notes and probably the nearest higher denomination as well. The actual effect was, however, precisely the one that Gresham's Law and this paper would predict: "These notes, however, failed to circulate. In spite of attempts to make their circulation easy, people preferred to keep them for the sake of interest."[6] Similarly, in the United States today demand deposits M' finance $13,552 billion dollars worth of purchases per annum ($= T_{M'}$) while time deposits M'' finance some $10 billion ($= T_{M''}$): in other words, $V' = 77$ and $V'' = 0.05$. In Canada, the velocity of non-interest bearing deposits is 43 and the velocity of interest-bearing chequable deposits (bearing only one half of the market rate) is 1.46.[7] Surely, the failure of adherents of the Golden Rules to offer supporting empirical evidence and to explain contradictory evidence merits notice.

3. It is striking that the supporters of the Golden Rules expect that a positive subsidy of holding money ($+r_x$) will increase spending and the general price level[8] while Silvio Gessell (endorsed by Keynes[9] and Fisher) did expect a negative subsidy on holding money (a stamp tax $-r_x$) also to increase spending and the general price level (or, reduce unemployment). And, should the former prove to be right, then a stamp tax on money should be suggested to the President as a deflationary measure for his Phase 3!

4. Given the analysis of this paper it is not surprising that C. S. Tsiang has recently concluded that "... for the sake of stability and efficiency of financial markets, we should keep the yield differential $[r_e - r_x]$ sufficiently high ..."[10] or that J. Stein has recently concluded that $r_d = r_e$ would put the economy on a knife's edge: "If anticipated deflation exceeds the rate of return on capital ..., investment ... is not profitable. If savings continue while investment stops completely, would not the rate of deflation increase? ... the instability of Friedman's proposal is apparent. ..."[11] In terms of this paper, Stein has failed to notice that spending of superlucrative money both for equilibrium-lucrative investment *and* for equilibrium-lucrative consumption must stop completely. But then to expect explosive increases in the purchasing power of an asset that is not used to purchase anything anymore is a contradiction in terms.

5. By obtaining the limits $r_x = r_e$ and $r_d = r_e$ to fully expected rates r_x and r_d this chapter's analysis of the flow of transaction services yielded by money provides a behaviour rationale for two analyses of equilibrium conditions governing the sources M and M' of these services: the limit

$r_x = r_e$ has been provided in a book by Pesek and Saving; the limit $r_d = r_e$, in a long-forgotten book by Irving Fisher.[12]
6. These three analyses—singly, and, *a fortiori*, in conjunction—provide theoretical explanation for and derive empirical support from two striking facts:

(a) The fact that we never—to my knowledge, unimproved by the advocates of the Golden Rules—observed a deposit or a bond yielding $r_x = r_e$ to circulate, to yield transaction services and

(b) the fact that we have never observed a continuing and thus fully expected hyperdeflation while we have observed many hyperinflations.

It seems safe to say that such intellectually undemanding things as $r_x = r_e$ or $r_d = r_e$ have never happened anywhere in the world by accident or design, to be cherished and perpetuated as golden forever after, either because they cannot happen or because the initial small steps towards the two limits have always proved so destructive as to be nipped in the bud.

8. CONCLUSIONS

This chapter explicitly relates various economic forces, including interest payments on money, to variables of overwhelming importance to our transacting society: to cash and cheque circulation, to barter transactions, and to self-sufficiency. Implicitly—since our transacting society makes out of the latter two items not viable alternatives—it also relates these forces to unemployment. In contrast, the dominant view leading to the Golden Rules and to the theory of Optimum Money focuses on quantitatively unspecified increases in real balances $\Sigma M/P$,[13] and merely notes quantitatively unspecified decrease in their average velocity V_a. Thus, for all we are told, the product $(\Sigma M/P)(V_a)$—that is, real money transactions $T_{\Sigma M}/P$—may increase, stay the same, or decrease. This, I suggest, reveals a very cavalier attitude towards a variable the size of which could not be reduced significantly without bringing our transacting society to a grinding halt.

It is sobering to realize that Sir Thomas Gresham (1519–79) and Irving Fisher (1867–1947) would hardly be surprised *either* with my focus on the circulation of money rather than merely on money *or* with the conclusion that bad money (of which resources devoted to bartering effort are a special form) will drive good money and, of course, optimum money out of circulation.[14] Thus, analytically this paper is thoroughly conservative while the Golden Monetary Rules and the theory of Optimum Money are thoroughly revolutionary. While the old frequently is replaced with the new, peaceful coexistence of both seems hardly tolerable. Either the old and the new may be reconciled; then those who assert the new without denying the old should reconcile the two. Or, the old and the new are not reconcilable; then one should be proven right and the other wrong. This chapter opts for the old, and views the new as merely another of the periodically recurrent schemes to provide society with free money.

NOTES

1. Irving Fisher, *The Purchasing Power of Money* (1911), p. 317.
2. Milton Friedman, *Price Theory* (1962), pp. 61–65.
3. The same prediction has been offered by Milton Friedman, *A Program for Monetary Stability* (1959), p. 73.
4. The opposite conclusion has been reached elsewhere. If $r_x = r_e$, "The transaction services rendered by demand deposits have become free goods, available without cost to the holders of demand deposits." M. Friedman and A. J. Schwartz, *Monetary Statistics of the United States* (1970), p. 114.
5. Cf. Abba P. Learner, *Economics of Control* (1944), p. 289: "When prices are *falling* it pays to hold on to money rather than to spend it quickly because waiting will enable purchases to be made later when prices are lower and one can get more for the money."
6. Fisher, *op. cit.*, p. 9.
7. *Federal Reserve Bulletin*, July 1971, p. A-15;. F.R. Bank of Chicago, "Activity in Time Deposits" (mimeo), 1968, p. 4; P. A. Polzin, *The Canadian Money Supply* (unpublished Ph.D. dissertation, East Lansing, Michigan, 1968), p. 126. (Note that V, V' and V'' are the weights that Fisher's theory of money assigns to monies M, M', and M''. This is worth pointing out in view of the claims that the problem of weighting monies is still virgin territory: cf. Friedman and Schwartz, *op. cit.*, pp. 151–3.)
8. Friedman and Schwartz, *op. cit.*, p. 114. (They claim that $dr_x > 0$ will cause $dP > 0$, which in terms of equation 6 means that $d(T_M + T_{M'}) > 0$. Since $T_{M'}$ is said to become a free good (cf. n. 4), the last must be assumed to be due to $dT_{M'} > |dT_M|$.)
9. John Maynard Keynes, *The General Theory of Employment, Interest, and Money* (1936), pp. 234, 357–8.
10. C. S. Tsiang, "A Critical Note on the Optimum Supply of Money," *Journal of Money, Credit, and Banking*, II (May, 1969), p. 279.
11. Jerome Stein, "The Optimum Quantity of Money," *Journal of Money, Credit, and Banking*, II (Nov. 1970), p. 417.
12. B. P. Pesek and T. R. Saving, *Money, Wealth, and Economic Theory* (New York, 1967), pp. 103–37 and Irving Fisher, *Appreciation and Interest* (1896), pp. 30–1.
13. M. Friedman, *The Optimum Quantity of Money* (1969), pp. 44.
14. Note that K. Brunner and A. H. Meltzer have concluded in "The Uses of Money," *American Economic Review*, LXI (Dec. 1971), p. 801: "The relatively high yield on money puts a premium on the search for assets that are close substitutes for the existing mediums of exchange—have similar information and transfer costs—and lower yield."

6 Banks' Supply Function and the Equilibrium Quantity of Money[*][1]

In 1935, Sir John Hicks issued his well-known call for a marginal revolution in monetary theory. Yet, in 1961, James Tobin had occasion to state that

> The intellectual gulf between economists' theory of values of goods and services and their theories of value of money is well known and periodically deplored. Twenty-five years after Hicks' eloquent call for a marginal revolution in monetary theory our students still detect that their mastery of the presumed fundamental, theoretical apparatus of economics is put to very little test in their studies of monetary economics and monetary models. As Hicks complained, anything seems to go in a subject where propositions do not have to be grounded in someone's optimizing behaviour and where shrewd but casual empiricism and analogies to mechanics and thermodynamics take the place of inferences from utility and profit maximization.[2]

In this chapter I want to accomplish two things. First, I shall show that considerations of profit maximization are given inadequate considerations in our current analysis of the determinants of the money stock. E.g., in the two recent influential books on the topic—by Cagan[3] and another by Friedman and Schwartz[4]—banks' resource costs are never quantified nor even mentioned; obviously, they must be viewed as irrelevant for the industry's equilibrium. Conversely, all studies known to me[5] into the costs conditions facing commercial banks fail to relate the results obtained to the equilibrium of the banking industry as a whole and to the equilibrium quantity of money. Yet, in the United States these resource costs amount to $10 billion per annum, to $13 billion if the return on capital is included, and to $15 billion if taxes are included.[6] It would be most surprising if these huge costs would not significantly co-determine equilibrium quantity of deposits and thus of money.

---

[*] From: *The Canadian Journal of Economics*, August 1970.

Second, I shall reformulate our current theory of the determinants of the money stock so as to incorporate resource costs into our analysis of the banks' supply function. We shall see that such reformulation affects substantially our analysis of past monetary developments and several major policy recommendations.

1. THE FUNDAMENTAL MONEY EQUATION

When we analyze market equilibrium in the case of most assets, we base our approach on the supply and demand apparatus of value theory. When, however, we shift our attention to an asset called money, the method changes drastically. The basic model that is said to determine equilibrium in the money market reads as follows:

$$C = H - r_1 D, \tag{1}$$

$$D = 1/r_2 C, \tag{2}$$

$$M = C + D, \tag{3}$$

where r_1 is the banks' reserve-deposit ratio and r_2 the currency-deposit ratio desired by the public. The symbol H denotes high-powered money (currency plus bank reserve R), exogenously determined by the Central Bank. Symbols C, D, and M denote the quantity of currency, deposits, and the sum of the two, the stock of money. The analytical basis for these equations is so well known as not to merit repeating. When we solve these questions simultaneously, we obtain the fundamental money equilibrium equation

$$M = H[1 + (C/D)]/[(R/D) + (C/D)] \tag{4}$$

or some alternative transformation of it.[7]

To connect this approach with those that follow, let me offer a geometric interpretation of this model. In Figure 6.1, place high-powered money on one axis and deposits on the other. Let the function $D_c D_c$ express the currency-deposit ratio and the function $S_h S_h$ show the supply of high-powered money. Should the banks hold zero reserves, equilibrium will be established where $D_c D_c = S_h S_h$. The equilibrium quantity of currency in public hands will be OH and the equilibrium quantity of deposits will be OD. If banks do hold reserve (say, if $r_1 = 0.5$), the supply of currency to the public becomes $S_c S_c$, with the vertical difference between $S_h S_h$ and $S_c S_c$ measuring the leakage of high-powered money into the banks' coffers. Equilibrium will be now established where $D_c D_c = S_c S_c$. The equilibrium quantity of currency held by the public is

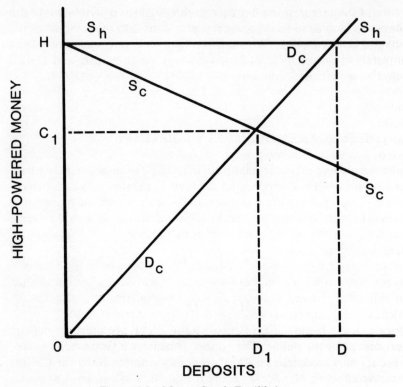

Figure 6.1 Money Stock Equilibrium

OC_1, the equilibrium quantity of deposits is OD_1, and the equilibrium quantity of bank reserves is C_1H.

According to this theory, the quantity of money is determined by (1) the level of high-powered money, (2) the reserve ratio, and (3) the currency-deposit ratio. In modern times the first two are mainly policy determined, so that the only genuinely endogenous variable in this model is the currency-deposit ratio. It has the task of summarizing the tremendously complex forces exerted on the money market by the public, the business sector, and commercial banks. This heavy burden the ratio is unable to bear, as is best evidenced by the fact that no one has, as yet, specified in a formal manner the economic determinants of this ratio. All that we do have are verbal and *ex post* speculations as to the probable causes of changes in it.[8] The ratio, rather than M, is the true unknown in the system. Given M, whatever the two other ratios do not explain, the currency-deposit ratio—by arithmetic necessity—must and does explain. Aside from this, the analysis summarized in equations 1 through 4 has two major shortcomings: (a) Determination of the equilibrium quantity of currency and deposit monies is completely divorced from the determination of the equilibrium price (i.e., "purchasing power") of these two assets. (b) Determination of the equilibrium quantity of deposit money is completely divorced from the resource costs facing the banks and thus from the supply function of bank deposits. For all we know, the purchasing power of money could halve while the resource cost of producing it doubled and the equilibrium quantity of deposits as specified in equation 4 would remain unchanged. In terms of price theory, this is most unusual. What is needed is a theory in which both the price of money and the cost of producing it are shown to co-determine the banking industry's equilibrium.

2. IS ALL MONEY A STOCK?

While the missing price variable makes the incorporation of banks' costs into the analysis impossible, the traditional view of money as a "stock" makes it seem either superfluous or secondary. However, I would submit that this view of bank money as a stock is analytically misleading (it misleads us into ignoring supply forces) and empirically false. Were all money a stock, it should be possible to abolish all producers of money after some desired stock is reached and to rechannel the resources used by the (former) suppliers to other uses. While this would be—at least conceptually—possible in the case of the "currency department," it would be clearly impossible in the case of the "banking department." By its very nature, bank money is constantly sliding into the abyss of non-existence, either as it is returned to the banks for conversion into currency or as rentals (or "loans") of it expire. This gives the banker-suppliers a constant opportunity to re-evaluate their output decisions in the light of the currently prevailing reserve costs (the reserve ratio) and resource costs. If bank money is a stock, it is not comparable to stock of Rembrandt paintings but rather to a river, constantly renewed in the mountains and constantly disappearing down in the valley, with the banker controlling the sluice.

In the United States, the average life span of a dollar of demand deposits is less than six days, and it seems to be getting shorter every year (Table 6.1). Veritably, the suppliers' (the bankers') job is never done, even though Table 6.1 tends to overstate the magnitude of the task that the banker faces. First, in many cases a withdrawal by one customer of a banker is merely a simultaneous deposit by another customer of the same banker. Second, as most other business firms, so the banker also has a stable of steady customers: those who demand the asset that he supplies at the beginning of the month, reduce their inventory of it in the course of the month, only to return for additional supplies when their next pay cheques arrive. But even so, the bankers' task is still quite monumental, as is shown by the fact that the performance of it absorbs annually, in the US, resources worth $15 billion. In view of this, what is the most fruitful approach of handling, analytically, bank deposit money?

One approach would be to view each $1 of bank deposits as a highly perishable product, with an average life span of less than six days, which the banker must constantly regenerate to keep his business in profitable existence and to lend verisimilitude to the notion that all money is a stock, in the case of which production costs do not matter. Another approach would be to view the asset supplied as one that is being produced and rented by the banker and the life span of which is not determined by the length of possession by one customer but by the length of existence of this asset in the hands of any customer. The resource cost that in the former approach would receive the name "production costs," in the latter approach simply receives the name "production, rental, and maintenance costs."

The latter approach would be akin to the one given to Xerox copiers: there we also do not say that a copier becomes destroyed when it is turned in only to be produced anew when it is rented again. In the case of demand deposits, however, which have no physical substance, the difference between the former and the latter approach is—empirically— impossible to establish. Thus, the difference between these two approaches is merely a difference in names that we give to observable phenomena; not a difference in substance. The choice of either approach is trivial and arbitrary since either approach describes correctly the economic facts that we are facing. Namely, that the continuing existence of bank money requires continuing activity of the banker without which

Table 6.1:   Average lifespan of $1 of demand deposit money in the US

Year	One New York bank	Six major banks	226 other banks	Entire sample of 233 banks
	\multicolumn{4}{c}{Life measured in days}			
1965	3.8	8.5	10.8	7.9
1966	3.5	7.7	11.6	7.2
1967	2.9	7.2	10.5	6.4
1968	2.8	6.6	10.1	6.1
1969	2.7	5.5	9.7	5.6

Source: Federal Reserve Bulletin, 1965–9, tables on bank debits and deposit turnover. (Figures for January of each year.)

the ever-changing stock—or, rather, the flow—of bank money would be destroyed in short order. For these reasons, I shall view bank money as a flow produced by the banker and apply to the analysis of it the standard tools of production theory.

3. DEMAND FOR MONEY: REAL OR NOMINAL?

The next issue to be faced is whether to analyze "nominal" quantities (as is done in equation 4) or whether to focus—as is frequently suggested—on "real" quantities. To demonstrate the validity of either approach, let me start in Figure 6.2 with the demand for nominal money. For simplicity, I shall provisionally assume that we face a one-money economy and that all money is bank money. Since production economics is the topic of this chapter, I shall label the demand function AR so as to remind the reader that from the standpoint of the supplier-banker a demand function is an average revenue function. The subscripts attached to the AR function indicate that real income and the real rate of interest are assumed to be given.[9] On the vertical axis we measure the market price P_m of each unit of nominal money in terms of some representative basket of goods and services *and* an index of the average revenue received by the banks $[1 - (1 + r)^{-t}]P_m$, where t measures the length of the rental period. A customer who sells the asset to others (intending to repurchase it when his rental period expires) receives, of course, the full market price P_m. The banker, as any other renter, does not receive from his customers this price but merely the average revenue the present worth of which is $[1 - (1 + r)^{-t}]P_m$. On the horizontal axis we measure the nominal quantity of money M supplied by the banker and demanded by customers per rental period t. Notice that in the case of money, which is not physically consumed over time, this flow quantity supplied and demanded *per* unit of time t is numerically identical with the inventory quantity (stock) held by the customers *at* any point of time within t. It is for this reason that, as long as demand occupies the centre of the stage and supply is ignored, analysis of bank money in terms of stocks will do equally well.

For expositive purposes, the AR function is drawn so as to exhaust all conceivable negative price elasticities of the demand for money, starting from minus infinity and ending with zero. Positive price elasticities are not considered since I accept the standard assumption that money cannot be an inferior good.

Next, let me undertake two elementary transformations of this function. As Friedman shows,[10] we may take either the price or the quantity

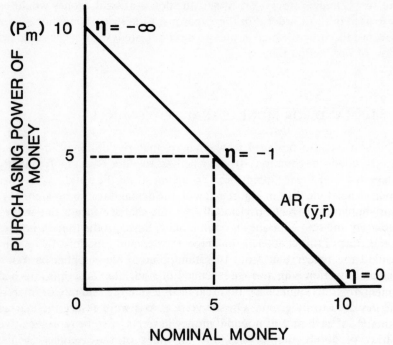

NOMINAL MONEY

Figure 6.2 Demand for Nominal Balances

to be the independent variables and derive from Figure 6.2 two alternative total revenue (*TR*) functions (Figures 6.3a and b). Except in the case of a monopoly, Figure 6.3b is more relevant and more often used, since each firm in any industry (and thus each bank) controls the quantity supplied while the price is market-determined.

Nevertheless, let us focus on the less relevant Figure 6.3a. The price of money measures the number P_m of representative baskets of goods and services that one unit of money sells for and, conversely, is able to purchase (thus the term "purchasing power" of money instead of the more usual term "price"). We may be more interested, however, in the reciprocal of this magnitude, in the number P_g (or in an index of this number) of units of money that must be paid for one representative basket of goods and services ("the general price level"). By definition, $P_m = (1/P_g)$. Simple transformation of Figure 6.3a into Figure 6.4 enables us to give expression to this preference of ours.

In price theory, the *TR* functions of Figure 6.3a and 3b are seldom used and the *TR* function in Figure 6.4 is never used. Monetary theory, however, makes frequent use of the *TR* function in Figure 6.4 and gives it the name "the demand for real balances." An example of such use is

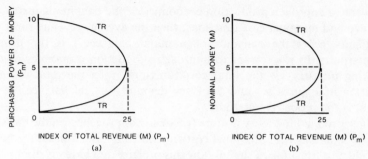

Figure 6.3   Indices of Total Revenue Function

provided by the work of Don Patinkin: inspection will reveal that my Figure 6.2 is consistent with his Figure II–2-b and that my Figure 6.4 is consistent with his Figure II–2-a.[11] The only difference is that Patinkin takes the *TR* function in Figure 6.4 to be a demand function and, on the basis of the argument stating that money cannot be an inferior good, concludes that this function must have only a negative slope (the heavy segment of *TR* in Figure 6.4). It then follows the only relevant part of the function shown in Figure 6.2 is the lower half (the heavy segment with elasticity, η, between minus unity and zero).

However, to discuss that would lead me away from my topic. My sole purpose in presenting Figures 6.2 through 6.4 was to show that analyses based on either real or nominal balances are equally valid, since they are merely alternative expressions of one and the same thing. Each function is a purely mechanical transformation of the other. Operationally they are equivalent, and cannot be identified in the econometric meaning of the term.[12] However, when using either concept of "demand" we must make sure that we relate it with a corresponding concept of supply: (a) if

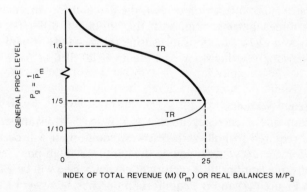

Figure 6.4   Index of Total Revenue or "Demand for Revenue Balances"

we want to approach production economics of the banking industry *via* average and marginal cost functions, then the average revenue function of Figure 6.2 ("the demand for nominal balances") is the proper counterpart; (b) if we want to approach production economics of the banking industry *via* the total cost functions, then the total revenue function of Figures 6.3 and 6.4 ("the demand for real balances function") is the proper counterpart.

Since production theory is more frequently approached on the basis of supply functions (i.e., marginal cost functions) and seldom on the basis of total cost functions, I shall follow this practice and base my discussion on demand for and supply of nominal balances in terms of their purchasing power. A reader who favours the analysis that proceeds *via* real balances in terms of the general price level may easily re-formulate the analysis that follows by undertaking the transformations leading from Figure 6.2 to Figure 6.4.

4. PRICE AND QUANTITY EQUILIBRIUM

With these two key issues behind us, we may now proceed. Using the demand function of Figure 6.2, let us re-formulate the model of equations 1 through 4 by adding

$$M_d = f(P_m). \tag{5}$$

The demand function that ensues[13] is reproduced in Figure 6.5 and is labelled $D_{c+d}D_{c+d}$ to reflect the fact that now we are dealing with a two-money world. There being nothing in the literature that would suggest that the structure of demands for currency and bank deposits changes with the general price level, I shall assume that the currency-deposit ratio is not a function of Pm. the demand for currency D_cD_c is then determined by this ratio, with the horizontal difference between $D_{c+d}D_{c+d}$ and D_cD_c functions measuring the demand for bank deposits D_dD_d. The supply of high-powered money is labelled as S_hS_h.

The Currency Market
Equilibrium in the currency market is now easy to establish. Should banks be required to hold zero reserves, equilibrium will occur where demand for currency D_cD_c equals the supply of high-powered money S_hS_h. Thus, the equilibrium quantity of currency held will be P_1C (equal to OH in Figure 6.1) and the equilibrium purchasing power of each unit

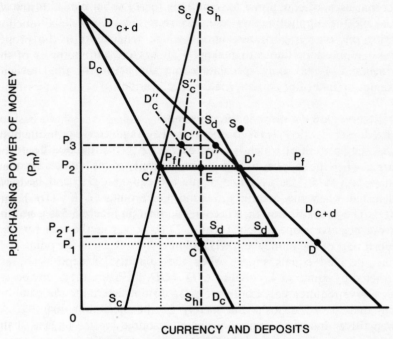

Figure 6.5   Money Market Equilibrium

of currency will be OP_1. Suppose, however, that the banks do hold reserves of currency. Assuming, as in Figure 6.1, a fifty per cent reserve ratio, we may construct in Figure 6.5 a supply of currency to the public function $S_c S_c$. At any P_m, the $S_c S_c$ function will be determined by the quantity of high-powered money in existence less the quantity of deposits demanded at the same P_m times the reserve ratio r_1; the supply of deposits is assumed to be irrelevant and automatically equal to the demand for them. Equilibrium in the currency market will then occur where $D_c D_c$ equals $S_c S_c$. Thus the equilibrium quantity of currency held will be $P_2 C'$ (OC_1 in Figure 6.1) and the equilibrium purchasing power of each unit of currency will be OP_2 units of representative baskets of goods and services.

The Deposit Market

What can we say about the deposit market? Isn't it imperative to specify the counterpart of the supply of currency function, the supply of deposits function, if we are to establish equilibrium in the deposit market? An affirmative answer would seem obvious were it not for the fact that users of equation 4 have nothing to say about banks' resource costs and the supply function resulting from them. Thus, they must be relying on some implicit assumption which renders consideration of banks' supply superfluous by making it always and automatically equal to demand. I may only speculate about the nature of this implicit assumption and offer two alternative specifications of it.

(a) Reserves are the only signification input

A fixed reserve ratio r_1 leads to a horizontal average reserve cost function S_dS_d, the position of which is given by $P_2 \times r_1$. This function becomes vertical when the supplies of high-powered money to the bankers become exhausted. At P_2 the available inputs are equal to $C'E$ and become exhausted when the quantity of deposits becomes $[C'E \times (1/r_1)]$ or $C'D'$. The S_dS_d function then becomes vertical (in Figure 6.5 it seems to have a negative slope merely because D_cD_c serves as the axis for the deposit part of the money market) and intersects D_dD_d at the point D'. Thus, demand equals supply when the quantity of deposits is, as predicted by equation 4, equal to $C'D'$ (OD_1 in Figure 6.1). Obviously the reserve requirements leading to S_dS_d do not determine *the* equilibrium quantity of deposits but merely fix the maximum quantity. A competitive industry facing average resource costs higher than $(OP_2 - P_2r_1)$ will never supply $C'D'$ and a monopolist equating marginal cost and marginal revenue may not supply $C'D'$ (see section 5).

Besides, this method of validating equation 4 breaks down completely in the zero reserve case. With $r_1 = 0$, $P_m r_1 = 0$, so that the S_dS_d function coincides with the horizontal axis throughout. We then become unable to explain the equilibrium quantity CD in Figure 6.5 (OD in Figure 6.1) predicted by equation 4. To cover even this special case, we must offer an alternative—and a more general—specification of the implicit assumption on which equation 4 rests.

(b) Fixed minimum price

The banker is subject to the convertibility clause that imposes on him the obligation to exchange on demand $1 of currency for $1 of deposits. The reverse, however, does not hold: he does not have to accept a deposit of currency if he does not want to. It is easy to see that this convertibility clause leads to the establishment of a fixed minimum price (purchasing power) of deposits.

Start with the currency leading to a price P_2 and quantity of currency P_2C'. Should the bankers supply more than $C'D'$ quantity of deposits, excess of supply over demand at this P_2 would drive the purchasing power of $1 of deposits below P_2: there would be a "discount" on deposits in terms of currency such as occurred in the last century in the

US when the convertibility clause was only imperfectly enforced. We then have an economy with three goods and three relative prices: (a) market determined price (purchasing power) of currency $P_m^c = P_2$ baskets of goods; (b) market determined price of deposits $P_m^d < P_2$ baskets of goods; (c) convertibility-clause determined $\$1C = \$1D$ which the bank must pay. Profitable arbitrage becomes possible and in the course of it deposits flow back into the banks to be exchanged for currency, or, indirectly, for financial assets that the banker must sell to obtain currency. Assuming zero cost of the arbitrage, this continues until P_m^d becomes equal to P_m^c, which occurs only when the quantity of bank deposits is reduced, with reserved ratio r_1, to $C'D'$ or, *with zero* reserves, to CD. In terms of price theory, we have a market containing (a) demand for deposits D_dD_d, (b) some unknown supply of bank deposits S_dS_d, and (c) a convertibility-clause induced fixed minimum price function P_fP_f, the position of which is determined by the equilibrium in the currency market (by P_m^c). The intersection of functions D_dD_d and P_fP_f will determine equilibrium, at the level predicted by equation 4, only if banks' and arbitragists' cost functions are implicitly assumed to be *always* irrelevant.

5. BANKS' SUPPLY AND THE FUNDAMENTAL EQUATION

The fixed minimum price constraint is superior to the fixed maximum quantity constraint (i.e., to the reserve constraint) in that it is a more general one. However, both suffer from identical shortcomings so grave as to indicate that the theory that must rely on either of them is not a valid one: (a) Both ways require us to assume that banks' resource costs are always irrelevant for banks' equilibrium. Since these costs in 1968 amounted to $\$10-\$15$ billion per annum and since, therefore, the market value of resources committed to banking was $\$166-\$250$ billion (if I assume 6 per cent interest rate), this assumption makes the two ways of validating equation 4 highly suspect. (b) Both ways, if they do explain banks' equilibrium, should lead to a price of deposits equal to P_f. Empirical evidence offered in section 6a shows, however, that the actual price charged by banks, including service charges, is $(1.16) \times (P_f)$, which must mean that resource costs do matter. (c) Even though both ways enable us to determine the industry's equilibrium, both lead to a "complete indeterminacy"[14] of the size of banks in this industry. Analytically this is unsatisfactory and empirically, contrary to observed facts.

However, the proof of the pudding is in the eating. Isn't the fact that equation 4 fully explains the stock of money throughout history an adequate proof that the banks' supply function does merit neglect? The answer is a negative one, since the banks' supply function plays the role of an *eminence grise* in equation 4. Ignored analytically, it co-determines equilibrium in the real world and creeps back into the analysis in the guise of the currency-deposit ratio. To see this, suppose that we are, initially, in equilibrium at the point D' so that the purchasing power of money is P_2 and the equilibrium stock of money P_2D'. If we face a *competitive industry* receiving zero profits, the industry's supply passes through the point D'. Next, unionization of bank employees increases sharply the costs facing the industry so that the banks start earning losses and the supply function now passes through a point such as S. Banks are forced to increase the price charged: either the market interest rate r_e or the service charge rate r_s. The former is, however, a shift parameter of the total demand for money function DD in Figure 6.2 and $D_{c+d}D_{c+d}$ in Figure 6.5. As stated in note 9, I assume that in full employment the banks are price takers as far as the real rate r_e is concerned. What they are free to change in my model is the service charge rate r_s. When the banks increase this rate, the relative cost of using bank deposits and currency changes, and this will cause a rightward shift of the D_cD_c and S_cS_c functions and an opposite shift in the demand for bank deposits function D_dD_d. The reduction in the quantity demanded of bank deposits must, at some level of service charges, match the reduction in supply of these deposits and result in a new equilibrium. Figure 6.5 is not suitable for finding it, however. Anticipating the result obtained in Figure 6.6, let me now merely assume that a new equilibrium will be found where $D_c''D_c'' = S_c''S_c''$ and where $D_d''D_d''$ equals the new supply of bank deposits $S_d''S_d''$. (Should we, in a more complex model, permit the market interest rate to change as well, demand for *all* money will decrease and thus the decrease in demand for deposits due to a higher r^s will be reinforced by a decrease in demand for deposits due to a higher r_e.)

Will this conclusion be affected if we assume, instead, some noncompetitive industry? Let us go to the other extreme and consider the case of a pure monopolist. Regardless of the level of reserves and resource costs, this monopolist would never supply even the initial quantity $C'D'$ since the demand function as drawn in Figure 6.5 happens to be less than unitary elastic at the point D', so that the marginal revenue yielded by the $C'D'$-th unit would be negative. If we now impose the above-specified increase in labour costs, the monopolist would supply still less than $C'D'$.

Obviously, either in the competitive case or in the monopolist case—and surely in the intermediate oligopoly cases—the much emphasized power of the policy-maker to control deposits through his control over bank reserves is far from complete. In terms of the $P_f P_f$ function, he does not control the purchasing power of money but merely the minimum purchasing power (i.e., the maximum price level). In terms of $S_d S_d$, by controlling the reserves ratio he does not control the quantity of deposits but merely the maximum quantity. In terms of banks' costs, he controls merely the minimum (average reserve) cost $P_m r_1$, but not the total average cost (reserve plus resource costs) which, in the case of any industry, co-determine the equilibrium output. [15]

This makes clear that the tautology of the fundamental equation 4 merely evades the issue of banks' resource cost and of profit maximization behaviour of bankers. As we have seen, either in the competitive or the monopolistic case an increase in resource costs shift the banks' supply function and reduces the initial quantity $C'D'$ to the quantity $C''D''$ or (in the monopolistic case) to an even smaller quantity. This causes the ratio of the now more expensive product to the cheaper product to fall; it causes the deposit-currency ratio to fall from $(C'D')/(P_2 C')$ to $(C''D'')/(P_3 C'')$ or less. Users of equation 4 will observe this consequence and conclude that the quantity of money and the price level changed because of a change in the *public's demand function*, in the deposit-currency ratio desired by the public. [16] Clearly, the equation does not have the power to predict an equilibrium, but merely to rationalize it *ex post*. And the method of rationalizing it is likely to mislead us into confusing supply and demand forces.

6a.   SPECIFICATION OF BANKS' PRICE AND COST VARIABLES

Sections 4 and 5 revealed the special implicit assumptions about banks' supply function contained in the current theory of determination of the equilibrium quantity of money. I believe that the mere act of spelling out these implicit assumptions makes us reach for some substitute theory in which banks' supply would be given an adequate consideration. In the case of bank money, however, our existing kit of tools is so rudimentary that it is necessary to start such endeavour by specifying the price and cost concepts to be used in the analysis. [17] One of the reasons for this rudimentary state is that neglect of supply forces failed to stimulate analytically defensible specifications of prices and costs of the banking industry. Another reason for this is that, in contrast with currency, bank money is not produced and sold outright but—like Xerox machines— produced and rented. In contrast to pure rentals found in price theory textbooks, rental agreements in the real world are frequently a complex mixture of once-for-all payment (such as a deposit) and of a stipulated flow of daily or annual charges complexly determined by formulae based on both time and rate of use. Let me consider the price mix facing the demanders of demand deposits.

(a) A depositor—representing r_1 fraction of a monopoly bank's customers—pays immediately \$1 of currency for \$1 of bank money.

(b) A borrower—representing $(1 - r_1)$ fraction of a bank's customers—deposits nothing. He obtains \$1 of bank money by promising to the banker to return his product at a specified time and to pay him in the meantime rental charges of $\$1 \times r_e$ (r_e is specified in Table 6.3). A borrower "deposits" his debt certificate.

It should be noted that with respect to the gross monopoly bank money supply, only r_1 fraction of a bank's customers are depositors. With respect to the net bank money supply (gross supply minus reserves of currency), a zero fraction of a bank's customers are depositors and all banks' customers are borrowers who deposited nothing, or their payees. It is for this reason that the orthodox term "depositor" is not employed in this chapter and the term "customer" appears instead.

(c) Bank money thus brought into existence then circulates among those willing to accept it. They all accept a burden of a complex set of service charges. Available statistical evidence (Table 6.3) expresses these charges most conveniently in terms of the service charge rate r_S that an average dollar of bank money yields to the bank per annum.

(d) Many customers and borrowers are subject to minimum and compensatory balances requirements, respectively. In their effects on the demanders these are indistinguishable from currency reserve requirements imposed on the bankers: the former increase the cost of using, just as the latter increase the cost of producing, bank money. Data on these requirements are not available at present.

Similarly, the firms supplying the asset rented typically face a complex mix of once-for-all production costs plus a flow of expenses resulting from the need to re-rent at frequent intervals the asset in question and from the necessity to maintain this asset in working order. In the case of a banker, the cost mix may be categorized as follows:

(a) Each \$1 deposit imposes on the banker the duty to deliver to the Federal Reserve System $\$1 \times r_1$ of currency.

(b) In the case of borrowers, the banker suffers the cost of investigating the credit-worthiness of the borrower and the quality of the asset serving as security ("appraising costs"), and insurance against default.

(c) The bank may lend its product indirectly by purchasing some already existing debt certificate from its owner. Such "investment" subjects the banker to the costs of managing his portfolio, brokerage charges, etc. Available statistical evidence lumps (b) and (c) together and expresses them, most conveniently, in terms of a cost rate r_i per dollar of earning assets. Since all other rates are, however, expressed in terms of costs per dollar of bank deposits, it is preferable to express this cost in the same way. Since earning assets are $(1 - r_1)$ fraction of deposits, the above cost per dollar of deposits is then $1 \times r_i \times (1 - r_1)$, where r_1 is the reserve ratio.

(d) The banker faces the cost of servicing the deposit accounts. Available statistical evidence expresses this again on an annual basis. I shall speak about maintenance costs of $1 \times r_m$ per annum per dollar of deposit.

(e) Finally, the banker faces several costs which the Federal Reserve System's cost analysis fails to quantify: insurance against default, return on capital invested, and taxes. Only the last item has been estimated; in Tables 6.2 and 6.3 it is labelled r_t.

For analytical purposes, this complexity of prices paid and costs incurred is most inconvenient, just as it would be inconvenient to speak about the price (or cost) of a Xerox copier as "$500 down immediately as a deposit and then $500 per month." Efficiency requires that we come up with a price and cost concept expressed in terms of one single *index* number. The standard approach of value theory is to express such mixes *either* as the sum of once-for-all equivalents of all items *or* the sum of per-year equivalents of all items. The first part of Table 6.2 shows the application of this standard method of expressing costs in terms of one common denominator, be it the immediate cost plus the discounted present value of the recurring costs *or* the annual opportunity cost of suffering the immediate cost plus the other annual charges.

Since this way of quantifying bank prices and cost is a new one, it may be useful to put some empirical flesh on the above abstract concepts. For this purpose, I am using a functional cost analysis prepared by the Federal Reserve Bank of Boston for 86 banks in 1965. In Table 6.3 I show the data needed for the calculation of the price and cost indices. These data, when substituted into the equations of Table 6.2, yield the price and cost estimates shown in the last column of Table 6.2. (Data for six other Federal Reserve districts and many other years are shown in Appendix A.)

The price and cost estimates given below are quite interesting. The fact that the market price of deposits is $1.16P_f$ shows—in terms of the analysis of Sections 4 and 5—that the policy-maker controlling reserves merely determines the maximum quantity of deposits but not the equilibrium quantity. The fact that the (incomplete) once-for-all average cost is $100.70 per $100 of deposits (the annual cost being $5.46 per $100) shows that all the proposed golden rule monetary policies based on the assumption of zero cost of producing money are empirically irrelevant.

Finally, the observation of proximity of market price and production costs of bank money ($P_m^d \approx C_d$ or, on an annual basis, $P_m^d r \approx C_d r$) has a bearing on the current debate as to whether this money is net wealth or merely the bankers' liability. (a) Such debate is possible in case of an asset with observed zero or negligible production costs since only then may such an asset be either net wealth (e.g., diamond accidentally found) or a liability (e.g., corporate bond). (b) Our observation of price-cost equality in the case of bank money renders such debate impossible since then such asset *must* be net wealth: no rational producer would sacrifice X baskets of resources (or, Xr baskets annually) to produce something which, when finished, merely adds X baskets of resources to his liabilities. In this case "the liability hypothesis" of bank money yields the unacceptable implication of a destruction of wealth while "the net wealth hypothesis" implies the standard transformation, through production, of one type of net wealth (banker's inputs) into another type of net wealth (bank money outputs) which the producer-banker then rents to the public.

Banker's alleged liability to his customers (called "depositors" even though they, with respect to the net bank money supply, deposited nothing) is then revealed to be merely his duty to accept back the product rented and to return to the former customer (or his payee) the customer's promise to pay rental charges and to return the product (or currency of equal value). Since everyone who rents his products to others has the

---

Table 6.2:   *Price and average cost indices*

(Per $100 of demand deposits)

Price index (discounted present value)
Depositor P_d $= \$100 + \$100\ (r_s^*/r_e) = \$116.79\dagger$
Borrower P_d $= \$100\ (r_e/r_e) + \$100\ (r_s^*/r_e) = \$116.79\dagger$
Average cost index (discounted present value)
Banker C_d $= \$100\ r_1 = \$100[r_i(1 - r_1)]/r_e + \$100(r_m/r_e) + \$100(r\text{-}_t/r_e) = \$100.70\ddagger$
Per annum price index
Depositor P_d' $= \$100r_e + \$100r_e^* = \$6.33\dagger$
Borrower P_d' $= \$100r_e + \$100r_s^* = \$6.33\dagger$
Per annum average cost index
Banker C_d' $= \$100r_1r_e + \$100r_i(1 - r_1) + \$100r_m + \$100r_t = \$5.46\ddagger$

Notes: * In time-series analyses the service charges would have to be adjusted for the volume of services that the customer receives (Table 6.1).
† These figures do not contain the cost of holding minimum and compensatory balances.
‡ These figures exclude insurance against default and the average return to banker's capital.

Table 6.3: Raw price and average cost data entering the two price indices, Boston banks, 1965.

(Data in $ per $100 of demand deposits)

(1) *Components of price*

Depositor's once-for-all payment	$100.00
Borrower's interest charges, per annum (r_e)	5.42
Service charges, per annum (r_s)	0.91
Minimum and compensatory balances	n.a.

(2) *Components of costs*

Banker's once-for-all reserve cost ($\$100 \times r_1$)	19.42
Investment costs, per annum and per $100 of earning assets ($r_i$)	1.15
Maintenance costs, per annum (r_m)	2.53
Taxes, per annum (r_t)	0.95
Insurance against loss, per annum	n.a.
Return to bank's capital, per annum	n.a.

Note: n.a. stands for not available
Sources: All figures come from B. P. Pesek and T. R. Saving, *The Foundations of Money and Banking* (New York, 1968), p. 160, except those for taxes, which come from estimates appearing in an M.A. thesis of Stephen M. Hagins (see Appendix A).

same duty, the existence of this duty cannot prove the validity of "the liability hypothesis" of bank money. In contrast, the fact of production costs equal to price can disprove it.

6b. IS C_d THE AVERAGE COST OF PRODUCING BANK MONEY?

Recently, M. Friedman published a paper[18] in which bank resource costs do receive recognition as co-determinants of the equilibrium quantity of deposit money and thus of total money. However, most of them are declared to be not the cost of producing money but a measure of the extent to which bank deposits are not money. His analysis leads him to recognize that money is society's net wealth while (interest-bearing) bonds are not (p. 28). Faced by a mixture of the two components, a joint product called interest-bearing demand deposit money, he applies the standard theory of joint products with variable proportions to isolate and measure the two components. I may draw on an equation that I offered elsewhere[19] to discuss efficiently the issues involved here:

$$\Delta w = (MD)/P - \Delta(M_d/P) - (Y_i/P_r). \tag{6}$$

(a) Friedman leaves out the second term (p. 41) since his definition of the money total does not exclude—somewhat unusually—reserves $\Delta(M_d/P)$ that must be immobilized to make the existence of demand deposits $(MD)/P$ possible.

(b) He assumes that bank money is "capable of being expanded with little real cost" (p. 42), which he measures by total service charges TS. Thus, the excess of total resource costs TC_R over TS must be spent as "indirect ways of paying interest on deposits":

$$TC_R - TS = (Y_i/P_r). \qquad (7)$$

(c) He probably uses much the same empirical evidence as I do in Table 6.3. There,

$$TC_R = \{[\$0.0253 + (\$0.015)(1 - 0.1942)]/(0.0542)\} \times (MD), \qquad (7a)$$

where $TS = (\$0.16) \times (MD)$, so that $TC_R - TS = (\$0.47) \times (MD)$. This is close to Friedman's estimate (p. 42) that

$$TC_R - TS \approx 0.5(MD)/P. \qquad (8)$$

(d) From equation 6 it then follows that, after demand deposits are purged of their interest-bearing component, their contribution to monetary wealth (w) measured in "equivalent"—i.e., homogeneous—units must be

$$\Delta w \approx (1 - 0.5)(MD)/P. \qquad (9)$$

Or, as Friedman puts it verbally, "As an arbitrary compromise, let us treat half of demand deposits as the maximum fraction that is equivalent to non-interest-bearing money" (p. 42).[20]

While I fully agree with the theory of equation 6 that is being applied here, I disagree with the empirical claim that is being made in equation 7. I can see no basis for the belief that TS measures the cost of producing bank money so that $TC_R - TS$ must be being spent on indirect interest payments. Empirically, this implies that those banks charging zero service charges—and there are many—are able to handle their demand deposit business at zero resource cost: this is patently false. My own, crude but direct, estimate of indirect interest payments led me to conclude that[21] in the United States

$$Y_i/P_r \approx 0, \qquad (7')$$

from which it follows that the contribution of bank money to total money measured in "equivalent"—i.e. homogeneous—units is

$$\Delta w \approx (MD/P) - \Delta(M_d/P) \qquad (9')$$

or

$$\Delta w \approx (MD/P) \qquad (9'')$$

depending on whether we measure money in public hands or inclusive of reserves immobilized by the banking system.

If $7'$ expresses empirical facts correctly, then not just TS but the entire resource cost TC_R measures the cost of producing demand deposit money; this is the assumption on which section 6a of this chapter is based. Obviously, however, neither the casual empiricism of equation $7'$ nor an assertion of equation 7 will do: only careful empirical research may settle this issue.

7. DEMAND FOR BANK DEPOSITS

To analyze the money market equilibrium by having, in one single framework of Figure 6.5, both the currency market and the deposit market is inconvenient. It will be useful to split the two. This has to be done with some care. The way of dealing with one good when there is a close substitute for it is well established in the price theory literature.[22] However, in this case we face two additional complications: (a) demand for deposits depends on the public holdings of currency and, given the quantity of high-powered money, these holdings decrease as the quantity of bank deposits increases if banks have to hold reserves. (b) The convertibility clause fixes the minimum purchasing power of deposits ($P_m^d \geqslant P_m^c$); in addition, business convenience seems to prevent a premium on deposits so that, as an expression of empirical facts, we may require $P_m^d = P_m^c$. It should be pointed out that the index $P_d > P_m^c$ introduces no inconsistency because the once-for-all component of P_d is equal to P_m^c. The excess contains merely the discounted present worth of the service charge component of P_d which is paid as it accrues by each successive holder to whom it accrues.

In practice, the construction of a demand function satisfying (a) $H = C + R$ and (b) $P_m^c = P_m^d$ is quite simple. The $D_c D_c$ function in Figure 6.5 was constructed for zero service charges so that $P_d = \$1$. The consumers will then demand, as Figure 6.5 shows, the $C'D'$ quantity of deposits. This quantity is shown as OQ_1 in Figure 6.6a and is associated with the price of money P_2 (or with the general price level $1/P_2$). Assume, next, that the function $D_c'' D_c''$ in Figure 6.5 (associated with $S_d'' S_d''$) is constructed for a higher service charge rate r_s' so that $P_d = \$1 + \$1 \ (r_s/r_e)$. The quantity demanded will be smaller and equal to $D''C''$. This quantity is shown as OQ_2 in Figure 6.6a and is associated with the price of money P_3. By constructing many such points and by

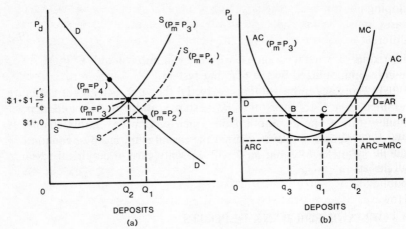

Figure 6.6 (a) Banking Industry, (b) One Commercial Bank

connecting them we obtain in Figure 6.6a the demand function DD satisfying, by virtue of its construction, both the restraints specified above. The purchasing power notations P_m have been added to its various points to remind the reader that the DD function shown is merely a projection of the DD function passing through a three-dimensional space.

8.   ONE BANK'S SUPPLY FUNCTION

What is the slope of the banks' supply function? Analytical focus on real balances and realization that it costs the suppliers nothing to add zeros to the existing bank accounts results in a widespread belief that in terms of nominal balances, the banking industry's supply function is a rectangular hyperbola: "It matters to no one, including the bankers, whether some index of nominal money and prices stands at 1, 100 or 1,000."[23] *If* the public's demand is then *also*[24] a rectangular hyperbola ("...it matters to no one..."), it follows that there can be no intersection of the demand and supply functions. "The nominal size of commercial banks is adventitious,"[25] just as the size of firms in some other industry would be adventitious if it were to face unitary elastic supply and unitary elastic demand. Yet, an individual banker would surely fail to recognize himself in this analysis: it matters to him very much whether the index of his bank deposit money stands at 1 or 100 or 1,000. Something must be wrong with an analysis that so sharply conflicts with facts as the supplier see them. As Friedman has shown, even if the *industry's* supply function is negatively sloping, each *firm's* quasi-supply function may be negatively sloping but it may also be positively sloping.[26] And these two alternative cases must be carefully distinguished since each carries completely different analytical and policy implications. Thus, I shall proceed more slowly and first inquire into the probable shape of each banking firm's supply function and only then consider the probable shape of the supply function of the entire banking industry.

The reasoning quoted above would hold (a) if there were only one type of money, (b) if there were only one monopolist banker so that the firm's and the industry's supply functions would be identical, and (c) if the public's demand were unitary elastic. The banker then could add zeros to all this assets and liabilities and nobody would care since prices facing the public and resource prices facing the banker would change *pari passu*. However, if there are two types of money, the public will desire to hold a balanced portfolio of each and even a monopolistic banker facing unitary elastic demand for *all* money would have to expend an ever-increasing quantity of resources to overcome sales resistance and to make his money relatively more attractive to the public. I.e., he would find it increasingly costly to change the public's choice of a specific currency-deposit ratio.

If there are several or many bankers, this conclusion would hold *a fortiori*. The reason for this is that each banker knows full well that what he does will have no perceptible effect on the economy and that, therefore, the index of prices will not move *pari passu* and become 1 and 100 and 1,000. As every supplier who is a small part of a big industry, the banker knows that the price per unit of assets that he supplies (P_m and P_d as defined in the previous section) and the price per unit of resource that he needs to produce one unit of assets supplied will remain unchanged regardless of what his contribution to the total quantity supplied is. An increase in the banker's output from 1 to 100 to 1,000 will require an ever-mounting quantity of resource inputs. With input prices constant, the banker's total cost function will be increasing. In addition, we may confidently expect that he will need an ever-mounting quantity of resources *per unit* of the asset supplied. With input prices constant to the banker, we may confidently expect that his average cost (C_d as defined in the previous section) will also increase.

Why should the latter outcome be expected with confidence? In contrast with the monopolistic banker in a one-money economy, our banker does not increase his supplies merely by adding zeros to all existing accounts. He must persuade those of his customers holding accounts in several banks to favour his bank more than before. Also, he must try to obtain new accounts either by inducing customers of other banks to shift to him or by persuading non-account holders to open an account. All this would be resource-costly even if his competitors were not simultaneously engaged in an effort to frustrate him and to increase their share of the business. Under these conditions, each additional deposit dollar supplied will have to be paid for by increasing advertising, costly shifts to loans with which the banker is less familiar than with those in his present portfolios, and acceptance of worse credit risks.

For all these reasons I feel justified in showing the *banker's average* cost function in Figure 6.6b to be negatively sloping for inefficient "small scale" production and to be positively sloping thereafter. Thus, I show his marginal cost function MC to be in the relevant range also positively sloping, both with respect to P_d and with respect to P_m. The P_m notation attached to the various functions in both Figure 6.6a and b remind the reader that they are merely projections of average and marginal cost surfaces located in three-dimensional space. It may be noticed that both functions are the sum of the average reserve cost or marginal cost functions plus the average resource cost or marginal resource costs functions. For simplicity, I am assuming that the banker's reserve needs do not change as his quantity supplied increases, so that ARC and MRC are drawn as horizontal functions, the position of which is determined by the reserve ratio ($\$1 \times r_1$). It may be, however, that even these reserve cost functions should be shown as positively sloping if acquisition of "marginal" accounts forces the banker to hold bigger and bigger reserves per dollar of deposits to service these accounts. The difference between the AC and the ARC functions then measures the average resource costs facing the banker: his expenditure on labour, machinery, and building.

9.　BANKING INDUSTRY'S SUPPLY FUNCTION

As Friedman has shown,[27] when we aggregate firms in the industry into the industry as a whole there are two functions that must be considered: the sum of the individual marginal cost functions ΣMC (the quasi-supply function) and the industry's supply function SS. The difference between them is given by the external economies or diseconomies which cause each firm's MC to shift as the industry as a whole expands output and which cause the industry's SS to have a different slope than has the ΣMC. In cases in which there is a fixed minimum price—as there is in the banking industry—the mutual relationship of ΣMC and SS functions acquires a crucial significance.[28] It thus becomes necessary to inquire into the external economies or diseconomies facing the banking firms.

As pointed out earlier, a bank monopolist operating in a one-money economy would have—as is expected frequently in the literature—a supply function that is a rectangular hyperbola. When we shift to several or many banks, this conclusion will continue to hold with respect to the

SS function though not with respect to the ΣMC function. Economies internal to a monopolist simply become external to each bank and cause each *MC* function, and thus the ΣMC function, to shift and result, again, in an *SS* which is a rectangular hyperbola. However, there are two facts about the bank money industry which make this orthodox outcome impossible: (a) even in a one-money economy, the above analysis ignores the risk element inherent in bank money production. In contrast with currency, the proportion $(1 - r_1)$ of bank money *must* be lent, and lent against a collateral of real non-money wealth guaranteeing repayment. If demand for bank money increases, with real wealth remaining constant, real bank money balances grow and thus the ratio of them to real non-money wealth rises. But, the thinner the collateral, the higher the risk insurance component of bank cost. In the case of a bank monopoly, this would be an internal diseconomy that would prevent the monopolist's *MC* (and thus *SS*) from being unitary elastic. In the case of several- or many-firms industry, this becomes an external diseconomy that shifts—as the industry's output expands—the ΣMC function by less than expected above, and thus causes the *SS* function to be less than unitary elastic.[29] (b) In the two-money economy case, this becomes joined by another diseconomy which results from the fact that banks must find it increasingly costly to change in their favour the currency-deposit ratio desired by the public. The denial that the industry's *SS* function is a rectangular hyperbola then must hold *a fortiori*.

However, what can we say about the *SS* function beyond the denial that it is unitary elastic? Since the problem has never been posed in these terms, our empirical knowledge about the size of external economies or diseconomies is non-existent. In what follows, I shall simply make the arbitrary simplifying assumption that the ΣMC function and the *SS* functions coincide. However, a reader who believes himself able to guess as to whether there are external economies or diseconomies should not find it difficult to incorporate this complicating factor into the analysis and revise what follows accordingly. As far as I am able to see, it will leave the substance of the analysis unchanged and merely complicate the presentation.

10. BANKING INDUSTRY'S EQUILIBRIUM

As pointed out in section 8, the standard conclusion that the size of each bank and of the industry (and thus of deposit money) is indeterminate without some exogenous constraint (usually, a reserve constraint) rests on the assumption that the demand for bank money, the ΣMC of producing bank money, and the *SS* functions are all rectangular hyperbolae. Once the existence of the real balance effect is recognized, this ceases to be true[30] about the demand facing the industry. The mere empirical fact of over 14,000 bankers of determinate size in the US and of fewer than ten major Canadian bankers of determinate size indicates that the ΣMC function cannot be negatively sloping. Finally, the risk element inherent in bankers' method of marketing money leads to external diseconomies which make it impossible for the industry's SS function to be a rectangular hyperbola. The alleged indeterminacy then disappears and only the well-formulated mechanics of price theory remain.

The intersection of the industry's supply SS with the consumer's demand DD in Figure 6.6a determine the price charged (P_d), the purchasing power of deposit (and currency) money $P_m = P_3$, and the service charge rate r'_s. These prices then face each individual banker and make his demand function appear as DD in Figure 6.6b. The intersection of DD with the relevant MC_{P3} causes each bank to supply Oq_2 and causes the industry to supply OQ_2 ($C''D''$ in Figure 6.5). We have obtained equilibrium for the banking industry and for the money market as a whole.

11. SOME INTERESTING IMPLICATIONS

To keep this chapter within tolerable size, it is impossible to deal adequately with empirical and policy implications of the proposed analysis. All that it is possible to do is to offer a very brief outline of some empirical and policy conclusions that could be reached by the ratios analysis only extremely awkwardly or not at all and thus illustrate the advantages of the proposed analysis:

(a) Free entry
As shown in Section 5, if we assume that resource costs are always irrelevant, then equilibrium in the industry is always determined by the maximum quantity constraint (S_dS_d in Figure 6.5) or by the minimum price constraints (P_fP_f) in Figures 6.5 and 6.6. This is analytically identical with "private cartel arrangements"[31] and the relevant part of price theory must be applied to establish the equilibrium of firms belonging to the industry.

As Figures 6.5 and 6.6a show, the industry as a whole will produce the quantity OQ_1 and the purchasing power of money will be $P_2 = P_f$. Not to complicate Figure 6.6b, assume that the AC and MC functions shown there are *now* drawn not for the equilibrium price P_3 but for the equilibrium price $P_2 = P_f$. An all-knowing regulator of the banking industry would order each firm to produce the quantity Oq_1 at the lowest possible average cost q_1A. With *free entry* alone, the number of firms will increase until each bank produces Oq_3 where P_fP_f intersects—at the point B—its negatively sloping AC function. This inefficient small-scale production causes the industry's resource inputs to increase from $(OQ_1) \times (q_1A)$ to $(OQ_1) \times (q_3B)$. With cost competition ("non-price competition") alone, each licensed bank's AC and MC functions start shifting up until one or the other or both intersect P_fP_f at each licensed bank's share of output Oq_1 (point C). The shifts of the functions show that each bank now wastes resources on inputs that are not socially necessary.[32] In reality we would expect, of course, a mix of both these inefficiencies.

This shows that the standard advocacy of free entry and free competition in banking is analytically schizophrenic: (1) in one water-tight analytical compartment it is assumed that the reserve constraint (determining maximum quantity) or the minimum price constraint solely determine the banking industry's equilibrium and override the industry's supply function and negligible cost of producing money: by this, the banking industry becomes a typical cartelized industry. (2) In another water-tight compartment, there is praised the virtue of free entry and free competition in banking "as in any other competitive industry."[33]

One cannot have it both ways simultaneously. As long as either of the two constraints is said to determine equilibrium quantity of deposits, the relevant part of the theory to apply is not the one showing welfare benefits of competition in a competitive industry, but the one showing welfare losses of intra-cartel competition in a cartelized industry.

(b) Degree of competitiveness

Regional monopolies enjoyed by some bankers in smaller towns in the United States and possible oligopoly of major Canadian bankers will cause the demand functions facing these bankers to be downward sloping and not horizontal as shown in Figure 6.6b. Equilibrium output of the monopolist banker will then be determined not by $DD = MC$ but by $MR = MC$. Major shifts of population towards the urban centres and great improvements in transportation, associated with the widespread use of automobiles in the twenties in the United States, will reduce the share of this monopolistic component of the banking industry; will lead to a shift of the industry's supply function to the right. Simultaneously, urbanization may—as frequently claimed—lead to an increase in the public's demand for bank deposits and a decrease in the demand for currency. In the money-ratios analysis of equation 4, these complex changes will be registered merely by a shift in the currency-deposit ratio desired by the public and will foster the notion that demand factors "seem paramount"[34] in explaining the change in the quantity of money.

(c) Changes in resource costs

Changes in resource costs facing the banks, given any specific level of competitiveness or lack of it, will in the money-ratio approach of equation 4 be misleadingly registered as shifts in the currency-deposit ratio desired by the public. This force may be quite significant since from 1960 to 1968, total annual resource costs of insured commercial banks in the United States increased from $5 billion to $10.1 billion (exclusive of return to capital and taxes).[35] Assuming equal change in demand and time deposits resource costs, this would suggest that the index of average resource cost of producing demand deposits rose from 100 in 1960 to 149.3 in 1968. It would be surprising if this increase in resource costs would not be important in explaining the drop in the deposit-currency ratio by 13 per cent and the drop in the deposit-*GNP* ratio by 21 per cent during the same period.

(d) Desirability of legal reserve requirements

In a recent inquiry conducted by the US Congress, one half of those invited to testify (including, unhappily, this writer) stated that open market operations obviate the need to change legally required reserves.[36] In terms of the above analysis, this is correct only if we make the assumption that the banks' supply function is sufficiently elastic. Suppose, however, that in any specific period of time this function is quite inelastic: the marginal cost function of individual banks rises steeply. In that case, an open market operation which shifts merely the $S_h S_h$ function in Figure 6.5 and thus the DD function in Figure 6.6 to the right will be less effective than an apparently (in terms of equation 4) equivalent reduction of reserve requirements which shifts both the DD *and* the SS functions to the right. In general, if we choose dH and dr_1 such that in terms of equation 4, $(dM/dH) = (dM/dr_1)$, in reality we must get $(dM/dH) < (dM_2/dr_1)$ since the reduction of banks' average reserve cost in the latter case must cause the currency-deposit ratio (r_2) to change so that $(dr_2/dH) > (dr_2/dr_1)$.

In the money ratio analysis it will appear that open market operations happen to be associated with partly offsetting changes in the currency-deposit ratio desired by the public, with the association depending on the momentary shape of the industry's supply function. But, such an automatic set of relationships between H, C/D, and R/D—depending on the slopes of DD and SS at some specific time and place—reduces the *predictive* power of the ratio analysis drastically.

12. CONCLUSION

I believe that reliance on the Marshallian scissors of demand *and* supply has proved as helpful in our analysis of the money industry and the equilibrium quantity of money that this industry supplies, as it has proved to be helpful in the rest of economics. I also believe that the analysis offered in this chapter represents a fairly straightforward application of our general theory of value. All that was needed was to organize, in an analytically useful manner, the economic facts that we face in the case of the money industry in general and in the banking industry in particular. Needless to say, it would come as a great surprise to this writer if major theoretical improvements were not found to be necessary; if this chapter will prove no more than a direction sign, I will be well satisfied.

Empirical application should not prove difficult. True enough, the price and cost concepts used are complex, but no more so than the concept of price and costs faced by a pure price theorist deciding to analyze an industry producing and renting some "real" asset; e.g., deciding to analyse the economics of Xerox Corporation, which produces and supplies office machinery to those who desire to rent it for a time period. A big advantage of monetary theorists is that banks are rigidly controlled and subject to the requirement of detailed reporting which is a matter of public record. As a result, there is a wealth of data available, waiting to be exploited by those able to organize this mass of data in an analytically meaningful way.

Faced by supply and demand analysis of the money industry in general and of the banking industry in particular and by empirical quantifications of the key analytical concepts, it should not take long before our students—to invert James Tobin's statement with which I started this paper—detect that their mastery of the presumed fundamental, theoretical apparatus of economics *is* put to use in their studies of monetary economics and monetary models.

Appendix Table 6.1: Estimates of price of demand deposits and of banks'
average costs

				Functional cost analyses utilized		
Bank Index						
1	Boston Federal Reserve	District,		1959	(Average of 83 banks)	
2	"	"	"	"	1960	(" " 82 ")
3	"	"	"	"	1961	(" " 81 ")
4	"	"	"	"	1962	(" " 70 ")
5	"	"	"	"	1963	(" " 79 ")
6	"	"	"	"	1964	(" " 84 ")
7	"	"	"	"	1965	(" " 86 ")
8	Atlanta Federal Reserve	District		1966	(Average of 19 banks with over $50 million in deposits)	
9	"	"	"	"	1966	(Average of 9 banks with over $200 million in deposits)
10	"	"	"	"	1966	(Average of 16 banks in Alabama)
11	"	"	"	"	1966	(" " 27 " " Florida)
12	"	"	"	"	1966	(" " 14 " " Tennessee)
13	Boston Federal Reserve	District		1966	(" " 78 ")	
14	"	"	"	"	1966	(" " 32 " with time deposits less than 30 per cent of total deposits)
15	"	"	"	"	1966	(Average of 29 banks with time deposits between 30 and 45 per cent of total deposits)
16	"	"	"	"	1966	(Average of 30 banks with time deposits more than 45 per cent of total deposits)
17	Chicago Federal Reserve District,			1966	(Average of 189 banks)	
18	Cleveland Federal Reserve District,			1966	(Average of 64 banks)	
19	Minneapolis Federal Reserve District,			1966	(Average of 150 banks)	
20	St. Louis Federal Reserve District,			1966	(Number of banks surveyed not available)	
21	Boston Federal Reserve District,			1967	(Average of 78 banks)	

Source: Stephen M. Hagins, "A Preliminary Investigation into the Supply of and Demand for Demand Deposits Produced by an 'Average' Bank," unpublished M.A. thesis (University of Wisconsin-Milwaukee, 1969).

Appendix Table 6.2: Discounted present value of price and average costs per $100 of demand deposit money

Bank Index (1)	Price (2)	Cost* (3)	Maintenance Costs (4)	Investment Costs (5)	Tax Rate (6)	Reserve Costs (7)
1	$133.32	$92.23	$37.75	$14.05	$20.23	$20.19
2	115.12	99.18	43.11	14.87	16.03	25.15
3	116.52	99.82	43.97	15.98	15.12	24.74
4	116.25	98.28	42.72	17.03	18.07	20.45
5	116.13	98.10	43.08	16.55	18.22	20.24
6	116.13	97.63	44.75	16.38	17.07	19.41
7	116.79	100.70	46.67	17.09	17.52	19.42
8	110.27	88.50	29.69	10.27	19.81	28.72
9	106.99	87.36	25.18	8.48	18.07	35.61
10	111.67	86.70	32.46	12.46	21.35	20.42
11	116.95	99.58	45.52	15.44	14.24	24.38
12	107.73	88.38	35.59	10.30	16.09	26.39
13	115.02	93.63	40.68	14.37	18.61	19.97
14	113.64	91.58	36.42	14.88	19.31	20.96
15	117.16	96.65	45.27	15.11	17.59	18.65
16	116.38	93.05	42.36	12.05	19.94	18.68
17	112.44	89.90	38.04	11.99	19.10	20.75
18	111.81	90.21	37.75	11.88	18.57	21.99
19	116.28	91.52	34.60	13.44	20.57	22.90
20	109.81	88.76	35.55	10.63	17.73	24.84
21	115.06	93.71	41.19	14.02	18.68	19.81

Note: * The sum of columns 4 through 7. Excludes risk insurance and return on capital invested.

Appendix Table 6.3:   *Annual price and average costs per $100 of demand deposit money*

Bank Index (1)	Price (2)	Cost* (3)	Maintenance Costs (4)	Investment Costs (5)	Tax Rate (6)	Reserve Costs (7)
1	$5.86	$4.77	$1.95	$0.72	$1.04	$1.04
2	6.16	5.30	2.30	0.79	0.85	1.34
3	6.06	5.19	2.29	0.83	0.78	1.28
4	6.91	5.34	2.32	0.92	0.98	1.11
5	6.39	5.40	2.37	0.91	1.00	1.11
6	6.50	5.46	2.50	0.91	0.95	1.08
7	6.33	5.46	2.53	0.91	0.95	1.05
8	6.55	5.26	1.76	0.61	1.17	1.70
9	6.71	5.48	1.58	0.53	1.13	2.23
10	6.94	5.39	2.01	0.77	1.32	1.27
11	7.28	6.20	2.83	0.96	0.88	1.51
12	6.82	5.59	2.25	0.65	1.01	1.67
13	7.07	5.75	2.50	0.88	1.14	1.22
14	6.89	5.55	2.20	0.90	1.17	1.27
15	7.15	5.90	2.76	0.92	1.07	1.13
16	7.07	5.65	2.57	0.73	1.21	1.13
17	6.40	5.11	2.16	0.68	1.08	1.18
18	6.79	5.48	2.29	0.72	1.12	1.33
19	7.02	5.53	2.09	0.81	1.24	1.38
20	6.31	5.10	2.04	0.61	1.02	1.42
21	7.27	5.92	2.60	0.88	1.18	1.25

NOTES

1. An earlier version of this much revised paper had been commissioned by the Banque National de Belgique and appeared as "La function d'offre des banques et le stock monetaire," in that bank's *Bulletin d'Information et de Documentation*, XLIV (Aug.–Sept. 1969), pp. 169–88. In preparing the revised version of this paper I have benefited from the advice of my colleague John Makin.
2. J. Tobin, "Money, Capital, and Other Shares of Value," *American Economic Review*, LI (May 1961), p. 26.
3. P. Cagan, *Determinants and Effects of Changes in the Stock of Money* (New York, 1965).
4. M. Friedman and A. J. Schwartz, *A Monetary History of the United States, 1867–1960* (Princeton, 1963).
5. Cf. the cost studies listed in note 17 and the articles on this topic in *Innovations in Bank Management: Selected Readings*, P.F. Jessup (ed.) (New York, 1969), pp. 219–84.
6. *Federal Reserve Bulletin* (May 1969), A-107.

7. Cagan, *Determinants*, p. 12, and Friedman and Schwartz, *Monetary History*, p. 791.
8. Cagan, *Determinants*, pp. 118–50.
9. One formal way of justifying this is to state that my model deals with a full employment economy (income is given) in which the money industry does not affect the real rate of interest. Cf. F. Modigliani, "Liquidity Preference and the Theory of Interest and Money," in *Readings in Monetary Theory*, F. A. Lutz and L. W. Mints (eds) (New York, 1951), 214. A more substantive way of justifying this exclusive focus on P_m is to say that the money industry, given demand, crucially determines P_m: without the industry there would be no money and thus no price of this asset. In contrast, the money industry is merely one of many factors co-determining the rate of interest r. The most efficient way of demonstrating this is to point out that this rate—in contrast with P_m—would exist even if the money industry did not exist, in a barter economy.
10. M. Friedman, *Price Theory: A Provisional Text* (Chicago, 1962), p. 21.
11. D. Patinkin, *Money, Interest, and Prices* (New York, 1965), p. 29.
12. In the case of money, we meet still other demand transformations. E.g., some writers (cf. note 23) speak about the relationship between M and P_g. Replacing, in Figure 6.2, the price P_m with its reciprocal P_g will cause the slope of the demand function to change from a negative into a positive one.
13. As in Figure 6.2, this function is given a general shape showing all elasticities. The same economic theory covers, of course, also the special case in which an industry faces, for example, a demand function of a uniform elasticity. Thus, those readers who reject the real balance effect and accept the homogeneity postulate (cf. Patinkin, *Money*, p. 28) should replace the function with a rectangular hyperbola.
14. Friedman, *Price Theory*, pp. 132–3.
15. These propositions are completely different from the orthodox proposition that banks restrict output when they start to hold "excess" reserves. (In terms of Figure 6.5, they are said to increase r_1 and by doing so force S_cS_c to the left and their own reserve cost function up over the initial S_dS_d.) That a difference exists is obvious from the fact that both $C'D'$ and $C''D''$ are associated with zero excess reserves and thus, in orthodox terms, both seem to be the maximum permissible quantities.
16. Cagan has shown that service charges are quite stable while the ratio keeps failing, from which the author deduces that other demand forces are of "paramount" importance (*Determinants*, pp. 123–4 and 132). However, once we shift our focus of attention from consideration of the money ratios to considerations of supply and demand (Figure 6.6), this reasoning is immediately revealed as a *non-sequitur*. A stable relative price associated with changing quantity *may* be due to an elastic and stable supply associated with sharply shifting and thus "paramount" demand, or it may just as well be due to an elastic and stable demand associated with sharply shifting and thus paramount supply, or it may also be due to simultaneous shifts of both functions irrespective of their slopes. In other words, the C/D ratio may be changed either by the actions of the public *or* those of the banks.
17. A number of bank costs estimates are available but all known to me suffer from grave shortcomings. For example, George Tolley offered a cost estimate for demand *plus* time deposits, based on aggregate Federal Reserve Bulletin data ("Providing for Growth of the Money Supply," *Journal of*

Political Economy, LXV (Dec. 1957), pp. 478–9). Subsequent functional cost studies indicate that these are two distinct products with vastly different cost conditions. F. W. Bell and N. B. Murphy in their book on *Costs in Commercial Banking* (Boston, 1968) do use functional cost studies. However, in the case of demand deposits their "basic unit of output in the [banking] industry is the account... It is especially difficult to understand why previous approaches to the problem of defining bank money did not consider the account" (pp. 12–3). To see the shortcoming of this approach, consider measurement of costs in the steel industry using dollar cost per customer instead of dollar costs per ton of steel. The second flaw of this study and of many others like it (cf. Jessup, (ed.), *Bank Management*, pp. 219–84) is that a bank is viewed as a "multi-product firm engaged in servicing demand and time deposit accounts, processing [various] loans, and providing many other services" (p. 12).

Out of total deposits, the $(1 - r_1)$ proportion is rented: the customer receives demand deposit money and the bank receives, in exchange, a customer's promise to pay interest and return the loan. To view these two as separate products makes just as little sense as to say that Xerox Corporation is a multi-product firm which (a) produces and maintains copying machines ("liabilities"), and (b) produces customers' promises to pay rent and return the machines ("earning assets").

I believe that this lends support to my above claim that "in the case of bank deposits our existing analytical kit of tools is rudimentary."

18. M. Friedman, *The Optimum Quantity of Money and Other Essays* (Chicago, 1969) pp. 1–50.

19. B. P. Pesek and T. R. Saving, *Money, Wealth, and Economic Theory* (New York, 1967), p. 110.

20. The second half of the value of demand deposits must therefore be "something else" than money (measured in uniform, currency-equivalent) units. But then the demand for and supply of pure deposit money $D_d D_d$ and $S_d S_d$ becomes converted into a demand for and supply of a joint product, pure money *plus* "something else," $D_{d+y} D_{d+y}$ and $S_{d+y} S_{d+y}$. The analytical problem to be solved becomes much more complex and far beyond the scope of this chapter (cf. also note 32.). Unhappily, it is precisely this issue which is also of some interest to readers in Canada, where some chequable deposits do pay interest. I say that they are merely of "some" interest because their velocity is negligible and thus their effect as money is negligible as well. (Cf. Paul A. Polzin, "The Canadian Money Supply," unpublished Ph.D. dissertation (East Lansing, Michigan, 1968), p. 126.)

21. Pesek and Saving, *Money, Wealth*, pp. 188–90.

22. Friedman, *Price Theory*, p. 24.

23. J. G. Gurley and E. S. Shaw, *Money in a Theory of Finance* (Washington, 1960), p. 256.

24. Note that Patinkin, *Money, Interest*, p. 29, shows this demand to be, actually, less than unitary elastic.

25. Gurley and Shaw, *Money*, p. 256.

26. The former implies no limit on a firm's size, while the latter does imply such a limit: Cf. Friedman, *Price Theory*, pp. 81 and 88. Also, given the minimum price $P_f P_f$ to which the banking industry is subjected, Friedman's Figure 40 on p. 90 (*Price Theory*) is especially relevant.

27. Friedman, *Price Theory*, pp. 80–93.

28. *Ibid*, Figure 40, p. 90.
29. This is never considered by the proponents of policies which would give the public a "satiation" level of real balances on the assumption that the cost of producing money is zero.
30. Patinkin, *Money, Interest*, p. 29.
31. Friedman, *Price Theory*, p. 29.
32. In the case of no industry would (a) such leftward movement along each firm's negatively sloping AC or (b) such upward shift in AC and/or MC (due, e.g., to advertising) be viewed as synonymous with transfers of "profits to the public in the form of services" or with "indirect interest payments"? (A. Meltzer, "Money, Intermediation, and Growth," *The Journal of Economic Literature*, VII (March 1969), p. 34, and M. Friedman, *Optimum Quantity*, p. 42.) Only in case (b) is some gain to the consumers possible, but it must be measured directly: cf. the conflict between equations 7 and 7'. And, should a gain be discovered, we start to face grave analytical difficulties outlined in section 6b.
33. Meltzer, "Money, Intermediation," pp. 34–5.
34. Cagan, *Determinants*, p. 127.
35. *Federal Reserve Bulletin*, 1961, p. 161; and 1969, p. 107-A.
36. US Congress, *Compendium on Monetary Policy Guidelines and Federal Reserve Structure* (Washington 1968).

Part Two:
Monetary Theory

7 Monetary Theory in the Post-Robertson "Alice in Wonderland" Era*

The thesis of this chapter is that current monetary and anti-inflationary recommendations rest on a theory of money, banking, and inflation with seriously inadequate foundations. One major reason for this failing is, I believe, the fact that the Keynesian revolution was able to discredit older monetary theories so completely as to push them out of texts and classrooms. As a result, modern monetary theorists are unaware of and therefore do not use some fundamental contributions made by older monetary theorists. For instance, current policy recommendations ignore some key things that Irving Fisher would have viewed as fundamental: a revolution in bank transactions technology that within a decade has trebled the inflation-making power of each dollar of demand deposits. The situation is like making agricultural policy recommendations without noticing that farmers have started to use hybrid seeds and balanced chemical supplements in addition to marginally-improved machinery.

Another major reason is that many theories now rest on assumptions that were introduced as purportedly only simplifying but are, in fact, conditions *sine qua non* for the validity of those theories. For instance, the dominant theory of demand for investment balances explicitly assumes, and I aver *must* assume, that the risk-averters cannot make (say) call loans and must make risky long-term loans. Or, the famous "bank money multiplier" that dominates all texts and is explored even in the most advanced treatises must rest—and frequently explicitly rests—on the indispensable assumption that bank resource costs currently exceeding $40.2 billion are an irrelevant supply force.

Still another reason for the strange state of current conventional knowledge is that monetary theory came to be dominated by macro-economics. For instance, several major economists have specified the size of investment balances on the basis of macroeconomic deductions,

* From: *The Journal of Economic Literature*, September 1976.

without noticing that microeconomic data—monthly banking statements to firms and households and the minimum (inactive) balances shown there—sharply conflict with these estimates. Or, two major economists have estimated the size of transaction balances on a macroeconomic basis, without anyone remarking that should individual households and firms hold only these transaction balances, they would have to spend their entire income within 0.05–2.00 days and remain cashless for the rest of the income period.

What follows is a sampling of items in which I attempt to list these and similar significant inadequacies of monetary theory, that cannot but be reflected in inadequate policy recommendations. The items in this sampling have been chosen because the empirical or theoretical proof needed is so elementary as to be fully understandable, even by non-monetary economists.

ITEM 1: TRANSACTIONS VELOCITY

Most money and banking texts contain chapters entitled, *eg.*, "The Old Quantity Theory" and "Modern Quantity Theory" [18, Hutchinson, 1971]. A representative description of the old theory is provided in a widely reprinted paper by Lawrence S. Ritter [26, 1963, p. 139]:

Before Keynes, prevailing monetary theory [had been] ... the Quantity theory of money. ... As expressed by Jean Bodin in 1569 ... and Irving Fisher, ... the velocity of money was held to be an institutional datum ... *V* and *T* were assumed to be given so that changes in the money supply would result in proportionate changes in prices.

In a recent paper in the *American Economic Review*, Joseph D. Gould and Charles R. Nelson describe the modern quantity theory as follows [14, 1974, p. 405]:

In the most naive form of the quantity theory of money this ratio— the velocity of money—is assumed to be constant. Such an assumption enjoys no empirical support, however, because the velocity of money clearly changes over time. More modern and sophisticated versions of the quantity theory treat velocity as a stable function of other variables...

Perhaps only the fact that Irving Fisher's book in which the old or naive theory culminates has been out of print for decades may explain these assertions. According to the sophisticated quantity theory to which the writers quoted above and many others refer, income velocity v is determined as follows:

$$v = f(r_b, r_e, 1/P \, dP/dt, w, Y/P; u) \qquad (1)$$

where r_b and r_e denote bank and equity yields, P the price level, t time, w wealth, Y permanent income and u both utility determining variables and technological conditions of production [8, Friedman, 1956, p. 11].

There seems to be a general agreement that Fisher belongs among the old or naive quantity theorists: He is so listed in many basic texts (*eg.*, H. D. Hutchinson [18, 1971, pp. 179–92]); Ritter lists him so in the above quotation; and Gould and Nelson assign sophistication to a much more modern writer. What justification is there for this consensus? Let me quote Fisher's statements about the variables that determine his transaction velocities, V and V' [7, 1971, p. 79]:

Having examined those causes outside the [quantity] equation which affect the volume of trade, our next task is to consider the outside causes that affect the velocities of circulation of money and of deposits.... These causes may be classified as follows:

1. *Habits of the individuals*[1]
   (a) As to thrift and hoarding.
   (b) As to book credit. $[r_b; r_e]$
   (c) As to the use of checks. $[p]$
2. *Systems of payments in the community*
   (a) As to frequency of receipts and of disbursements. $[s]$
   (b) As to regularity of receipts and disbursements. $[v]$
   (c) As to correspondence between times and amounts of receipts
        and disbursements. $[x]$
3. *General causes*
   (a) Density of population. $[y]$
   (b) Rapidity of transportation. $[z]$

After offering this list of the determinants of velocity, Fisher goes on and discusses each one of them in rich detail. Elsewhere he specifies that [7, 1971, p. 168]: ... a change in the volume of trade, when it affects the *per capita* trade, affects velocity of circulation as well. $[n]$
He also states that [7, 1971, p. 68]:

During ... depression, velocities (V and V') are abnormally low. People are less hasty to spend money or checks when the dollars they represent are rising in purchasing power. $[1/P \, dP/dt]$

At still another place, Fisher states that [7, 1971, p. 167]:

.. the rich have a higher rate of turnover than the poor. They spend money faster, not only absolutely but relatively to the money they keep on hand. ... This is what we should expect; since, in general, the larger any operation, the more economically it can be managed. ... We may therefore infer that, if a nation grows richer *per capita*, the velocity of circulation of money will increase. $[Y_c/P]$

In summary he writes [7, 1971, p. 182]:

Innumerable causes *outside* the equation of exchange may affect M, M', V, V', and the Q's and through them affect the p's. Among these outside causes are the price levels in surrounding countries.

Surely a far cry from claiming that velocity is an institutional datum, in any run. In terms of symbols (that I have added in brackets) Fisher's theory of velocity V (or, V') as quoted above may be written as follows:

$$V = g(r_b, r_e, 1/P \, dP/dt, Y_c/P; n, p, s, v, x, y, z) \qquad (2)$$

(where Y_c denotes current income).

This makes it clear that Fisher has expected proportionality between money and prices only in the special case of a purely monetary disturbance that leaves the equilibrium values of the real variables in equation 2 unchanged. This is hardly a sin because in the same Keynesian special full employment case the same conclusion about proportionality is reached. Special cases aside, Fisher's velocity may be claimed to be an institutional datum in *any* run only by those willing to argue that he has not been aware of the business cycle and that he has expected such variables as the price level, real income, and interest rates to be also institutionally given. As far as Fisher's determinants of velocity are concerned, it may be noted that he employs all but one of the variables that the modern quantity theory employs plus seven others, which are of demonstrably major importance in our period of extremely significant advances in corporate and household cash management. Fisher focuses in great detail on revolutionary changes in transactions technology which modern theory ignores, such as:

1. Credit cards, some with overdraft privileges (Fisher's "book credit" in both cases);
2. Once-a-month payments to which they lead (Fisher's "correspondence between times and amounts of receipts and disbursements" and "regularity of receipts and disbursements");
3. Chequeless transfers of wages and salaries by computer that reduce this type of float to zero;
4. Magnetic ink character recognition and massive introduction of computers able to read these codes and to process cheques speedily;
5. Lock-box system of mail delivery of cheques to locations as close as

possible to the payer's domicile and pick-up of these cheques for deposits and telegraphic transfer of deposits by such banks as Continental Illinois National Bank (acting for 180 other banks) every twenty minutes;
6. Extended disbursement float system of drawing cheques on very remote banks;
7. Society for Worldwide International Financial Tele-Communications that has reduced international cheque-clearance time from some three days to five-to-twenty minutes;
8. The Federal Reserve System's (F.R.S.) chartered fleet of ten jets and forty "props" that transport cheques from one Federal Reserve Bank (F.R.B.) to another;
9. F.R.S. Regional Processing Centers which, in Washington area, have reduced the collection period from four days to twelve hours (all of the above items representing Fisher's "rapidity of transportation");
10. Quadrupling of transactions within a decade (*Appendix A*) which, given much smaller increases in the price level and in population, must mean significant increases in real *per capita* transactions in equation 2.

The net effect of these measures and countermeasures is surely crucial for any explanation of the revolutionary changes in the transaction velocity of demand deposits from 37–42 in 1964 to 98–111 in 1974 (*Appendix A*). Thus, all are surely very important for any explanation of the inflation that we have suffered during this decade.

Finally, may sophistication be found in the shift from transaction velocities V and V' to income velocity v? I don't think so. It is this shift of focus that is responsible for the fact that innumerable journal articles and Congressional testimonies blame all sorts of culprits for our inflationary problems, but never mention the powerful and perhaps crucial engines of inflation represented by the above-listed changes in bank transactions technology that have tripled the inflation-making power of each dollar of demand deposits within a decade. Whether equation 1 or 2, income velocity or transactions velocity, will prove to be more stably related to the independent variables that determine them and thus will prove to be a better policy-making tool, only an empirical comparison—not assertions—can tell.

The best that may be said about the modern theory is that it has bowed to realities. While Fisher's *total transactions* [7, 1971, p. 186], which are also key in William Baumol's [2, 1952] and James Tobin's [29, 1956] theories of transaction balances, and *all prices* at which these transactions are undertaken [7, 1971, pp. 186–7] both remain unknown, a fragment of total transactions consisting of income transactions (GNP) and a fragment of these prices consisting of prices of income goods (implicit deflators) are available, ready-made, for testing. But, if we make virtue out of necessity by denigrating the old and extolling the new, we shall never know whether Fisher's much broader theory of the role of money and of the transmission mechanism that connects money with the rest of the economy (*eg.*, stimulation of production and/or financing of stock market speculations) would not yield us better monetary policies.

ITEM 2: THE LIQUIDITY TRAP

Even the dependent variable V in equation 2 and the variables P and T that enter Fisher's tautology are still unknown, with the exception of Fisher's extremely crude "guesstimates." Some key independent variables that determine V and V' are still unknown today (*e.g., per capita real trades*). Thus, the theory that V and V' are stable functions of other variables could not and has not yet been tested. Nevertheless, it has been dismissed as naive and has been replaced to a small extent with the modern quantity theory and to a large extent with John Maynard Keynes's theory of demand for money which states that

$$M = L_1(Y) + L_2(r) \qquad (3)$$

where M and Y denote money and income and r "the relation between the current rate of interest and the state of expectations" [21, 1936, p. 199]. In modern restatements, L_1 is understood to represent demand for transaction balances and has been investigated by such writers as Baumol and Tobin. The theory of demand for "investment balances" L_2 rests on the liquidity preference function as a behaviour towards risk.

This theory, both in Keynes's somewhat casual exposition and in Tobin's rigorous analysis, relies on the formula specifying the present value of a bond A_2 (Tobin's notation) that yields an interest income I and repayment E:

$$A_2 = I[1 - (1 + i)^{-m}]/i + E[(1 + i)^{-m}] \qquad (4)$$

This formula shows that the more distant the maturity m of a bond, the bigger $\partial A_2/\partial i$, and the more costly any increase in the interest rate i will be for the investor. To avoid this loss, the investor who thinks that the current rate is too low will wait it out by holding non-interest-bearing investment money balances L_2 (A_1 in Tobin's notation) rather than interest-bearing but risky financial assets A_2.

The numerical example by which Keynes illustrated his liquidity preference theory [21, 1936, p. 202] and most of the paper in which Tobin rigorously explores this theory (and transforms unobservable r into observable i) both rest on the assumption that the maturity m

in equation 4 equals infinity [30, 1958, p. 67]: "To simplify the problem, assume that there is only one monetary asset other than cash, namely consols."

This is not the case in our world. Thus, towards the very end of his paper Tobin gives the appearance of shifting his analysis to our world of "bonds and other debt instruments differing in maturity, debtor, and other features." The full sentence, however reads as follows [30, 1958, p. 82]:

The argument is not essentially changed, however, if A_2 is taken to be the aggregate share invested in a variety of non-cash assets, eg., bonds and other debt instruments differing in maturity, debtor, and other features. The return R and the risk σ_g on "consols" will then represent the average return and risk on a composite of these assets.

Here m that is infinite is converted into an m of some significant size.

"Consols" or "aggregate shares" A_2 do not represent a simplifying assumption but a *conditio sine qua non* for the liquidity preference theory. Let there exist only one additional interest-bearing financial asset A_2^* with zero or negligible maturity m^*. With $m^* = 0$, $\partial A_2^*/\partial i = 0$: any risk of a capital loss resulting from a change in the interest rate, that is scaring risk-avoiders into the holding of sterile "investment balances" $L_2 = A_1$, disappears. Of course in our economy we don't even know consols or composite shares, and we do know a huge number of various financial interest-bearing assets $A_2^j (j = 1,2, \ldots, n)$ with maturities m^j as small as zero, all of which *are* available separately. The consumer may choose call loans, government and corporate bonds expiring tomorrow and any day thereafter, savings deposits maturing every thirty days, etc. In other words, in our real world the risk-avoiders may always choose some interest-bearing asset A_2^j that makes holding of any sterile "investment balances" $L_2 = A_1$ a profit minimizing decision.

It seems wasteful to force generations of students to learn the liquidity preference theory of demand for investment balances—so dominant that in many texts it has become a synonym for the theory of demand for total money—even though this theory has been proven to hold only in Alice's Wonderland where the consumers must buy representative cross-sections of financial assets which are not sold separately.[2] This theoretical conclusion will be empirically reinforced in the next two items, which will offer evidence proving that currently no financial asset meets the specifications of "investment balances" found in Tobin's paper. Even if it were to be proven valid for our world, the theory would remain inoperative for want of a subject.

ITEM 3: PURE TRANSACTIONS BALANCES

Whatever the merits of the liquidity preference theory, empirical testing requires specification of investment balances L_2. Correspondingly, testing of the Baumol–Tobin theory requires specification of transaction balances L_1. In some cases such specifications rest on arbitrary decisions, such as are those claiming that money balances in some boom year (1926, 1929) are all transaction balances and that the then observed transaction velocity is constant over time (which, as note 4 shows, is false) and may be used to estimate transactions and thus investment balances in other years. There is only one book, to my knowledge, that gives specific economic criteria to be used for a quantification of "transaction balances" L_1 and thus, *ipso facto*, of investment balances L_2. Milton Friedman and Anna J. Schwartz first share with the reader their belief that the observed size of currency and demand deposits cannot constitute L_1 only [11, 1970, p. 107]:

In the United States in 1966, this total [currency plus demand deposits] was equal to the value of four months' personal disposable income, about one month's in currency and three months' in demand deposits. Roughly two-thirds of currency and two-fifths of the demand deposits were held by individuals and the rest by business. On the average, therefore, individuals held in currency about three weeks' of income, in demand deposits about five weeks', or a total amount equal to two months' disposable income. Is it plausible that anything like this large a sum was held for the narrow medium of exchange function of money alone—that is, for mechanical transaction needs?

Next they apply to the United States the income velocities observed in countries that have experienced hyperinflation (in which investment balances are surely zero) such as Hungary, Greece and Poland in the twenties [11, 1970, p. 108]:

Applied to the United States, this experience would imply that, for individuals and businesses combined, roughly one to two days' income is the hard core, as it were, of what might be called transaction balances proper, and one to two months' income is the level of balances that can be maintained for extended periods without serious transaction difficulties.

It seems preferable to base our decisions not on these somewhat far-fetched deductions but on the actual size of the "mechanical transaction needs" faced by the spending units in the *United States today*. Because data on currency transactions are missing, I shall focus only on cheque transaction needs and demand deposits that satisfy them.

Demand deposit balances equal in value to three months' of income may appear excessive only to those whose sole focus on income velocity has caused them to forget that spending units don't buy income goods alone. Firms also buy intermediate goods and non-income goods, and households also buy non-income goods such as stocks and bonds, old masters, antiques, old houses, used cars, furniture, appliances and all those items we find in classified sections of the daily papers. Table 7.1 based on figures from the *Federal Reserve Bulletin*, shows that transactions financed by cheques amounted in 1974 to $20,978–$23,603 billion. Once *all* this transacting activity is considered, the proposed "hard core transaction balances proper" of "individuals and businesses combined" (row 2, column 2, table 7.1) are revealed as grotesquely inadequate. These balances would be able to finance actually undertaken cheque transactions only if they were able to change hands every 46–103 minutes (row 6, table 7.1); allowance for eight hours of sleep and Sunday rest reduces this to 26–59 minutes. This is not a product of a sophisticated modern monetary theory; this is science fiction. Or rather, this is horror fiction in which all spending units give up all productive activity to specialize in undertaking innumerable miniscule transactions (e.g., purchase one fifth of an egg), in the course of which they write innumerable cheques against their miniscule balances. The only respite they get is when they make a fast trip to their banks at least every 26th to 59th minute to deposit cheques received so as to prevent cheques issued from bouncing.

Are the no serious difficulties with transaction balances any more reasonable? To argue so would require us to claim that current household plus business deposit balances exceed by 71–242 per cent (row 3, Table 7.1, and *Appendix A*, row 3) the transaction needs of the nation. Surely, all that we know about what has been called "The Scrooge Instinct" of corporate cash management and about our own and our friend's cash management tells us that this is nonsense. Is there any corporate treasurer who would last for a week if his reports to the management would show that the sterile balances he keeps exceed by 71–242 per cent the transaction needs of the corporation? And he would not last even that long should he simultaneously report that he is engaged in a very expensive effort (e.g., lock-box system, extended disbursement float system, etc.) aimed at making these sterile balances even more excessive.

Financial pages and monetary theory don't pay any attention to household cash management. Lacking facts, casual empiricism must suffice. The fact that I and all my friends are quite careful about writing cheques at the end of the month suggests that households are not holding balances exceeding their transaction needs by 71–242 per cent. This gets some support from unique data obtained for 242 randomly selected household depositors by my student Michael Tretheway [32, 1976, p. 19]

Table 7.1:   Transaction balances, 1974 (Billions of Dollars)

	Observed magnitudes	"Hard core" case	No "serious difficulties" case
1. Personal disposable income	$979.7		
2. Proposed transaction balances		$2.7–$5.4	$81.6–$163.3
3. Proposed demand deposits transaction balances		$2.1–$4.1	$62.2–$124.4
4. Total cheque transactions	$20,978–$23,603		
5. Observed turnover of demand deposits	3.3–3.7 days		
6. Proposed turnover of transaction demand deposits		46–103 minutes	0.9–2.1 days

Notes:
Row 1: *Federal Reserve Bulletin* [5, June 1975, p. A-55].
Row 2: Row 1 multiplied by 1/365 and 2/365 (column 2) and by 1/12 and 2/12 (column 3).
Row 3: Row 2 allocated by the use of the 1974 currency-deposit ratio.
Rows 4 and 5: *Appendix A*.
Row 6: Row 3 divided by cheque transactions (row 4) per minute per day, respectively.

which show that they, in a month preceding summer vacations, held a minimum demand deposit balance equal only to 0.315 of the value of cheques written during this month, and to 0.019 of cheques written in the past year. And even these small amounts certainly don't measure investment balances. One part of them will represent a provision against float. Another part of them will reflect scarcity of short-term investment opportunities. Frequently, a shift out of a demand to a time deposit may await one's leisure after the tenth of each month and is profitless entirely if the amount is needed for transactions before the end of the next month.

One may look at the same issue in an alternative—more Fisherian— way. The proposed "no-serious-difficulties" demand deposit transaction balances would require that the existing turnover of deposits be increased from the current level of 3.3–3.7 days to the proposed level of 0.9–2.1 days (rows 5 and 6, Table 7.1). All that we know about current transactions technology indicates that this is impossible. Mail delivery of many cheques takes two to three days, at best. Deposits of all cheques received surely must take at least a day if done personally, and another two to three days when mail is used. Cheques received by stores are deposited personally or picked up by armoured cars once a day. Staggered billing days used by corporations, and insurance contracts signed every day of each month, force the consumers with monthly incomes to hold transaction balances covering these bills on the average for fifteen days longer than they would have to hold them with a better synchronization of receipts and disbursements. Only very accurate bookkeeping, beyond the ability of many households, would make it superfluous to hold an end-of-the-pay-period balance that does not contain a safety cushion against embarrassing and costly errors.

These well-known facts about the purely technical limits upon the speed of turnover of deposits indicate that the current demand deposit turnover every 3.3–3.7 days (every 1.8–2.1 working-time days) is so amazingly fast as to make inescapable—I believe—the conclusion that current demand deposit balances are being operated at or close to peak efficiency and that they are therefore either pure transaction balances or, to be conservative, 99 and 44/100 per cent pure transaction balances L_1.

ITEM 4: EQUILIBRIUM STOCK OF BANK MONEY

In Item 2 we have seen that the theory of *demand for investment balances* has not as yet been proven, and in Item 3 we have seen that it would be empirically inapplicable even then: demand deposit balances are pure transaction balances and currency—in view of serious fire and theft risks—cannot be anything else.[3] Time deposits are, by Tobin's specification, on the other side of the dividing line: they are interest-bearing financial assets A_2 that risk-preferers will hold in preference to sterile investment balances $L_2 = A_1$. All the excellent theories of *demand for transaction balances* initially offered by Baumol and Tobin are currently empirically inapplicable because they employ transaction T as a lynchpin, and these are unknown. What about the post-Keynesian theories of demand for total balances? Some of them casually mention and none of them builds into the demand function transactions T which, according to all existing theories, are the key determinant of demand for the transaction part of total balances.[4] On these grounds alone, all the post-Keynesian theories of demand for total balances are difficult to accept: they and the Baumol–Tobin theory of demand for the dominant transaction part of these total balances cannot be valid simultaneously (cf. also note 20).

Another problem is that when it comes to the explanation of the equilibrium quantity of most money balances, of bank deposit balances, *all* the above demand theories are abandoned. In all textbooks, and in many advanced treatises (frequently written by the very same authors who have offered the above demand theories elsewhere [10, Friedman and Schwartz, 1963, pp. 776–808] and frequently even in one and the same book [20, Johnson, 1972, pp. 53–96, 136–40]), the explanation of the quantity of bank money is said to be the famous "bank money multiplier"

$$D = H \times 1/(r_1 + r_2) \tag{5}$$

where D denotes deposits, H high-powered money or "the monetary base," r_1 the currency-deposits ratio desired by the public, and r_2 the reserves-deposits ratio maintained by the banks. The multiplier is always defended on the basis of bank mechanics, and is never given any price theoretic supply-demand rationale. However, simple arithmetic will show that it is actually the equilibrium solution $D_d = D_s$ of the following demand for and supply of bank deposits functions:

$$D_d = (1/r_1) \times (H - R) \tag{6}$$

and

$$D_s = (1/r_2) \times R \tag{7}$$

(where R denotes bank reserves).

These two equations are, to put it very mildly, grossly deficient. On the lowest level of generality it may be said that the multiplier analysis always treats r_1 and r_2 as independent of each other, even though it should be obvious that $\partial r_1 / \partial r_2 > 0$. If r_2 is increased, the assets-deposits ratio falls, the volume of bank interest payments or services financed by these assets falls, the demand for D falls, and thus r_1 increases. Also, the above demand function is totally unrelated to all known demand for money functions and is price-theoretically most suspect. Except in the case of perfect complements, no other branch of economics claims that the demand for some asset is a constant fraction of the quantity of some other assets. Clearly, currency and deposits are not perfect complements but imperfect substitutes.[5]

Let us now look at the other blade of the Marshallian scissors: No theory of supply worthy of its name would dare to ignore what the multiplier and the above supply function ignore: bank interest and resource costs (Table 7.2) that in 1974 have amounted to the huge sum of $68 billion. *All* textbooks and many advanced and celebrated treatises [3, Cagan, 1965; 10, Friedman and Schwartz, 1963, pp. 776–808] base their analyses of the equilibrium stock of bank deposits on the multiplier and never mention let alone quantify, banks' costs.[6] In many cases, discreet silence is even replaced with denials that bank costs exist. One such statement reads as follows [18, Hutchinson, 1971, p. 92]:

Unlike the manufacturer, who must pay to hire the resources needed to produce his product [emphasis mine] the banker can merrily create the "product" that provides his income—money for loan—by the mere stroke of a pen. What a wonderfully simple means of amassing profits! "You give me your IOU for $100,000 and I will reciprocate by giving you mine for the same amount, providing you agree to pay me $6,000 of interest for doing so." What a seemingly effortless way of earning a living!

The author goes on to point out that there are, nevertheless, "a few flies in the ointment" that keep the bankers "from expanding the money supply to infinite proportions in their quest for added profits" [18, 1971, pp. 92–3]. These flies in the ointment are said to be the ratios r_1 and r_2 in equation 5.

Unfortunately, there are a few bumble-bees in this ointment as well. The zero-cost banker's Elysium exists only in the Wonderland of monetary theory. Any banker knows that *exactly like* any other manufacturer or service supplier, he must hire resources and struggle daily with labour costs, energy costs, computer costs, building costs, and taxes. And he also knows that in his quest for infinite profits, to increase his deposits by a fraction of a percentage point above his current equilibrium would involve him in additional costs that would reduce his profits below their present equilibrium level. He would have to accept worse credit risks to place his deposits into circulation, supply more expensive services to all his depositors to keep them there, advertise more, etc. ... The bank costs of $68.1 billion indicate that a banker creates his product by the stroke of a pen writing "Demand Deposit $100,000" in the same way in which a telephone company creates its product by the stroke of a pen that assigns the number 963-4554 to a customer, and in the same way in which a football team creates its product by each turn of the press printing season tickets.

With $638.5 billion of deposits in existence in December of 1974 [5, Feb. 1976, p. 87] and with commercial banks cost (tautologically equal to total revenues) net of direct charges (row 1 minus rows 2 and 3 in Table 7.2) amounting to $65.3 billion, the average cost of $1 of deposits is $0.102. Since allocation of costs to two joint products is notoriously difficult, assume merely for discussion purposes that they are the same in the case of demand and time deposits.[7] The banker must then tell the prospective borrower, not the utter nonsense implicit in the bank money multiplier, but something completely different:

Exactly like any other producer I must pay to hire resources to exist. You give me your IOU and I will give you $100,000 of bank demand deposit money which

Table 7.2:   Income and expenses of insured commercial banks, 1974 (Dollar amounts in millions)

	1974	Per cent of change 1973–74
Total operating revenue (tautologically equal to total costs)	68,160	28.5
Trust department income	1,506	3.1
Service charges on deposits	1,326	10.0
Total operating expense	58,910	32.9
Salaries and wages	9,797	14.2
Pensions and other employee benefits	1,788	15.1
Interest on deposits	27,888	40.6
Interest on borrowed money	6,903	56.8
Interest on capital notes and debentures	283	11.2
Net occupancy expense	2,052	15.1
Provision for loan losses	2,285	80.7
Other expenses	7,910	18.7
Current operating expenses	9,250	6.2
Taxes on operating earnings	2,083	– 1.8
Net current operating earnings	7,167	8.8

Source: F.D.I.C. [4, 1975, Table C].

will, on the average, cost me annually $10,221 to service. Unless your IOU promises to yield me annually the same amount, I will be on a road to bankruptcy.

Even worse, price theory tells us that should the banker's marginal cost function be above his average cost function, he will ask to be paid not $10,221 annually but more than that. This is extremely likely because there is no evidence that banks are natural monopolies, and there is evidence that to attract *additional* bank borrowers, depositors, and reserves is costly.

At present, all professors of money and banking spend weeks teaching the multiplier analysis of bank money that implicitly and sometimes even explicitly[8] ignores $68 billion of banks costs. And, both their advanced treatises (see Cagan [3, 1965] and Friedman and Schwartz [10, 1963, pp. 776–808]) and their policy recommendations show that this is not being taken for a mere simplifying assumption, good enough for the beginner. Can the reader think of one congressional testimony, or of one report of the Shadow Open Market Committee, or of one journal article that would explain the wide divergence between the F.R.S.'s stated objectives with respect to the money stock and its actual performance by the fact that its policies fail to take into account major changes in the regulated industry's revenues, labour costs, energy costs, capital costs, taxes, etc.?

The same professors then depart to teach their other classes, ready to flunk any student who would ignore orthodox costs-revenues analysis and try to replace it with the multiplier analysis: who would try to explain (say) the nominal value of Hertz cars by (1) the ratio r_2 of till cash to Hertz cars desired by or forced upon the corporation and (2) the ratio r_1 of currency to Hertz cars desired by the public. Even though arithmetic success of the multiplier approach would be guaranteed here as well, no student would even think of applying such a tautological and mechanistic approach to any industry for which he has some empirical feel.

ITEM 5: BANKING SECTOR'S WEALTH

While bank costs are typically ignored as a factor determining the quantity of money and thus as something that should be of crucial interest both to the theorist and the policy-maker, in 1969 they have been finally recognized—in a most peculiar way—as a factor determining national "income originating in the banking industry" and thus "the capitalized value of [this] income stream" [25, Patinkin, 1969, p. 1151], the banking sector's wealth or net worth.[9] In a frequently quoted and thus seemingly definitive paper Don Patinkin specifies the revenues and costs of a hypothetical bank as shown by Table 7.3. The flow of Net Profits ($250) shown in this table is then discounted to the present and is entered as Net Worth ($5,000) into the T-account of the banking sector. These two amounts are then given the following verbal explanation [25, 1969, p. 1151]:

Table 7.3: Income statement (Patinkin's Table II-9) of the banking sector

Net interest from loans (= $285,000 × 0.05)	$14,250
less depreciation	$ 2,000
less other operating costs connected with bank money (including possible interest payments)	$12,000
Net Profits	$ 250

Source: Patinkin [25, 1969, p. 1150]..

This does not mean that the banking industry is not a productive sector of the economy. On the contrary, Table II-8 indicates that it has net worth of $5,000, representing the capitalized value of the income stream which it generates [$250 in Table 7.3]. Similarly, the standard procedure for estimating income originating in the banking industry (*viz.*, imputing interest-income to holders of demand deposits, and an offsetting charge for the banks' services [27, Ruggles and Ruggles, 1956, pp. 60–4]) will show it to be making a positive contribution to national income.

Both Richard and Nancy Ruggles and official accounts agree with Patinkin that "operating costs" consisting of interest income passed on (a specific treatment given to intermediaries) and of supplies purchased from other firms (a treatment given to *every* "industry") should be subtracted: see the subtraction on the income side Tables 14 and 15 in Ruggles and Ruggles [27, 1956, p. 62]. But, neither agrees that all other "operating costs" should be subtracted so that national income generated by the banking industry[10] would consist only of Net Profits obtained by the owners of "monopoly rights or goodwill" [25, Patinkin, 1969, pp. 1153, 1155]. Official accounts show that the banking *industry* does generate national income consisting of all the returns on the firms' capital—only a small fraction of which will be Net Profits of the owners of monopoly rights—plus the incomes of bank employees. The term "the sector" is used in the official accounts for concepts different from "the industry"; a concept that would meet the needs of monetary theory is illustrated in the official accounts by "Gross Auto Product" (see *Surv. Curr. Bus.* [33, 1973, p. 24]), which shows gross expenditures. Application of this concept to banking would show the banking *sector*[11] (similarly defined by gross expenditures on its services) as contributing to the GNP some $40 billions (Table 7.5). The sectoral contribution to the national income is unknown, but will lie between this amount and the industry's contribution to national income (Table 7.4). When we shift to stocks, it is obvious that the industry's wealth will consist not only of the present value of monopoly rights (as Patinkin claims) but also of the present value of the income flows shown in Table 7.4. Out of this wealth, only the wealth of the banking firms is given by the *Federal Reserve Bulletin* and amounts to $66 billion in historical prices [5, August 1975, p. A-14). Its present value must be a multiple of this amount.

Patinkin's method of measuring national income that the banking sector generates and thus of wealth or "net worth" that this sector owns is so grotesquely at variance with the official method—agreement with which he claims—that there simply must be some misunderstanding: he cannot be trying to measure the same thing that the official data do measure. And, indeed, he is not. The difference is to be found in the way he set up his hypothetical numerical example. There he chops off—by empirical assumption—almost all the sector's physical wealth and thus the income it yields and there he chops off—by definition—all those engaged in the banking sector except the final suppliers, the banks. He accomplished this by basing his entire analysis on the assumption that six different economic concepts are three pairs of synonyms: wealth and wealth at the margin, the firms and the sector to which they belong, and interest in the form of money and in kind.

1. Wealth and wealth at the margin are not synonyms
In one closing sentence Patinkin states that [25, 1969, p. 1152]:

... the question at issue ... [is] the proper measure of wealth of an economy at a given point of time; *or, more specifically* [emphasis mine], the proper measure of wealth for the analysis of the real-balance effect ...

The latter is said to consist of wealth that banking adds "at the margin" [25, 1969, p. 1152], without drawing upon and thus reducing resources of the other sectors (monopoly rights). It is amazing to read that the problem is to measure a sum, *or*, more specifically, one addend entering this sum: how much less specific could one be? Patinkin's
(a) earlier quoted statement where he speaks about wealth without any qualifier added (about the former wealth),
(b) his use of T-accounts and their *terminus technicus* "net worth", which measure and denote only the former wealth and are incapable of measuring the latter (otherwise, all the learned articles estimating the size of monopolies in the US would be superfluous),
(c) his claim of agreement with our official income accounting, which always measures income and never its component, monopoly income,
(d) and his use of the words "or, more specifically" that connect wealth with monopoly wealth

Table 7.4: National income originating in the banking industry including the F.R.S. (in billions of dollars)

National income by industry	1970	1971	1972	1973
Banking industry plus the F.R.S.	16.4	16.1	17.5	10.7
Compensation of Bank and F.R.S. employees	8.8	9.6	10.3	11.5
Corporate profits before taxes	5.9	5.3	n.a.	n.a.
F.R.S. profits*	3.6†	3.3	n.a.	n.a.

Sources: Survey of Current Business [33, 1974, pp. 17, 36, 39].
    * These profits plus wages of the F.R.S.'s employees would have to be subtracted to obtain National Income contributed by private banking.
    † The three components exceed the industry's total because data on numerous small adjustments (up and down) employed by the Department of Commerce are not available.

all indicate that he has unknowingly adopted the notion—which his hypothetical numerical example is *forced* to meet—that the two wealths are synonyms. They are not. A banker who uses his paid-in capital to buy a bank building ($66 billion in historical cost) certainly adds something to the former wealth and nothing to the latter; as Patinkin correctly shows, only his Monopoly Rights $5,000 (due to the monopoly income $250 in Table 7.3) do both. Why does Patinkin treat the two wealths as synonyms? I suspect because in all advanced treatises, including his own [24, 1965, pp. 296–304], the above $66 billion (pre-inflation dollars) of bankers' real capital is always implicitly assumed away: out of sight, out of mind (or, *vice versa*).

2. Firms, an industry, and a sector are not synonyms

By an unlucky chance, the explicit notion that the two wealths are synonyms finds full support from the implicit notion that the term "the firms" is a synonym for an industry and a sector. In the body of Table 7.3 (his Table II-9) Patinkin clearly shows receipts, costs, and income of the firms (in his case, we have a one-firm industry). In his above-quoted verbal discussion of it, this income is claimed to belong to the industry or the sector; the reader is free to choose which of the two Patinkin "really" means. Finally, as shown in the heading of Table 7.3, Patinkin settles for the sector. If so, then these results follow: impose (a) the assumption that the banks own zero capital and (b) the claim that the banking sector is the sum only of the banks, and it follows that the banking sector's income and wealth consist only of the banks' monopoly "Net Profits" and monopoly wealth.

The use of three terms when describing one and the same set of figures does reflect the current state of the art, but is most confusing. In the official accounts firms producing products worthy of separate classification *plus* their employees are defined as an industry (Table 7.4). The term sector is reserved for classification by legal organization (corporate, government, etc.). This is clearly not what economists want to stress when they speak about a sector. As to what they do exactly mean is hard to say because—as Patinkin's text illustrates—the empirical content of the theoretical concept "the banking sector," discussed in books and journals for decades, has not yet been considered.

In contrast with official accounting, economists in general use the term sector when describing all those who produce final goods by use: the consumption sector, the investment sector, etc. Here, a sector is said to contain *all the inputs* that went into the production of consumption goods, investment goods etc. This is a content that—I believe—empirical specification of the banking sector should copy. Except for those few who want to study banks, monetary theorists are interested in the quantity of the money in use. This is determined by *all the inputs* needed to produce and maintain money: banking firms, bank employees, and suppliers of raw materials to the extent that they service the banking industry. To do otherwise is to subject our analysis of the banking sector to the vagaries of firms' capital–labour ratio (focus on firms) and of vertical integration (focus on industry). The only sector as just described that may be found in the national income accounts is represented by the automobile firms, their employees, and their suppliers. With the term "sector" reserved for other uses, the label "Gross Auto Product" has been chosen [33, 1973, p. 24]. The banking sector as defined above would yield Gross Bank Product (and its subdivisions, NNP, NI, etc.).

I believe I have shown the way that Patinkin deals with banking firms conflicts with the official treatment given to the banking industry; it also conflicts with the Pesekian[12] notion of a sector as something broader than an industry.

A student who wishes to focus solely on firms (as Patinkin does in the body of our Table 7.3) would expose himself to the vagaries of the capital–labour ratio and of vertical integration. Only data about the sector, as defined above, show the total amount of resources that the society devotes to a given use (banking, automobiles). And, it is these data that anyone intent on a costs-revenues price-theoretic analysis of banking and of the equilibrium supply of bank deposits must have.

3. Interest in money or in kind are not accounting synonyms

Patinkin's method of quantifying the banking sector's income and wealth is (independently) reinforced by his notion that interest income in money *or* in kind are both "offsetting" transfers; analytically, synonyms. Notice his use of this term in his initially quoted statement and the fact that in our Table 7.3 he lumps interest in money and in kind together in his deduction $12,000. If so, then $14,250 of gross receipts minus $2,000 of depreciation minus $12,000 in interest in money or in kind transfers indeed yields a sectoral income of only $250 and sectoral wealth of only $5,000.

The trouble is that monetary theorists seem not to have noticed that there is a fundamental difference between interest in money and in kind:

Sector A receives $14,250 (or 14,250 bushels of wheat), sets aside $2,000 (or, 2,000 bushels) for depreciation, passes on $12,000 (or, 12,000 bushels) as interest in money (or, in kind). It, indeed—even according to standard income theory—generates only $250 (or, 250 bushels) of income. Unfortunately, the parenthetical statement never happens in the United States. What does actually happen?

Sector B receives $14,250 of money interest, sets aside $2,000 for depreciation, and uses $12,000 to hire resources to produce—let me stress, *to produce*—$12,000 worth of goods and services to pass on as interest in kind.

Sector B may be visualized as owning two hats. While wearing one, the banker receives and passes on $14,250 of money interest: no income is generated. The depositors then turn right around and purchase from the banker, who now wears the hat of a producer (indistinguishable from, say, an accounting firm or tax advisory service) $14,250 worth of his good or service. When the banker wears this second hat, the banking sector generates income exactly like any other productive sector and is so treated in national income accounts: $14,250 gross receipts minus $2,000 firms' depreciation minus unknown other bank factors' depreciation—which, however, must be only a very small part of their gross income $12,000. *The sector* generates income much in excess of $250 assigned to it by Patinkin.

To sum up. As far as *national income* generated by banking is concerned, only the evil spells cast by the combination of the orthodox litanies "interest in money or in kind" and "interest receipts and payments are offsetting" may explain why Patinkin, as shown in Table 7.3, lumps both together in his deduction $12,000 to arrive at the remainder, at his measure of bank national income. By this aggregation he treats as indistinguishable *Sector A* where a small boy is hired for a dollar to deliver $11,999 from *Sector B* that produces $12,000 worth of goods and services for the depositor or from any mix of the two. And, only these two evil spells may explain why monetary theorists, economists all, have agreed for almost a decade with this conclusion that is unprecedented in the annals of economics: that both a complete idleness by and a mightily productive effort of a sector have the same—zero—effect on the national income that this sector generates. If "exorcism" [21, Keynes, 1936, p. 352] was ever needed, it surely is badly needed here.

As far as the present value of this income flow is concerned, i.e., as far as *sectoral* wealth is concerned, only a third, complementary, evil spell of the orthodox litany "bank assets minus bank liabilities equal zero net worth," the T-account version of which orthodoxy covers *all* elementary texts and innumerable advanced treatises (e.g., [16, Gurley and Shaw, 1960; 24, Patinkin, 1965]) may explain why Patinkin—perhaps unconsciously to be sure—has made banking fit this crime by subjecting it to the salami tactic: by defining the banking sector as the sum of the firms, he chops off the sector's hired resources, and by assuming away the firms' capital, he chops off the owned resources, and *presto*: with the exception of negligible monopoly rights (in an industry with 14,000 firms) one is conveniently back in the Alice-in-Wonderland world of a zero-net-worth sectoral T-account that is the foundation of our banking theory. [13]

One reason why all these evil spells have proven impervious to criticism is that they have been cast in an empirical vacuum. Every undergraduate even vaguely interested in some other sector will *start* his studies with data about this sector's contribution to out GNP and NI, about the factor incomes earned in this sector, about various types of capital invested by firms in this sector, about supply costs and demand revenues, etc. Such empirical knowledge should serve to impose self-discipline upon those who try to work out theories and discipline over them by the readers after these theories are published. In contrast, many professors of money and banking *retire* without ever having seen such empirical evidence about the sector of their choice; much of such evidence has not yet even been prepared. [14] In such an empirical vacuum, anything goes; or, rather, stays on and on.

ITEM 6: BANKS' RESOURCE COSTS.

That the depositors are receiving some services from the banks is not denied by monetary theory, though casual mentions of them and complete lack of quantification (such as provided by Tables 7.2 and 7.5) surely must lead to the impression that these services are minor and incidental to the main task of the banks. Yet, it is easy to show that they are so big as to endow bank deposits with a yield that is comparable with the yield obtainable by any other asset. In Item 4 it has been shown that in 1974 the quantity of bank deposits amounted to $638.5 billion and that it costs banks $65.3 billion to maintain these deposits in working order, partly to furnish direct benefits to the depositors (account keeping, acceptances of deposits and withdrawals at the counters, etc.) and partly to manage asset portfolios—without such activities the continuing existence of bank deposits would become impossible (akin to, say, the maintenance of cables by the telephone company). This total of $65.3 billion consists of $27.9 billion of interest payments and of $37.4 billion of resource costs for which depositors don't pay separately in extra charges.

This means that in 1974 the total cost, and thus total paid plus imputed yield, of each dollar of bank deposits amounted to 10.2 per cent. If we add some $4 billion as the imputed cost of holding reserves, this average yield increases to 11.2 per cent. [15] Such yield compares well to the yield that an investor could obtain in 1974 on any other asset. This conclusion would hardly surprise any price theorist who knows that a competitively-produced asset with a yield smaller than the market yield would simply not be held by a rational consumer.

As a result, students are forced to master literature about "the optimum quantity of money," about the role that it would play in economic growth, and about the bliss of satiation with money that would ensue if costless money were to yield the market rate of interest (e.g., [1, Ahmad, 1975; 19, Johnson, 1970; 35, Weber, 1975]) which is no more relevant than would be literature about optimum growth in a world of decreasing returns to scale where the entire wheat crop may be grown in a flower-pot. The major part of the money stock, bank money, is already yielding the equilibrium rate; in the case of currency, interest payments are impractical on technical grounds.

ITEM 7: PAYMENTS FOR BANK SERVICES

When bank services are recognized, they are claimed—even by the official accounts—to be received by the depositors "without payment" (Table 7.5)—as imputed interest income—even though it is possible to observe innumerable businessmen holding borrowed working demand deposit balances who are receiving, month after month, bank services that these deposits yield and who are paying to the banker, month after

Table 7.5: *Gross national product generated by the banking sector** (in billions of dollars)*

Gross national product	1970	1971	1972	1973
A. *Personal Consumption Expenditures*				
Personal Business				
2. Bank service charges, trust services, and safe deposit box rentals	$ 2.1	$ 2.3	$ 2.4	$ 2.6
3. Services furnished without payment by financial intermediaries except insurance companies	$14.6	$15.6	$17.3	$19.0
B. *Bank Services to Firms* (which enter the values of consumption, investment, government, and export final goods produced by these firms)	n.a.†	n.a.†	n.a.†	n.a.†

Source: Survey of Current Business [33, 1974, p. 24].
   * *Sector* defined here as the sum of the Banking Industry plus the suppliers of it, to the extent that they supply the Industry.
   † Given the known structure of household and business deposits, this unknown amount must be a size similar to the one in Row A-3.

month, a fee ("interest") for the use and servicing of their balances. Of course, failure to notice that some depositors are themselves paying for the services that they are receiving and insistence on the notion that in *all* cases one person (the borrower) pays what a different person (the lender) receives "without payment" are essential for upholding the notion that banks are exclusively intermediaries between different spending units.

1. The intermediary theory of costless banking

All money and banking texts employ an exposition based on the pure Intermediary Theory of Banking. According to C. A. Phillips's 1921 rationalization, the private sector ceases to demand $10,000 of currency and deposits it, the banker sets aside $2,000 and frustrates the public by lending $8,000 of unwanted currency back, the public retaliates by depositing this $8,000 of unwanted currency, etc., until finally the banker has borrowed $50,000 of currency and the public holds $50,000 of deposits. [16]

The observable fact here is that the bank is a pure intermediary that has borrowed $50,000 and has lent $40,000. It collects interest in the form of money from the borrowers and passes all of it (i.e., the bank has zero resource costs), also in the form of money, to the depositors-lenders. The banking sector's T-account then reads as shown in Table 7.6.

Note that a competitive sector is assumed here and in the upper half of Table 7.7:

1. A monopsonist will pay his depositors less: his liability to pay interest *I* in equation 8 and thus his liabilities in Table 7.6 fall; his Net Worth (Monopsony Rights) increases by the same amount. Total Assets remain unchanged.
2. A monopolist will charge his borrowers more: his interest earnings *I* in equation 4 and thus his Earning and Total Assets increase—for all we know, quadruple; his Net Worth (Monopoly Rights) increases by the same amount. Liabilities remain unchanged.

In Accounting Wonderland both theorists and bank examiners ignore cost and income flows and rely on what the latter, here and now, know to be economically totally irrelevant *face values* of Assets and Liabilities (*E* and *B* in equations 4 and 8). These do not change. To force the T-account to show the non-competitive case nevertheless, they simply tack to face values non-competitive Net Worth ("Charter" [11, Friedman and Schwartz, 1970, p. 113; 25, Patinkin, 1969, p. 1146]). This unbalances the accounts, and so the very same item is simply tacked to the other side as well. Total Assets allegedly must increase—which they may not—but no more than double (which they may).

Table 7.6:   Intermediating banking sector

Assets:		Liabilities:	
Reserves	$10,000	Deposits (earning imputed income,	
Earning Assets	$40,000	the value of intermediating service)	$10,000
		Deposits (earning explicit income)*	$40,000
		Net Worth:	None
Total assets	$50,000	Total	$50,000

Note *Of course, each dollar of deposits yields a composite of the two.

2. Intermediary-direct-supplier theory of banking

Even though the litany "interest income in money or in kind" treats the two as indistinguishable, a fundamental change clearly occurs when the banking sector produces—let me stress, produces—for the depositors-lenders interest income in kind. As we have seen in Item 5, the current incomes earned by the factors that constitute the banking sector measure the national income that is contributed by the sector. Correspondingly, the present value of the future flow of this income represents the wealth of the banking sector. In essence, the bank becomes a conglomerate of a pure bank depicted by Table 7.6 and of a productive enterprise indistinguishable from, say, a C.P.A. firm or from H & R Block's tax advisory firm. If money interest payments are zero, the banking sector's T-account is then obtained by consolidating two T-accounts of two sectors that would exist if the conglomerate were to split and perform its two functions separately (Table 7.7).

While paying lip service to interest income in kind that the lower half

Table 7.7:   Intermediating banking sector producing interest income in kind

	Assets:		Liabilities	
	Reserves	$10,000	Deposits (yielding	
Pure Intermediary	Earning Assets	$40,000	imputed income)	$50,000
			Net Worth:	None
	Assets:		Liabilities:	None
Direct Supplier			Net Worth:	
			Present Value of the	
			Flow of Bank Services	$40,000
	Resources plus			
	Monopoly Rights	$40,000		
	Total assets	$90,000	Total	$90,000

of Table 7.7 depicts, all advanced treatises theorize about the banking sector on the basis of the zero-costs, zero-interest-income-in-kind, upper half of Table 7.7 (e.g., [16, Gurley and Shaw, 1960, pp. 135–46; 24, Patinkin, 1965, pp. 296–304]). In one isolated instance, negligible interest income in kind is permitted by replacing, in the upper half of this table, a negligible fraction (0.3 per cent) of earning assets with resources that produce income in kind in the lower half of Table 7.7 [25, Patinkin, 1969, p. 1149]. As a result, modern theory in its formal specification of the banking sector (a) ignores entirely or, in one case, almost entirely interest income in kind that the sector is supplying (in the case of over $200 billion of demand deposits, the sole and equilibrium income), (b) ignores known net worth of the banking firms amounting to $66 billion in pre-inflation prices, and (c) ignores still unknown net worth of all the other factors engaged in the sector. A very crude stab in the dark suggests that the *total sectoral net worth ignored* amounts to some $300–$500 billions.[17] It is easy to visualize the quality of subsequent theorizing about a sector that is so grotesquely misrepresented even with respect to its most fundamental economic characteristic.

3. Non-intermediary direct-supplier theory of banking
Demand deposits earn only income in kind. This income could consist exclusively of the bankers' intermediating service—of finding safe borrowers for the depositors-lenders—only if the latter would have zero alternative investment opportunities and thus had to accept zero explicit net return on their loans. As time deposits show, this is not the case in our world. It thus follows that the banker must be supplying the demand depositors to a major extent (given by the time deposit rate) or fully with some *service other than intermediation*—like a C.P.A. firm or H & R Block's tax advisory service. Unless it is shown that the intermediating and the non-intermediating services are inseparable joint products (which has not yet been done or even considered by our theory that insists that the banker is strictly an intermediary), it is entirely possible that the banker is supplying his demand depositors only with this non-intermediating service (like a C.P.A. firm) without engaging in *any* intermediation whatever. The Non-Intermediary Direct-Supplier Theory of Banking becomes at least a theoretical possibility.

Postulate an economy in which *the banker absolutely refuses to borrow* (and thus to intermediate), and in which the private sector either refuses or is incapable of lending; indeed, in which—perhaps—currency to be lent does not even exist. The banker invests $50,000 worth of his resources (if money does not exist, resources worth 50,000 bushels of wheat) into factors of production needed by his firm. He then approaches local businessmen with a proposition. Not to lend the banker anything. God forbid! He suggests that *they borrow* from him his new product that will prove more convenient in use than gold (if it exists) and which will be either "bank notes" currency or a bookkeeping substitute for it, "deposits" (or both). He persuades them to come in, sign $50,000 worth of promises to pay annually for this service, at a stipulated time return $50,000 of his bank notes or his "deposits" that they are renting, and circulate these units of accounts among themselves in the meantime. His T-account will then be the same as a T-account of any other pure service industry (Table 7.8). [18]

The theory that has been proposed that one part of our banking business does not consist of intermediation at all and does consist only of direct supply of a good (medium exchange) and a service (accounting) to the demanders has been emphatically rejected [25, Patinkin, 1969; 11, Friedman and Schwartz, 1970, p. 113]. The rejection, however, has not been based on some theoretical proof that the debtless type of a bank discussed here is impossible, nor on some empirical proof that such a type of a bank does not happen to exist in our world. One rejection rests on an already discussed hypothetical numerical example manipulated so as simply not to show this type of a bank; the other rests on a two-sentences-long assertion containing no economic analysis whatever [11, Friedman and Schwartz, 1970, p. 113].

Banks are engaged in financial intermediation when they issue promises to pay dominant money bearing no interest that are in excess of the amount of dominant money they hold in their vaults. These promises to pay are properly regarded as debts of the banks.

This is a simplistic view of a fragment of a complex problem: if we observe (e.g.) a celebrity to sign a promise to pay (while his autograph sells for twice as much) do we "properly" conclude that he has acquired a debt (rather than discreetly sold his autograph cheap)? Only careful economic analysis may decide whether bank promises to pay lend support, in specific times, places and instances to one of the two Intermediary Theories of Banking (in which case banks do have debts, as in Tables 7.6 and 7.7) or the Non-Intermediary Theory of Banking (in which case they don't, as in Table 7.8). Economic analysis is needed to decide whether a promise to pay is (1) either a promise of a banker-debtor to pay $1,000 of currency, or (2) a promise of a debtless banker and lessor of *his* medium of exchange (a) either to take his asset back from the lessee in exchange for his rental agreement, or (b) to purchase his asset back from anybody for $1,000 of currency, to be recovered from the lessee at the contractually stipulated time. [19] (Notice that in the "real" sector many firms *also* promise "Your Money Back Unless Fully Satisfied" and nobody claims that these firms have debts equal in value of their products in the public's hands, nor that they are intermediaries

Table 7.8:   Non-intermediating banking sector

Assets:		Liabilities	None
Reserves	$10,000	*Net Worth*	
		"Deposit" money supplied"*	$50,000
Other Resources plus			
Monopoly Rights	$40,000		
Total assets†	$50,000	Total	$50,000

Notes: * Alternatively: present value of bank services supplied.
          † Paid for by the customers' service contracts, "Earning Assets $50,000."

because they have not enough cash on hand to honour all these "debts" simultaneously.)

It may be also noticed that the allegedly decisive promise of the banker to pay currency is purely incidental; it merely increases the attractiveness of, and thus profitable demand for, bank money owned by the third type of bank in a two-money world by making shifts back and forth easy. In a cashless society of the future—which is currently a distinct technical and empirical possibility as more and more stores are being equipped with electronic banker tellers—demand deposits will, exactly like currency today, promise to pay to the holder nothing, because there will exist nothing to pay. And, bank time deposits will promise to pay the only medium of exchange left: bank demand deposits. May a fundamental conclusion about the nature of an industry rest *entirely* on a feature which is so incidental that it is easy to visualize its disappearance without anybody caring?

However, instead of relying on the usual factless theorizing, let us continue our reliance on the evidence of our senses. Let's visit a bank. Any day we may see a time depositor and a penniless businessman short of working balances that he will need in his planned business entering their bank. The time depositor checks his banker's credit rating, enters proudly, plunks his money on the counter, and sternly demands his time deposit, his evidence that he is lending money to the banker. The businessman enters humbly and after a credit check (in terms of the former theory, a prospective lender is being subject to a credit check by a prospective borrower) is found meritorious, signs a promise to pay interest for the loan of a "deposit" working balance and starts to depart. This is the moment for the monetary theorists to make their belated appearance. With an eagle eye they notice that both these people are leaving with things called "deposits," look up the definition of deposits in a dictionary *et voila*: they know that both the time depositor and the businessman have just lent money to the banker for his intermediation to others, are depositors-lenders, and fit the Intermediary Theory of Banking.

Should the theorist stop the businessman and tell him about his instant metamorphosis from a humble borrower into a proud lender, the businessman would—justly—consider him to be mad. He knows that before entering the bank he did not have a penny to his name and thus could not lend anything to anybody, could not deposit anything, could not possibly become (as the time depositor has become) a depositor-lender within the meaning of the Intermediary-Direct Supplier Theory of Banking. And he knows equally well that he certainly had no intention—as many textbooks insist [18, Hutchinson, 1971, p. 92]—to visit his "intermediating" banker and start to serve to him as an intermediary in return: had no intention to exchange IOU's with him, to borrow from him long and turn around and lend him the borrowed amount short. In fact, the debt certificate that he has signed may be a call loan, while the deposit working balance obtained he may use for decades. The businessman knows that he went to the bank to borrow a working demand deposit balance and to start using it exactly like he went to his father-in-law to borrow a till-cash working balance and to start using it in his business. As far as he—and I—can tell, these two transactions are indistinguishable both in their economic characteristics and even in their outward appearances (which would become even more visibly identical if the bank would send the businessman home not with his borrowed bank "deposit" but with his borrowed bank notes currency). The businessman has borrowed money from both and has lent money to neither; neither lender thus owes him anything.

The businessman could also point out that the time depositor has sacrificed an asset that has performed a service for him and has exchanged it for an idle and useless deposit book, to be put into a safe-deposit box; he will get paid for this sacrifice. In contrast, the businessman was penniless, had nothing to lend, and had to borrow a working "deposit" balance that will start serving him just as busily as his borrowed till cash, machine, or telephone. And, he will start to pay for the use and servicing of his borrowed working balance just as he will start paying for the servicing of his phone number or for his rented piece of equipment. And, should he fail to keep up with his payments, all three firms will come and wipe him out: the banker and alleged borrower will simply cancel the businessman's alleged loan to him (wipe out his "deposit"), the phone company will disconnect his phones, the rental outfit will cart back its machinery.

Nevertheless, in the Alice-in-Wonderland world of modern monetary theory the decision has been made that a sterile time deposit book and the businessman's working demand deposit balance are indistinguishable: both loans to the banker. It has been therefore decided that the Non-Intermediary Direct-Supplier Theory is incorrect—cannot explain any part of the banking business. Has the world really been made safe again for the Intermediary Theory of Banking—a theory so divorced from reality as to claim that a penniless businessman who borrows his deposit working balance from a bank and his till-cash working balance from his father-in-law actually is a lender to (or, a borrower-lender from-and-to) the banker, while he is simply a borrower from his father-in-law. And, a theory so divorced from reality that it claims—in the same breath—that the banker creates his money by the stroke of his pen, *and* is strictly an intermediary who cannot lend his new money without borrowing it first, *and* does borrow it—acquires a demand deposit liability—by the very act of lending his stroke-of-a-pen demand deposit to his indebted customer. With a theory like that to be saved, a distinct aversion to a debate is fully understandable.

CONCLUSION

This is merely a *small* sampling of major difficulties that permeate not the periphery but the very supply-demand core of monetary theory. Clearly, sometime in the past monetary theory took several wrong turns. One wrong turn came when it started to rely exclusively on macroeconomics. Investment balances are being deduced from macroeconomic evidence without anybody checking these deductions by looking at microeconomic evidence, at minimum balances shown in monthly bank statements received by firms and households. Or, US transaction balances are being deduced from half-a-century old macroeconomic evidence about foreign countries, without anybody checking these deductions by looking at microeconomic evidence about the size of the task that these balances must perform here and now. Or, any fall in the ratio of national income to the money stock is interpreted to mean that money is a luxury consumer good, without anybody noticing that households and firms are using more and more frantically this producer's good in its grimy task of facilitating our economic intercourse. Or, the conclusion is reached that income velocity is today suspiciously high and thus our measure of the money stock probably too low and that an expensive search for an error should be undertaken by the F.R.S. Such a search would be recognized as superfluous if only one would pay attention to precise data showing that firms and households now use each deposit dollar three times as efficiently as a decade ago, which makes the observed increase in income velocity entirely credible: many fewer dollars are now needed to purchase income goods.

As far as banking theory is concerned one major false turn came when out monetary theory came to be dominated by a legalistic, economically irrelevant, concept of Assets, Liabilities, and Net Worth (wealth) based on face values; something to which practical men of affairs such as bank examiners or accountants of those corporations that promise to the customers their money back unless fully satisfied never pay any attention to. And, it has become dominated by a fragment of legally prescribed T-accounts of the banking firms that leaves all of the banking sector's resources unaccounted for. Another false turn came when the bank money multiplier proved, in its form of a tautology, so seductively successful as to start to dominate the analysis even in its form of an equilibrium condition. Somehow nobody has noticed that price theoretically this multiplier tautology rests on the notion that huge bank resource costs are irrelevant for the suppliers. As a result of this victory, the F.R.S. is currently the *only* regulatory agency in Washington that is receiving a stream of policy recommendations that never take into account the regulated industry's costs and revenues. Can these be any more valuable than those that would go to the I.C.C. and be based on the assumption that the transportation industry levitates freight at zero cost from place to place?

Another false turn came when monetary theory came to be dominated by the quest for rigour and precision obtainable only by mathematical models. Form frequently wins over content: it has become prestigious to perform elegant manipulations with equations the economic content of which has been pushed into the background. To replace verbal analyses of economists like Fisher, Schumpeter, and Keynes with models, one has to make many precise assumptions which, at first, are understood to be either grossly simplifying or to be made necessary by our lack of knowledge of key facts; but which, with the passage of time, acquire a life of their own and hide the need to measure the unknown but key facts and to work out new theories that would reflect them. Thus, in modern theories, the commodity market and the money market—the IS and LM functions—hang together only if we disbelieve empirical evidence that in the case of the latter income is not a proxy for transactions. Or, the liquidity preference theory of demand for investment balances may be so dominant today only if we really believe that the consumers must buy representative cross sections of financial assets that are not sold separately. Or, the multiplier theory of bank money may dominate texts and, recently, be given so much space by the journals only if we really believe that the banker has volunteer workers labouring in charity-donated buildings. In the end, the necessity or the convenience of making assumptions at sharp variance with observed facts has been made criticism-proof by the claim that realism of assumptions does not matter:

that the proof of the pudding is in the eating and that statistical testing will do what it cannot do, perform the economists' job for them.[20]

Still another false turn is to be found in the totality of Keynes's successful effort to discredit monetary theorists who have preceded him: the old is seldom so bad as it seems to the innovator. This excessive success has caused the Keynesians and non-Keynesians alike to use a demand for money functions that in their essential components are entirely Keynesian in nature. And, in their empirical work modern theorists go even further and out-Keynesian Keynes. It is hard to believe that intensely practical Keynes would have agreed that all our economic intercourse and transaction balances that have the grimy task of facilitating it are unimportant, and that therefore the demand for money is dominated either by his liquidity preference or by income that finances holdings of this luxury good. Finally, the totality of Keynes's success has caused all texts to relegate pre-Keynesian monetary theories to a historical chapter where they are treated with condescension and are made to look so naive as to seem unworthy of the student's notice, not to speak of Ph.D. theses or journal articles. This is a pity. The world of monetary theory has not collapsed, but neither had it been born in Cambridge in 1936 or in Chicago and New Haven twenty years later.

The problem gets compounded when some of the wrong pieces in monetary theory's jig-saw puzzle get surrounded by pieces that are made to fit to perfection: consider (e.g.) the perfect fit of the earlier discussed three pairs of alleged synonyms, or of the zero-bank-cost money multiplier with the zero-income and zero-wealth theory of the banking sector. This makes any attempt to reform individual pieces extremely difficult. First, any such effort must either be or seem naive when compared with the sophistication that has been lavished on such sterile tools as is the bank money multiplier. Second, any such reform effort becomes immediately and understandably suspect because any reshaped piece will conflict with all the neighbouring pieces—which, of course, have been *made* to fit the wrong piece. This places a would-be reformer under the impossible obligation to re-shape a great number of pieces simultaneously or forever hold his peace.

What is needed is recognition that important parts of monetary and banking theory rest on theoretical and empirical assumptions that are indefensible; e.g., that we must not use theories that equate idleness with productive effort or inconspicuously assume away hundreds of billion dollars of bank resources. Energies will then be shifted away from further attempts to refine irrelevancies or to pave with gold additional stretches of blind alleys, and towards efforts to rectify these shortcomings. Also, such recognition may cause editors and referees to abandon the attitude of *nolite tangere circulos meos*: some of the apparently perfect circles may—just may—consist of doodling. It is clearly better to give attention to discussions of even very crude theories pointing in the right direction than to highly sophisticated elaborations of theories resting on theoretical and empirical assumptions satisfiable only in Alice's Wonderland.

APPENDIX A

Table 7.9: Cheque transactions in 1964 and 1974 (billions of dollars)

	1964	1974
1. Demand deposits in metropolitan areas	$103.5	$173.2
2. Demand deposits in rural area	$ 18.6	$ 39.6
3. Total demand deposits	$122.1	$212.8
4. Cheque transactions in metropolitan areas	$4,619.4	$20,978.2
5. Cheque transactions in rural areas (estimate row 2 times row 11)	$0 – $ 543.1	$0 – $ 2,625.5
6. Total cheque transactions	$4,619.4 – $5,162.5	$20,978.2 – $23,603.7
7. Turnover* of demand deposits in metropolitan areas in days	8.1	3.0
8. Turnover of demand deposits in rural areas in days (estimate)	$12.5 - \infty$	$5.5 - \infty$
9. Turnover of all demand deposits in days	8.6–9.8	3.3–3.7
10. Velocity V' in metropolitan areas	44.6	121.1
11. Velocity V' in rural areas† (estimate)	0–29.2	0–66.3
12. Velocity V' of all demand deposits‡	37.9–42.3	98.6–110.9

Sources: Rows 1, 4, 11: [5, July 1972, p 634; 5, Feb. 1975, A-13].
Row 3: [5, Dec. 1964, p. 1553; 5, July 1965, p. 979; 5, Feb. 1964, p. 87].
Row 5: Row 2 times Row 11.
Row 10: Row 4 divided by Row 1.
Row 12: Row 6 divided by Row 3.

Notes: *Turnover equals 365 divided by velocity.
† Based on one extreme assumption that rural areas don't transact at all, and another extreme assumption that they transact as much as metropolitan areas not containing financial centres.
‡ Velocity not corrected downward for cheques cashed, nor upward for cheques endorsed on second parties to buy goods or services.

NOTES

1. The three items listed here are most frequently used to misrepresent Fisher:
   (a)   It is claimed that his term "habits" implies long-term stability and that

therefore the three items listed here are impervious to short-run economic forces. Yet, the term "habit" is merely the old-fashioned equivalent of the modern term "tastes" that are said in our demand theory to determine the demand *function* (and not to fix the quantity demanded). That this is a fair interpretation is demonstrated by the fact that Fisher's contemporary Alfred Marshall uses the same term, "habits," in exactly this demand *function* sense [22, 1949, p. 110].

(b)   It is often claimed that it took a modern theory to recognize $\partial V/\partial r$ even though the author of *The Rate of Interest* [6, 1907] must have taken it for granted that "thrift" and "book credit" (elsewhere, "time credit")—that determine V and V'—are, in turn, determined by the interest rate.

2. Recently, an effort has been made to salvage this theory on the basis of the risk and uncertainty attached to the transaction costs of getting out of and back into money [34, Waul, 1975]. Shall we be consistent and apply this approach to *all* assets temporarily idle because of uncertain and high transaction costs of getting out of them and back into them again (e.g. hammers or Christmas ornaments stored in basements)? Shall we have two demand functions, one for goods active on Christmas day and one for investment balances of Christmas ornaments?

3. Item 6 will show that demand deposits cannot fall under the scope of the liquidity preference theory for still another, also empirical, reason. They yield 10 per cent *per annum* in the form of bank services. Thus, they are not sterile money assets $L_2 = A_1$ that the risk-averters have been scared into temporarily holding by the risk of a future interest rate increase that befalls income-earning assets.

4. Modern focus on income as *the* determinant of demand for money cannot be bailed out by the orthodox claim (e.g., [17, Horwich, 1965, p. 36; 19, Johnson, 1970, p. 383; 28, Stein, 1971, p. 63]) that income is either equal to or a proxy for transactions. The ratio of transactions to income has been shown to be *highly* unstable from 1919 to 1968 [13, Garvy and Blyn, 1969, p. 65] and has exploded between 1968 and 1974 (Appendix A).

5. The two equations and the resulting multiplier will be, *trivially*, adequate as determinants of the *nominal* stock of money [10, Friedman and Schwartz, 1963, p. 776] and all other nominal stocks in the special full-employment case of a change in the general price level and no change in relative prices, when all assets *are* in a way perfect complements. If all prices double, the consumers will want to keep a balanced portfolio of the nominal values of *all* assets (including, incidentally, $H - R$ and D): r_1 and all other such ratios will be constant and will seem to be the sole determinant of demand for any one asset. And, if the values of all the inputs and of the outputs double, the producers will be unaffected: r_2 and all other such ratios of any one input (regardless how insignificant) to each output will be constant and seem to be the sole determinant of supply of this output. The bigger the general price level variability and the smaller the relative prices variability, the better will the multiplier look statistically.

6. I do not claim that costs are *never* mentioned: merely that they have never even approached the mainstream of banking theory. And, in the few exceptions known to me, they are frequently paid only lip service. For instance, Patinkin in his book does mention that the supply of bank money is a function of the wage rate and the interest rate. Then he adds that the

former is assumed to be constant, so that his supply function will contain only the latter rate [24, Patinkin, 1965, pp. 301–2].
A fragment of bank costs is introduced only to be assumed away, and for *what* a reason! Economists in branches of economics where supply analysis is taken seriously would be aghast to hear that a horizontal supply of an input function justifies the removal of this input from the supply of a product function.

7. Application of the assumption that the cost of maintaining one dollar of time deposits by commercial banks is the same as that of the Mutual Savings Banks (MSB)[23, 1973, p. 49] leads to the conclusion that each dollar of demand deposits earns more than one cent more, and of time deposits one cent less. This may be perhaps partly explained by Regulation Q that leads to excess profits on time deposits and their dissipation in a competitive effort to attract demand depositors.

8. In a frequently reprinted and quoted paper by Tobin, costs are casually considered on one-and-a-half pages, but irrelevant conclusions about their relationship to the multiplier are drawn [31, 1963, p. 416]:

> Without reserve requirements ... deposits ... would be limited by [MC = MR]. ... When reserve requirements and deposit interest rate ceiling are effective, the marginal yield of bank loans ... exceeds the marginal cost of deposits to the banking system.

Under the conditions of $MC < MR$, the multiplier analysis is shown to hold. But, there cannot be any ceiling on interest in the form of services paid on demand deposits. When the F.R.S. controls merely r_2 and H, it imposes the supply ceiling $D_s \leqslant (1/r_2 \times H)$ that cannot be effective because demand D_d has always been, by a huge margin, below it. Thus, $MC < MR$ has never been imposed, and the multiplier analysis has never been imposed, and the multiplier analysis has never been valid. Equilibrium $D_d = D_s$ has always been determined, endogenously, by $MC = MR$; by the MC of bidding away the input R from the holders of $H - R$ (co-determined by the fixation of H and r_2) *plus* the MC of bidding away other inputs from other sectors. (Note that the multiplier would start to hold in a cashless society where $H = R$.)

9. Immediately thereafter, discussion of even this issue has slid back to the Wonderland of zero-cost banking. For two most recent examples in one single issue of a journal and for the bibliography that they offer, see S. Ahmad [1, 1975] and W. E. Weber [35, 1975].

10. Note that I am speaking here about the "banking industry" and not about the "banking sector." More about this later.

11. I use the term *sector* in the "Pesekian" or "Pickwickian" sense because I don't know a better term.

12. See note 11.

13. I agree with one referee that the problem stems from the fact that what Patinkin "really" wanted to measure was not total wealth or "net worth" as (say) Ruggles and Ruggles or standard accounts measure it, but only that part of it that is subject to the real balance effect: wealth at the margin or monopoly rights. Unfortunately, even in this he has failed because of his erroneous banks-sector synonym. The *sector* will have monopoly wealth even if firms are fully competitive, provided that other factors in it are monopolists: e.g., the printer of bank cheques.

14. Indeed, this empirical vacuum must have become a security blanket for those who have spent their lives teaching the zero-bank-costs bank money multi-

plier and zero-net-worth bank T-accounts. I deduce this from the rejection of my recent application to the National Science Foundation in which I have declared myself willing to undertake the tedious task of assembling both official and industrial data and prepare—decades too late for monetary theory—empirical evidence about the contribution of the banking sector to our GNP and NI.

15. This is the lender's (depositor's) *gross* yield, which includes the cost of finding and servicing suitable borrowers. But, one should not try to be overly nice. Reported common stock yields also contain the cost of buying and selling, and the explicit or imputed costs of studying, frequently daily or hourly, the performance and outlook of suitable corporations making use of the investor's funds.

16. It is puzzling why this C. A. Phillips 1921 rationalization of bank inter-mediaries still dominates and wastes at least one chapter in each text. Elsewhere in economics one always explains equilibrium output of any asset by the demand for it, and not by non-demand for something else. The quantity of corporate bonds or of life insurance contracts is always explained by the demand for $50,000 worth of these assets. It is never explained by the decision of the public to get rid of $10,000 of money by buying these assets, by the sellers' decision to frustrate the public by spending most of the proceeds, by the public's retaliation in the form of renewed spending of the unwanted money for these assets, etc., until finally all the unwanted $10,000 of money has been absorbed as additional working balances by the sellers (while the assets sold, purely incidentally, have reached the level of $50,000). The only advantage of the non-demand approach to demand is that it is one more way of endowing our monetary theory with a "profitable" aura of "the occult" [12, Galbraith, 1975, p. 4].

17. Resource costs of commercial banks of $40 billion discounted to the present by the use of 10 per cent rate yield $400 billion. Add to this amount wealth of the Savings and Loan Associations and of the Mutual Savings Banks, and subtract gross overstatement of the value of the human wealth component in all three items caused by the fact that humans are mortal: that in their case *m* in equation 4 is small and that production costs and depreciation are not accounted for.

18. To capitalize on the reputation of genuine intermediaries or to meet legal requirements governing "banks," the entrepreneur may keep two sets of books and in the published version interpose the entries on the right side of Table 7.8 and show as his assets not his resources but his contracts with his customers that pay for these resources: he may publish Table 7.6 instead. "From the standpoint of economic analysis" this second set of books is "demonstrably wrong" [25, Patinkin, 1969, p. 1143], but of course the banker does not care about economic analysis: in his "business decisions" he will know what the true score is.

19. Two concepts, liability and wealth that remains after the former is subtrac-ted, play crucial roles in monetary and banking theory. But, as my earlier discussion of the non-competitive banking case and the above quotation both illustrate, monetary theory labours under the evil spell of a completely non-economic concept of a liability based on mere face value, both in the case of currency and of bank money.

Theoretically, weighty conclusions are based on the claim that currency H is a non-interest-bearing Liability of the government [24, Patinkin, 1965,

p. 288]; empirically, a grotesque Asset ("Cumulated Deficits" [24, 1965, p. 296] of a wastrel) is invented to offset it, and thus to force national wealth accounts to balance. Yet, everybody knows and accepts the textbook formula according to which a liability L is determined by interest costs I, face value B, and time to maturity n

$$L = I[1 - (1 + i)^{-n}]/i + B(1 + i)^{-n} \qquad (8)$$

and everybody knows and—verbally—stresses [24, 1965, p. 364] that in the case of currency $I = 0$ and $n = \infty$, so that $L = 0$. It's only that in Alice's Wonderland known formulae and known facts never happen to meet: $H \equiv L \equiv B$. The same error, as discussion of Table 7.6 has shown, afflicts bank deposits D. In the case of Table 7.8 the worst one could say is that the banker has a small liability

$$L = A[B_1(1 + i)^{-n} - B_2(1 + i)^{-m}] \qquad (9)$$

where A is the probability of the repurchase clause being exercised, and n and m the timing of net repurchases B_1 and net recoveries B_2 of these costs from the lessees. Of course, I would argue that the promise to pay in this case merely gives rise to the need to hold inventory of yet another factor of production needed to bank money in working order, and that its annual burden is measured by the factor cost $R \times i$.

20. The fact that empirical tests of many theories that are based on vitiating assumptions yield high correlation coefficients—and thus fail to be rejected—makes one wonder about the discriminatory power of statistical tests when it comes to uncontrolled macroeconomic experiments in the social sciences. Is it humanly possible to invent a theory based on vitiating assumptions that are strong enough to garner statistical rejection for this theory? (Besides, as every swain knows, not to be rejected is in most cases a far cry from being successful.)

REFERENCES

1. Ahmad, S. 1975. "The 'Paradox of Bliss' and Money as Net Wealth," *Journal of Money, Credit, and Banking*, August 1975, 7(3), pp. 385–90.
2. Baumol, William J. 1952, "The Transactions Demand for Cash: An Inventory Theoretic Approach," *Quarterly Journal of Economics*, Nov. 1952, 66, pp. 545–56.
3. Cagan, Phillip 1965. *Determinants and Effects of Changes in the Stock of Money, 1875–1960*. New York: National Bureau of Economic Research; distributed by Columbia University Press.
4. Federal Deposit Insurance Corporation 1975. *Bank Operating Statistics, 1974*. Washington, DC.
5. *Federal Reserve Bulletin*. 1964, *50*; 1965, *51*; 1972, *58*; 1975, *61*; 1976, *62*.
6. Fisher, Irving 1907. *The Rate of Interest*. New York: Macmillan.
7. —— 1971. *The Purchasing Power of Money*. Reprints of Economic Classics. New York: Kelley, [1911].
8. Friedman, Milton 1956. "The Quantity Theory of Money—A Restatement," in *Studies in the Quantity Theory of Money and Other Essays*. Edited by Milton Friedman. Chicago: University of Chicago Press, pp. 3–21.

9. ———— 1969. *The Optimum Quantity of Money*. Chicago: Aldine.
10. ———— and Schwartz, A. J. 1963. *A Monetary History of the United States, 1867–1960*. Princeton, NJ: Princeton University Press.
11. ———— 1970. *Monetary Statistics of the United States*. New York: National Bureau of Economic Research; distributed by Columbia University Press.
12. Galbraith, John Kenneth 1975. *Money*. Boston: Houghton Mifflin.
13. Garvy, G. and Blyn, M. R. 1969. *The Velocity of Money*. New York: F.R.B. of New York.
14. Gould, J. P. and Nelson, C. R. 1979 "The Stochastic Structure of the Velocity of Money," *American Economic Review*, June 1974, 64(3), pp. 405–18.
15. Grossman, H. I. and Policano, A. J. 1975. "Money Balances, Commodity Inventories, and Inflationary Expectations," *Journal of Political Economy*, Dec. 1975, 83(6), pp. 1093–1112.
16. Gurley, J. G. and Shaw, E. S. 1960. *Money in a Theory of Finance*. Washington, D.C.: Brookings Institution.
17. Horwich, G. 1964. *Money, Capital, and Prices*. Homewood, Ill.: Irwin.
18. Hutchinson, H. D. 1971. *Money, Banking, and the United States Economy*. Second edition. New York: Appleton Century Crofts [1967].
19. Johnson, Harry G. 1970. "A Note on the Theory of Transactions Demand for Cash," *Journal of Money, Credit, and Banking*, August 1970, 2(3), pp. 383–4.
20. ———— 1972. *Macroeconomics and Monetary Theory*. Chicago: Aldine.
21. Keynes, John Maynard 1936. *The General Theory of Employment, Interest and Money*. New York: Harcourt, Brace.
22. Marshall, Alfred 1949. *Principles of Economics*. Reprint of eighth edition. London: Macmillan [1920].
23. National Association of Mutual Savings Banks 1973. *Savings Banks Journal*, Oct. 1973.
24. Patinkin, Don. 1965. *Money, Interest and Prices*. Second edition. New York: Harper and Row [1956].
25. ———— 1969. "Money and Wealth: A Review Article," *Journal of Economic Literature*, Sept. 1969, 7(3), pp. 1140–60.
26. Ritter, Lawrence S. 1963. "The Role of Money in Keynesian Theory," in *Banking and Monetary Studies*. Edited by Deane Carson. Homewood, Ill.: Irwin, pp. 134–50.
27. Ruggles, Richard and Ruggles, Nancy D. 1956. *National Income Accounts and Income Analysis*. Second edition. New York: McGraw-Hill [1949].
28. Stein, J. L. 1971. *Money and Capacity Growth*. New York: Columbia University Press.
29. Tobin, James 1956. "The Interest-Elasticity of the Transactions Demand for Cash," *Review of Economics and Statistics*, August 1956, 38(3), pp. 241–7.
30. ———— 1958. "Liquidity Preference as Behavior Towards Risk," *Review of Economic Studies*, Feb. 1958, 25, pp. 65–86.
31. ———— 1963. "Commercial Banks as Creators of 'Money'," in *Banking and Monetary Studies*. Edited by Deane Carson. Homewood, Ill: Irwin, pp. 408–19.
32. Tretheway, M. 1976. "Theories of the Demand for Money: Evidence from Individual Demand Deposits," unpublished M.A. Thesis; University of Wisconsin-Milwaukee.

33. US Department of Commerce 1973, 1974. *National Income Issue. Survey of Current Business*, July 1973, 53(7), and July 1974, 54(7).
34. Waul, R. N. 1975. "Net Outlay Uncertainty and Liquidity Preference as Behavior Toward Risk," *Journal of Money, Credit, and Banking*, August 1975, 7(3), pp. 499–506.
35. Weber, W. E. 1975. "Monetary Assets, Net Wealth, and Banking Structure," *Journal of Money, Credit and Banking*, August 1975, 7(3), pp. 331–42.

8 In Defence of Neoclassical Monetary Theory*

One chapter in Don Patinkin's *Money, Interest and Prices* (New York: Harper and Row, 1965), entitled "Critique of Neoclassical Monetary Theory" (pp. 162–98) is considered of such crucial importance for the book and for its *Integration of Monetary and Value Theory* (subtitle of the book) that it now dominates our literature. In this Note, I propose to show that the "Critique" is invalid, that the neoclassical theory[1] has been well integrated, and that the celebrated "real balance effect" is a mere theoretical refinement of uncertain empirical relevance.

THE "CRITIQUE" REPRODUCED

The neoclassical error is said to be an "Invalid Dichotomy" which has the real sector determine relative prices and the monetary sector, the absolute prices. Patinkin criticizes it by using a verbal argument and a formal model (Fig. VIII, p. 179, reproduced here as Figures 8.1 and 8.2). The verbal argument is best summarized by its outcome, which one can also trace in the Figures. In one market experiment, assume a haphazard equiproportionate change in money prices:

(1) By virtue of the homogeneity postulate, this does not change relative prices on which supply and demand functions in the real sector depend. Thus, the market continues to be in equilibrium: see the *ss* and *dd* function in the figures. The market is in a metastable equilibrium and the price level there is indeterminate. By Walras's Law, it should also be indeterminate in the money market (p. 176).

(2) The neoclassical analysis of the money market rests on either Fisher's or Pigou's quantity theory, both of which yield a determinate price level

---

* From: *Quarterly Review of Economics and Business*, Summer 1982.

(functions *SS* and *DD* in Fig. VIII-b here, Figure 8.2). By Walras's Law, it *should* also be determinate in the real market (p. 178).

A second market experiment, based on an increase in the quantity of money, yields the same conclusion. Thus, the author concludes both discussions with the refrain: "Hence a contradiction" (pp. 178, 179). The real balance effect is said to eliminate it (p. 21):

It must also be emphasized that, for the simple exchange economy with which we are now dealing, the assumption that there exists a real-balance effect in the commodity markets is the *sine qua non* of monetary theory. For as we shall see below (p. 176), in the absence of this effect the absolute level of money prices in such an economy is indeterminate: that is, no market forces exist to stabilize it at a specific level.

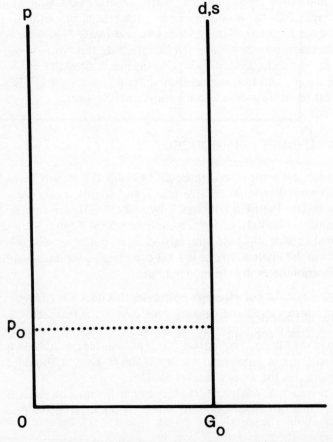

Figure 8.1   Amount of commodities demanded and supplied (per annum)

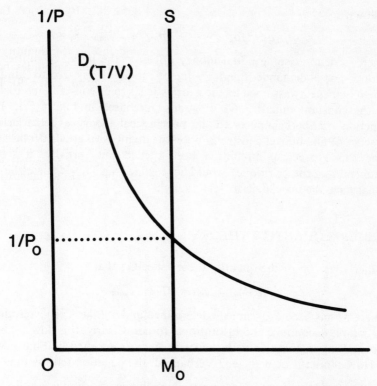

Figure 8.2   Nominal Amount of Money Supplied and Demanded
(at a point of time)

This statement—variously paraphrased—is repeated so frequently that it seems fair to deduce that the author considers it to be *the* crucial *leitmotif* of the book.

Formally, the money market in Figure 8.2 is specified (p. 177) in terms of the Cambridge k as follows:

$$kPT_{(at\ a\ point\ of\ time)} = M_{(at\ a\ point\ of\ time)}, \tag{1}$$

where the left side depicts the demand for the stock of money DD (with k and T assumed constant) and the right side the exogenous stock of money SS.[2] At the same time, Patinkin's figure is said (p. 163) to apply *also* to the Fisherian version of the quantity theory by virtue of the *alleged* identity

$$V \equiv 1/k \tag{2}$$

What about the goods market in Figure 8.1? Let me accept the function ss there as correct and focus on the other function. The economic content of the demand function dd must be specified as follows:

$$0 \leqslant (fp_1q_1 + fp_2q_2 + \cdots + fp_nq_n)_{(per\ annum)} \leqslant \infty, \tag{3}$$

where p denotes some initial money prices, q the initial quantities of various goods demanded, and f a factor ranging from zero to infinity. The q is allegedly assumed by the neoclassicists to be constant and to add to the constant quantity G_0 of goods purchased in Figure 8.1. The function dd there imputes to the neoclassical theory a belief in the absence of any budget constraint upon the quantity of goods demanded. Had this geometric imputation been spelled out verbally, it seems doubtful that the "Critique" would have gained such a wide acceptance. What have the neoclassicists really taught?

FISHER'S QUANTITY THEORY

Fisher's version of the quantity theory specifies that

$$MV_{(per\ annum)} = PT_{(per\ annum)}, \tag{4}$$

where M has been exogenously determined and V (like k) is determined by complex economic and institutional forces. Clearly, this flow analysis has nothing in common with the stock analysis depicted by Figure 8.2.

How should it be depicted? Verbalized, the equation tells us that

(1) The holders of money are determined to spend—supply to sellers of goods—a constant amount of money MV per annum. This is depicted by the inelastic (flow) supply of money per annum function SS in Figure 8.3. (2) By arithmetic necessity, the corollary of (1) is that the holders of money will purchase (demand) a constant money value PT of real goods per annum. This is depicted by the unitary elastic (flow) demand for goods function dd in Figure 8.4 (not by the inelastic dd function in Figure 8.1).

This function may be expressed in symbols as follows:

$$(\overline{PT})_{(per\ annum)} = (fp_1q_1 + fp_2q_2 + \cdots + fp_nq_n)_{(per\ annum)} = (\overline{MV})_{(per\ annum)}. \tag{5}$$

Instead of advocating the budget "constraint" ranging from zero to infinity (imputed to him by the function dd in Figure 8.1), Fisher in his famous equation has explicitly specified a very rigid budget constraint: constant MV.

The suppliers of goods for money per annum—the demanders of money in exchange for their goods—do not care for what absolute price they will sell their good and turn around and purchase the good they want. Only their stock of resources—the suppliers' budget constraint—and relative prices determine their supply of G in Figure 8.1 and of T in Figure 8.4. The ss functions in both figures are inelastic. By arithmetic necessity, the holders of goods thus have a demand for money per annum function DD in Figure 8.3 that is unitary elastic. Velocity is *not* a co-determinant of it.[3]

Reconsideration of Patinkin's two market experiments will reveal that equilibria in Fisherian Figures 8.3 and 8.4 *are* simultaneously and consistently determined in both markets; Walras's Law is *not* violated. It is not true that neoclassicists of the Fisherian persuasion held a theory with a "...dichotomy...involved in a basic internal contradiction" (p. 176).

In Fisher's theory, the goods market (where goods are sold for money, at the exchange rate P) and the money market (where money is sold for goods, at the exchange rate $1/P$) are not merely two integrated markets. By arithmetic necessity, correctly perceived by Fisher's tautology

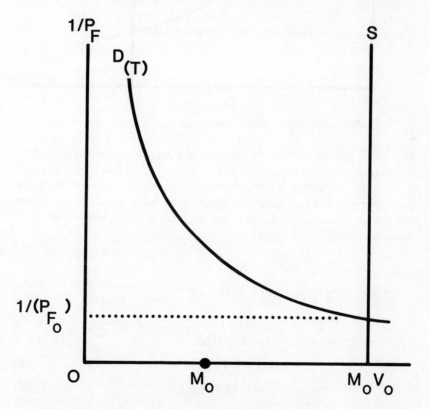

Figure 8.3 Nominal Amount of Money Expenditure (per annum)

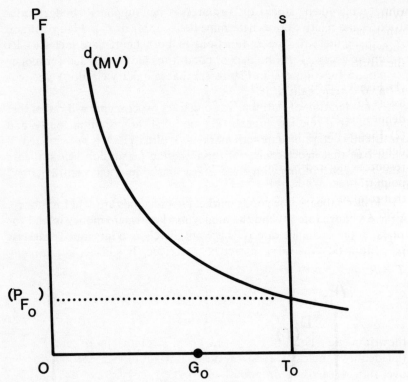

Figure 8.4   Amount of Assets Demanded and Supplied (per annum)

$MV = PT$, any two-goods model can yield only one single market. One may choose to depict it either by Figure 8.3 or Figure 8.4; to show both is an optional *pleonasm*. Two functions depicting one single market and two obverses of these functions depicting the very same market do not add up to two pairs of functions depicting two markets which a theoretician needs to integrate.

A. C. PIGOU'S QUANTITY THEORY

Patinkin claims (p. 163) that the Fisherian and Cambridge versions of the quantity theory should be specified as

$$MV = PT, \text{ and} \tag{6}$$

$$M = kPT, \text{ so that} \tag{7}$$

$$V \equiv 1/k. \tag{8}$$

With one of the theories being a mere mechanical transformation of the other, he believes that by showing an inconsistency in the one he has shown it in the other. This widespread myth could not be further from the truth. On a very low level of generality one could argue as follows:

(1) Fisher defines his T as the total of all real resources and financial assets (offsetting debts and liabilities) traded per annum, and explicitly defines his P_F as the price index of these assets traded.

(2) Pigou, on the very page quoted by Patinkin as his source (p. 176), defines his T—which he in fact (significantly) labels R—as "the total resources enjoyed by the community," which are measurable only at a point of time. While he does not define his price level, is there any doubt that total resources in existence must be evaluated by all their prices and yield P_P?

Pigou makes misunderstanding of his *difference* with Fisher impossible by explicitly stating (on the very same page quoted by Patinkin) that $T \neq R$, and thus $V \neq 1/k$. With

$$MV = P_F T \text{ and} \tag{9}$$

$$M = KP_P R, \tag{10}$$

the arithmetic relationship between V and k is much more complex than the identity 8 indicates. And it is not a constant but variable relationship over time, as division of labour and markets develop and the ratio T/R changes.

However big the confusion there is in the orthodox claim that $V \equiv 1/k$, it retreats into insignificance once we consider a much more fundamental problem. Fisher considers flows per annum, while Pigou considers stocks at the point of time. Equations 9 and 10, if we want (for comparative purposes) to tear them out of the contexts of their authors' discussions, must be written as

$$MV_{(per\ annum)} = P_F T_{(per\ annum)} \tag{9'}$$

and

$$M_{(at\ a\ point\ of\ time)} = kP_P R_{(at\ a\ point\ of\ time)}. \tag{10'}$$

Thus, V is a rate while k is a pure number, and the two are incommensurable. There is not, and cannot be, any mathematical relationship between them. We face not one theory expressed in two alternative ways, but two totally different theories.

Pigou focuses on the consumers' balanced portfolios. They may desire to hold (for example) one fifth of their resources (at a point of time) in the form of money (at the same point). Or, to reflect more recent theories, they may desire to hold (for example) one fifth of their income at a point of time (measured at annual rate) in the form of money (at the same point of time)[4]: $k = 1/5$. However:

(1) in a stodgy society, demanders and suppliers prefer to trade goods very seldom so that they turn over this money only twice a year ($V = 2$). (2) in a restless society, they may prefer to trade goods very frequently so that they turn over their money twelve times per year ($V = 12$).

In other words, any given k is consistent with a V ranging from zero to infinity. And, the two theories have vastly different implications: $2 \times M$ causes either $2 \times P_F$ or $2 \times P_P$, with the latter being consistent with $0 \leqslant dP_F \leqslant \infty$.

Figure 8.2 does depict Pigou's monetary theory. It seems incredible that Figure 8.1—with its absence of a budget constraint—should depict Pigou's price theory. But even so, the price variable in the former would have to be the price of all resources; in the latter, the trading price. The quantity in the former would have to be specified at a point of time; in the latter, per annum. Juxtaposition of the two figures is impossible, and thus it cannot prove that the neoclassicists of the Pigouvian persuasion held a theory with a "...dichotomy involved in a basic internal contradiction" (p. 176).

CONCLUSION

The real balance effect does not introduce logical consistency into the neoclassical model by integrating its analysis of the real and money markets; it introduces a mere theoretical refinement that may, or may not, prove to be empirically significant.[5] With money being one part of the net wealth of the community, we must expect decreases in the price level (increases in this wealth) to cause increases in the demands for "luxury" goods, and decreases in the desire to save. The effect of the real balance effect on the relative prices of luxuries and necessities has as yet not been explored; the effect of it on the consumption-saving ratio seems to be of some significance. However, given the insignificant proportion of real balances in total wealth, we would—a priori—not expect this effect to be of policy significance. It is lucky that it is *not* true that the effect is *the* instrument that integrates, holds together, the goods market and the money market; a weaker reed would be hard to imagine.

NOTES

1. The definition of "neoclassical" writers varies from writer to writer. Thus, it needs to be said that the "Critique" is said to apply to such writers as "...Leontieff, Haberler, Marschak, Samuelson, Tinbergen, and Boulding..." (p. 625) as well as to Keynes's *General Theory* (pp. 634–7); in fact, to all pre-Patinkin writers.
2. I have added the specification of the time dimension to the equation and in the figure because this will become a major concern later.
3. The neoclassical price theorists have then elaborated upon the properties of the demand for goods function that appears in the center of Equation 5 (with the supply function given the same treatment). They have proposed that *in equilibria* (I stress, in equilibria) $q_1 = a_1(fp_1/fp_n),...,q_{n-1} = a_{n-1}(fp_{n-1}/fp_n)$. They have added "the homogeneity postulate."
4. In Figure 8.2 "velocity" has not a time dimension, and thus is merely a ratio. In contrast, modern income velocity *could* have a time dimension: it could be a rate, the speed at which M moves (is spent for income) per annum. Empirically, however, this is false because a substantial and variable fraction of income is not purchased for money (for example, all imputed incomes). Not to do violence to the generally accepted meaning of velocity of an item (as the measure of *the motion* of this item) the term "income velocity" should be dropped in favour of "income-money ratio."
5. It revises the neoclassical homogeneity postulate in note 3 by adding to it a *ceteris paribus*: "money wealth constant."

9 Monetary Policy, Taxes, and the Rate of Interest*

I. INTRODUCTION[1]

In the classical analysis, emphasis is placed on the proposition that the supply of and demand for "real" saving lead to a unique rate of interest that cannot be affected by changes in the quantity of money. This doctrine also asserts an automatic tendency toward full employment provided that the requirement of full wage flexibility is satisfied. Keynes in his *General Theory*[2] challenged the part of the doctrine that asserts that there is an automatic tendency toward full employment. Pigou,[3] Haberler,[4] and Scitovsky[5] replied by introducing an additional variable, wealth, into the saving function, and have shown that this variable will restore the automatic tendency of the system toward full employment.

Metzler further extended the revision of the classical doctrine by the introduction of wealth into the demand for money function.[6]

His analysis indicated that in a model containing wealth the rate of interest becomes partly real and partly monetary: (1) A simple increase in the quantity of money leaves the rate unaffected and thus the rate is a real phenomenon. (2) Changes in the quantity of money accompanied by open-market operations do affect the rate of interest and thus the rate becomes a monetary phenomenon in the sense of being co-determined by the quantity of money outstanding and by changes in this quantity.[7] The first result, however, is the consequence of a definition of wealth that includes only money and equities (titles to streams of income fixed in real terms). In this article we extend the analysis by including bonds (titles to income streams fixed in money terms) in our definition of wealth. This enables us to consider open-market operations more realistically, because central banks typically buy and sell not equities but government

* From: *Journal of Political Economy*. August 1963.
Coauthor: Thomas R. Saving

bonds. We demonstrate that with this extension of the definition of wealth, every monetary change now affects the rate of interest whether or not it consists of a simple increase in the quantity of money or is brought about by open-market operations. The introduction of wealth into the model, and defining wealth to include bonds, changes the classical real theory of the rate of interest into one that is fully monetary.

In addition, our model considers explicitly the effects of open-market operations on the levels of personal and corporate taxes that are necessary to finance interest payments.[8] We shall see that, in contrast to an analysis that ignores either the fact that an open-market purchase of bonds lowers the quantity of taxes needed to pay interest on these bonds,[9] or the fact that changes in the price level change the real burden of these taxes, the effects of monetary policy on the rate of interest depend on whether personal or corporate taxes are changed. Indeed, it would be possible to keep the quantity of money and bonds unchanged and simply change the tax mix to affect the rate of interest. Thus one could argue that, once we introduce bonds and the taxes necessary to pay interest on these bonds, the theory of the rate of interest becomes "monetary" and "fiscal" as well: fiscal in the sense that if everything else is held constant, the rate of interest will depend on the distribution of taxes between personal and corporate taxes.

The Model

The Commodity Market	The Money Market	Identities
(1) $s = s(r,m,h,y_n)$	(4) $m = m(r,h,y_n)$	(6) $y_n = d - t_1 + g$
(2) $i = i(r,t_1)$	(5) $m = M/P$	(7) $h = y_h - t_2$
(3) $s = i$		(8) $P_g = T_1 + T_2$
		(9) $Pt_1 = T_1$
		(10) $Pt_2 = T_2$

List of Symbols

s = real saving
i = real investment
r = rate of interest
m = real quantity of money
h = real net human income
y_n = real net non-human income
t_1 = real corporate taxes
t_2 = real personal taxes

g = real government interest payments
d = real corporate earnings
y_h = real gross human income
T_1 = nominal corporate taxes
T_2 = nominal personal taxes
P = price level
M = money supply (in nominal units)

2. THE MODEL

In our model, equations 1 and 2 express the relationships in the commodity market. Taxes imposed on both human income and on income yielded by wealth are introduced explicitly. Equation 3 asserts that in full employment, assumed throughout, saving and investment are equal. The next two equations express the situation in the money market: equation 4 expresses the demand for money, [10] and equation 5 asserts that the demand for money measured in real terms will equal the supply of money (exogenously determined in the case of a simple increase in the quantity of money, otherwise determined by open-market operations). [11]

The remaining equations, 6–10, are definitional in character. [12] In equation 6 we are assuming that all corporate earnings are distributed as dividends.

Equation 8 asserts that the government exists only to collect taxes to be disbursed as interest payments and to buy and sell bonds. This limited view of government activity is due to the fact that this is the only aspect of it that we want to explore in this chapter. If other government receipts and expenditures were assumed to occur, but their amounts were held constant throughout our analysis, the results obtained would not be affected.

The signs which we attached to the various partial derivatives are specified in Table 9.1.

The signs are those customarily employed by economic theory: Saving increases with an increase in the rate of interest (a) and with the level of human income (b); since the existence of saving is by itself a proof that the saver has less wealth than he desires, savings decrease with an extraneous increase in one of the items constituting wealth, namely, with real money (c), bonds, and equities. Given the levels of prices and of the

Table 9.1: List of partial derivatives

(a) $\dfrac{\partial s}{\partial r} > 0$	(d) $\dfrac{\partial s}{\partial y_n} < 0$	(g) $\dfrac{\partial m}{\partial r} < 0$
(b) $\dfrac{\partial s}{\partial h} > 0$	(e) $\dfrac{\partial i}{\partial r} < 0$	(h) $\dfrac{\partial m}{\partial h} > 0$
(c) $\dfrac{\partial s}{\partial m} < 0$	(f) $\dfrac{\partial i}{\partial t_1} < 0$	(i) $\dfrac{\partial m}{\partial y_n} > 0$

rate of interest, saving therefore decreases with items that are indexes of the level of wealth: the income yielded by bonds and equities (d). Investment decreases as either the return on capital falls (e) or as taxes imposed on the returns to capital increase (f). The demand for money for asset purposes decreases with increases in the rate of interest, which make this non-interest bearing wealth less attractive to hold relative to interest-bearing wealth (g). The transaction demand for money increases with any increase in human income (h). Since both the transaction demand for money and the asset demand for money increase with increases in non-human income, the total demand for money must increase with increases in non-human income (i). Finally, since the source of income spent should not affect the quantity of money necessary to support these expenditures, we may state that the absolute size of the partial derivatives relating only the transaction demand for money with net human and net non-human incomes are the same. However, the partial derivative (i) contains both the transaction demand for money and the asset demand for money. Consequently, we may write[13]

$$\frac{\partial m}{\partial y_n} > \frac{\partial m}{\partial h} > 0. \tag{11}$$

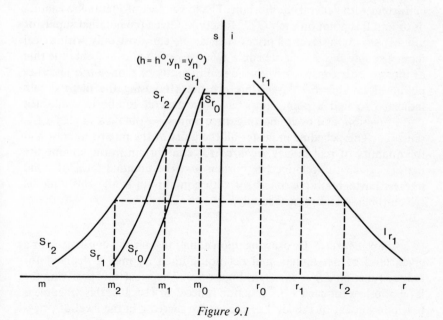

Figure 9.1

3. ANALYSIS OF EQUILIBRIUM

1. Commodity market. From equation 1 we can construct a set of saving functions $S_{r_i}S_{r_i}$ relating the level of saving to the level of real money (Fig. 9.1). Each *SS* function is constructed for some particular level of the rate of interest; the set of functions is constructed for given levels of net human and net non-human income. Similarly, from equation 2 we can construct an investment function $I_{t_i}I_{t_i}$, given the level of corporate taxes. Figure 9.1 can then be used to construct a schedule $C^*_{(P=1)}C^*_{(P=1)}$ (Fig. 9.2), which shows all the pairs of the rate of interest $(r_0, r_1, ..., r_n)$ and the quantity of real money $(m_0, m_1, ..., m_n)$ required for equilibrium in the commodity market (equation 3). The subscript specifying the level of prices for each C^*C^* function is necessary because this schedule is not independent of the level of prices. An increase in the level of prices will (a) redistribute net income from non-human to human income [14] and thus (by virtue of derivatives [b] and [d] in Table 9.1) shift the set of *SS* functions in Figure 9.1 leftward, and (b) decrease corporate taxes and thus (by virtue of derivative [f] in Table 9.1) shift the $I_{t_i}I_{t_i}$ function in Figure 9.1 rightward.

Given the nominal supply of money, only one level of prices is consistent, in equilibrium, with a given real quantity of money (equation 5); consequently, only one point, A, along each $C^*_{(P=n)}C^*_{(P=n)}$ function is consistent with general equilibrium. The lower part of Figure 9.2 enables us to find this point on each C^*C^* function. Given the nominal supply of money, say M, a level of prices such as P_1 can exist only with a real money supply m_1. As the schedule $C^*_{(P=1)}C^*_{(P=1)}$ indicates, only the rate of interest r_1 is consistent with the real quantity of money m_1; all other points along this C^*C^* schedule are not. By using the method just indicated to find a point consistent with general equilibrium on each C^*C^* function, and by connecting these points, we obtain a single C_MC_M schedule. This schedule indicates all the pairs of the rate of interest and the quantity of real money *required* for equilibrium in the commodity market (given the relative tax burden and the nominal level of bond interest payments) and *consistent* with equilibrium in the entire model (given the nominal money supply).

2. Money market. By drawing upon equation 4 we can construct, for a given level of net human and net non-human income, a demand for money function $L^*_{(P=1)}L^*_{(P=1)}$ in Figure 9.3. The subscript specifying the level of prices for each L^*L^* function is necessary because this schedule is not independent of the level of prices. An increase in the level of prices will redistribute net income from non-human income to human income

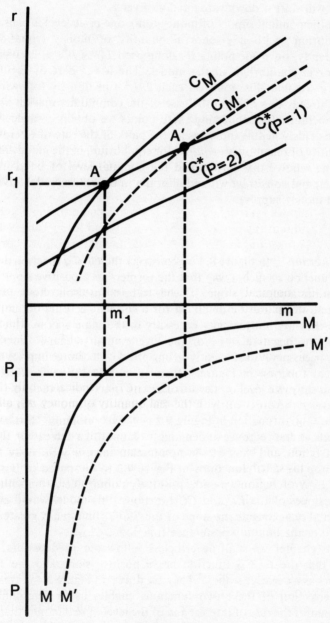

Figure 9.2

(cf. note 14) and thus affect the position of the L^*L^* function: a price increase will shift it downwards and vice versa.[15]

Given the nominal supply of money, only one price level is consistent, in equilibrium, with a given real quantity of money (equation 5). Consequently, only one point, B, along each $L^*_{(P=n)}L^*_{(P=n)}$ is consistent with general equilibrium in the model. The lower part of Figure 9.3 enables us to find this point on each L^*L^* function by following the method already described in the case of the commodity market and the C^*C^* functions. By connecting these points we obtain a single $L_M L_M$ schedule. This schedule indicates all the pairs of the rate of interest and the quantity of real money *required* for equilibrium in the money market (given the relative tax burden and the nominal level of bond interest payments) and *consistent* with equilibrium in the entire model (given the nominal money supply).

3. Equilibrium.　In Figure 9.4 we construct the $C_M C_M$ function and the $L_M L_M$ function in such a way that the former has a positive slope while the latter has a negative slope. It needs to be pointed out, however, that while these slopes can be defended for a society like ours on empirical grounds they are not logically necessary in the same way in which, for instance, the negative slope of the Friedmanian demand function is logically necessary. A sufficiently strong effect of a change in price on the investment function in Figure 9.1 and a sufficiently weak effect of a change in the price level on the set of saving functions in the same figure could reverse the order of the C^*C^* functions in Figure 9.2. This would make the $C_M C_M$ function in Figure 9.2 negatively sloping.[16] Similarly, a sufficiently strong response of demand for money to a decrease in the real value of bonds and thus of the non-human income yielded by bonds could cause the L^*L^* functions in Figure 9.3 to be spaced so far apart that the $L_M L_M$ function would be positively sloping. Yet, even with these peculiar slopes of the LL and CC functions, this model would possess static stability as long as the slope of the $C_M C_M$ function is greater than the slope of the liquidity preference function $L_M L_M$.

In this chapter we shall nevertheless follow our predecessors[17] and assume that the $C_M C_M$ function has a positive slope and the $L_M L_M$ function has a negative slope.[18] They are drawn in Figure 9.4 in this way. The intersection of these two functions enables us to determine one unique pair of the rate of interest and of the level of real money that must exist if there is to be equilibrium simultaneously in the commodity market and in the money market.

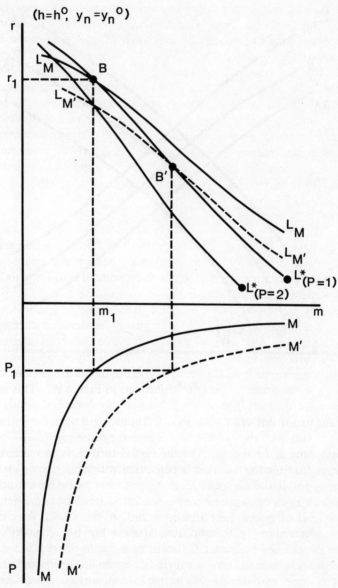

Figure 9.3

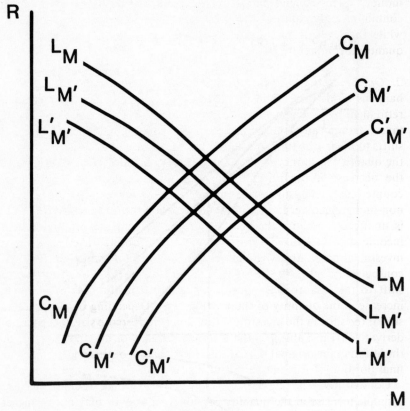

Figure 9.4

4. EFFECTS OF MONETARY POLICY

1. Simple Increase in money.   By the very nature of its derivation each point along the $C_M C_M$ function is consistent with only one quantity of real money and hence one price level. Now if we increase the quantity of nominal money to M', each amount of real money will be consistent with a higher level of prices, necessitating a shift in the $C_M C_M$ function to $C_{M'} C_{M'}$, (derived in Fig. 9.2 and transferred to Fig. 9.4). The difference between the old and the new CC functions is due to lower real taxes on human and non-human income (obviously an equiproportionate reduction). The same reasoning applies to the $L_M L_M$ function, which shifts to $L_{M'} L_{M'}$, (derived in Fig. 9.3 and transferred to Fig. 9.4). Therefore, if only the quantity of money is increased in a model containing bonds, the rate of interest must decrease while the level of prices must increase, though not necessarily proportionately to the increase in the quantity of money.[19] This conclusion is different from that derived from a model containing only equities: there the rate of interest remains unchanged while the level of prices rises proportionately to the increase in the quantity of money.[20]

2. Open-market purchase of bonds: lower corporate taxes. What happens if the increase in the quantity of money is accompanied by a retirement of the same amount of bonds and by a decrease in corporate taxes? Graphically, the money market's $L_M L_M$ function in Figure 9.4 shifts to the left by the same amount as in the case of a simple increase in the quantity of money (to $L_{M'} L_{M'}$); there is no additional shift because the decrease in wealth due to lower interest payments is precisely counterbalanced by an increase in wealth due to lower corporate taxes on non-human income. In the commodity market the SS function (Fig. 9.1) is unaffected because the net human income and the net non-human income are unchanged. However, lower corporate taxes make new investment more attractive than before, and the $I_{t_1} I_{t_1}$ function (Fig. 9.1) consequently shifts to the right. This causes the $C_{M'} C_{M'}$, function to shift to the left from the position it attained in the case of a simple increase in the quantity of money (Fig. 9.4). Depending on the absolute size of the shift in the investment function (the absolute size of the partial derivative [f] in Table 9.1) the CC function may or may not lie more to the left than the original $C_M C_M$ function (because of this uncertainty, the final position of it is not shown in Fig. 9.4).

Consequently, the rate of interest must be higher than would result from a simple increase in the quantity of money; it may or may not be higher than the original interest rate. This again, is a conclusion different from the one reached on the basis of a model containing only equities.[21] The price level must be higher than it would have been in the case of a simple increase in the quantity of money. The increase in the price level may, however, be more or less than proportionate to the increase in the quantity of money.

3. Open-market purchase of bonds: lower personal taxes. If the quantity of money is increased through open-market purchases of bonds, and if lowering of personal taxes is selected as a means of decreasing the resulting government budgetary surplus, the set SS in Figure 9.1 shifts to the left both because of the higher net human income (cf. partial derivative [b] in Table 9.1) and because of the lower net non-human income (cf. partial derivative [d]). Consequently, the $C_{M'} C_{M'}$ function in Figure 9.4 shifts to the right from the position that was reached in the case of a simple increase in the quantity of money to $C'_{M'} C'_{M'}$. The LL function in Figure 9.4 shifts to the left. First, one part part of the shift is identical with the shift that occurred in the case of a simple money increase (from $L_M L_M$ to $L_{M'} L_{M'}$). Second, lower personal taxes increase the real value of net human income, pushing the LL function to the right, and lower government interest payments decrease the real value of net non-human income, pushing the LL function to the left. By virtue of equation 11 the leftward shift predominates and the function shifts to, say, $L_{M'} L_{M'}''$.

Consequently, the rate of interest must be lower in this case than any one of the three rates already discussed: the original rate, the rate resulting from a simple increase in the quantity of money, and the rate resulting from open-market operations combined with lower corporate taxes. The price level will be higher than the original one.[22] It might be noted that, even though the rate of interest is the lowest in the case of open-market operations combined with a decrease in personal taxes, it does not necessarily follow that this policy will be more conducive to economic growth than would be open-market operations combined with lower corporate taxes. In the case of the lower corporate tax alternative, we obtain a higher rate of interest but at the same time a higher marginal efficiency of capital function; in the case of the lower personal tax alternative, while we have a lower rate of interest we at the same time continue to operate along the original marginal efficiency of investment function. Whether investment will be higher or lower if the personal tax alternative is selected cannot therefore be predicted on a priori grounds.

4. Open-market operations: equiproportionate reduction in both personal and corporate taxes.   The last policy we want to consider is based on open-market operations combined with an equiproportionate decrease in both personal and corporate taxes. This case is similar to the case of a simple increase in the quantity of money; in that case, too, both personal and corporate taxes were decreased equiproportionately but for a different reason (an increase in prices). If we now, in addition, decrease even the nominal level of taxes equiproportionately, there will be a further shift in the LL and the CC functions in the same direction as in the case of a simple increase in the quantity of money. These shifts must stop short of the positions reached by the LL and CC functions in the case in which only personal taxes were decreased, because in the present case part of the given tax decrease benefits net non-human income. Therefore the LL and CC functions expressing the equiproportionate decrease in taxes accompanying open-market operations in Figure 9.4 must lie between the functions $L_{M'} L_{M'}$ and $L_{M'}' L_{M'}$ and between $C_{M'} C_{M'}$, and $C_{M'}' C_{M'}'$ respectively. The new rate of interest reached must be lower than in the case of a simple increase in the quantity of money; consequently it must be lower than in the case of open-market operations accompanied by a reduction in corporate taxes; and it must be higher than the rate resulting from open-market operations accompanied by a reduction in personal taxes. About the price level no more may be said than that it must be higher than the original one.

5. SUMMARY OF RESULTS

In Table 9.2 we present in summary form our conclusions as to the effects of various monetary and fiscal policies on the rate of interest and the level of prices. These results are obviously different from those that would be yielded by the classical theory. The difference is due, we may state by way of recapitulation, to three separate causes:

1. Our model contains the wealth effect as introduced by Pigou, Haberler, and Scitovsky. This effect is based on the assertation that the level of saving will be affected if the real value of government non-interest-bearing debt (money) changes and, by extension, if the level of government interest-bearing debt (bonds) changes. The existence of this effect in our model is demonstrated by *the presence* of the partial derivatives (c) and (d) in Table 9.1.
2. The model contains a redistribution effect. The decisions to hold money and to save are supposed to be affected by a shift of income from human to non-human income and vice versa. The existence of this effect in our model is embodied in the difference between the partial derivatives (b) and (d), on the one hand, and between the partial derivatives (h) and (i), on the other. These differences are due to the fact that human and non-human incomes are not traded in a perfect market.
3. The model contains bonds. The significance of bonds is twofold. First, bonds are another item through which the wealth effect may operate. Second, bonds by their very nature necessitate taxes and through these taxes they affect the investment function and the saving function.

The first difference, consisting in the presence of the wealth effect is a *conditio sine qua non* in our model: without it, we would not have a model that assures an automatic tendency toward full employment, we could not assume that the sum of net human and net non-human income is constant, and the entire analysis would fall to the ground. However, it will be useful to allocate part of the difference between the neoclassical model and our model to the presence of the redistribution effect and the remaining part to the mere presence of bonds. This can be done by setting the difference between the derivatives (h) and (i) and between the derivatives (b) and (d) in Table 9.1 equal to zero. The remaining difference must be due only to the presence of bonds in our model. When the preceding analysis of the four monetary policies is revised along these lines we obtain the following conclusions (which the reader may easily check for himself): (1) the interest rate resulting from a simple money increase or from open-market operations combined with a reduction of personal taxes will be higher than the original rate of interest; (2) the rate resulting from open-market operations combined with an equiproportionate reduction in both taxes will be still higher; and (3) the rate resulting from open-market operations combined with the reduction in corporate taxes will be highest of all. The same ordering is obtained for the level of prices. As Table 9.2 indicates, when the redistribution effect and the presence of bonds operate jointly, the resulting rate of interest is lower than the original rate of interest in three cases out of four (the exception being the corporate tax case). From this it follows that at least in three cases out of four the redistribution effects cause the rate of interest to decline. Geometrical analysis is not powerful enough to decide the fourth case. However, mathematical comparison established that what is true about the three cases is true about the fourth one as well: in the case of open-market operations combined with a reduction in corporate taxes the distribution effects make the resulting rate of interest lower than it would be in the absence of these effects.

This conclusion appears significant and worth special mention. In aggregative models it is commonly assumed for the sake of simplicity that redistributive effects are absent. We have already seen that this assumption is equivalent to the claim that human and non-human wealth are traded in a perfect market. In addition, our analysis indicates that the assumption of a perfect market for human and non-human wealth, or the equivalent assumption of no redistributive effects, introduces a

Table 9.2: *Comparison of price levels and interest rates resulting from various policies*

Basis for comparison	Policy Compared							
	Price Level				Interest Level			
	SMI	OM–C	OM–P	OM–E	SMI	OM–C	OM–P	OM–E
Initial equilibrium	+	+	+	+	−	?	−	−
Simple money increase (SMI)	xxx	+	?	?	xxx	+	−	−
Open-market operations combined with a decrease in:								
Corporate taxes (OM–C)	xxx	xxx	?	?	xxx	xxx	−	−
Personal taxes (OM–P)	xxx	xxx	xxx	?	xxx	xxx	xxx	+
Equiproportionate change in both taxes (OM–E)	xxx	xxx	xxx	xxx	xxx	xxx	xxx	xxx

systematic bias into the results obtained. The bias is due to an equally *systematic* preference for non-human over human income (cf. equation 11 and the signs of the partial derivatives [b] and [d] in Table 9.1).

6. CONCLUSION

As we pointed out in the introduction, the classical conception of the rate of interest was that it is a completely "real" phenomenon, unaffected by changes in the quantity of money. The introduction of the wealth effect into the saving function and, subsequently, into the demand for money function affected this conclusion. In a model that contains only equities this rate becomes partly "real" and partly "monetary" in the sense that changes in the quantity of money do not affect it while changes in the quantity of money combined with changes in the quantity of equities due to open-market operations do affect it. However, defence of the "real" nature of the rate of interest is still possible because one can argue that the open-market operations are simply two distinct policies that happen simultaneously: a change in the quantity of money (which leaves the rate unaffected) and a change in the wealth held by private individuals (which does affect the rate). Since the classicists never denied that a change in the level of real wealth will affect the rate of interest, they could argue that the argument based on open-market operations cannot affect the claim that the rate of interest is a "real" phenomenon. The introduction of bonds into the model makes this defence impossible because in this case increases in money and thus prices necessarily affect the level of real wealth. Therefore, even a simple increase in the quantity of money will affect the rate of interest; the rate of interest becomes monetary.[23]

Finally, our analysis enables us to discuss the relationship between the rate of interest and the fiscal policy followed by the government. From our discussion it follows that a decrease in corporate taxes accompanied by an increase in personal taxes must cause the rate of interest to increase, and vice versa, even if all other things remain the same. Thus in our model the theory of the rate of interest becomes not only monetary but fiscal as well. "Neutrality" of *either* the monetary *or* the fiscal measures of the government with respect to the rate of interest, and thus with respect to economic growth, cannot be achieved.

MATHEMATICAL APPENDIX

A. Solution of the model

The model can be differentiated and solved simultaneously for dr, dm,

dh, dy_n, dt_1, dt_2, dg, ds, di and dP in terms of dT_1 and dT_2, and dM (since y_h and d are constants, dy_h and dd are equal to zero). For our purposes we need only consider the derivatives (dr/dm) and (dP/dm) for the four cases considered in the chapter. Let us denote the determinant of the system as:

$$\Delta = \left[\left(\frac{\partial s}{\partial r} - \frac{\partial i}{\partial r} \right) \left(\frac{\partial m}{\partial h} - \frac{\partial m}{\partial y_n} \right) - \frac{\partial m}{\partial r} \left(\frac{\partial s}{\partial h} - \frac{\partial s}{\partial y_n} \right) \right] t_2 - \frac{\partial m}{\partial r} \frac{\partial i}{\partial t_1} t_1$$

$$+ \left[\left(\frac{\partial s}{\partial r} - \frac{\partial i}{\partial r} \right) + \frac{\partial s}{\partial m} \frac{\partial m}{\partial r} \right] m.$$

Then we can write the relevant total derivatives for each of the cases as follows:

1. Simple increase in the quantity of money $(dT_1 = 0,\ dT_2 = 0)$.

$$\frac{dr}{dM} = \frac{- \frac{\partial s}{\partial m} \left(\frac{\partial m}{\partial h} - \frac{\partial m}{\partial y_n} \right) t_2 - \left(\frac{\partial s}{\partial h} - \frac{\partial s}{\partial y_n} \right) t_2 - \frac{\partial i}{\partial t_1} t_1}{P\Delta}, \tag{A1}$$

$$\frac{dP}{dM} = \frac{\left(\frac{\partial s}{\partial r} - \frac{\partial i}{\partial r} \right) + \frac{\partial s}{\partial m} \frac{\partial m}{\partial r}}{\Delta}. \tag{A2}$$

2. Open-market operations—reduction in corporate taxes $(dM = -\ Pdg/r$; $Pdg = dT_1$, so that $dT_1/dM = -r$; $dT_2 = 0$).

$$\frac{dr}{dM} = \left(\frac{dr}{dM} \right)_{(1)} + \frac{r \left[- \frac{\partial i}{\partial t_1} \left(\frac{\partial m}{\partial h} - \frac{\partial m}{\partial y_n} \right) t_2 - \frac{\partial i}{\partial t_1} m \right]}{P\Delta}, \tag{A3}$$

$$\frac{dP}{dM} = \left(\frac{dP}{dM} \right)_{(1)} + \frac{r \frac{\partial m}{\partial r} \frac{\partial i}{\partial t_1}}{\Delta}. \tag{A4}$$

3. Open-market operations—reduction in personal taxes $(dM = -\ Pdg/r$; $Pdg = dT_2$, so that $dT_2/dM = -r$; $dT_1 = 0$).

$$\frac{dr}{dM} = \left(\frac{dr}{dM} \right)_{(1)} + \frac{r \left[\left(\frac{\partial m}{\partial h} - \frac{\partial m}{\partial y_n} \right) \left(\frac{\partial i}{\partial t_1} t_1 - \frac{\partial s}{\partial m} m \right) - \left(\frac{\partial s}{\partial h} - \frac{\partial s}{\partial y_n} \right) m \right]}{\Delta P},$$

$$\tag{A5}$$

$$\frac{dP}{dM} = \left(\frac{dP}{dM} \right)_{(1)} + \frac{r \left[- \left(\frac{\partial s}{\partial r} - \frac{\partial i}{\partial r} \right) \left(\frac{\partial m}{\partial h} - \frac{\partial m}{\partial y_n} \right) + \frac{\partial m}{\partial r} \left(\frac{\partial s}{\partial h} - \frac{\partial s}{\partial y_n} \right) \right]}{\Delta}.$$

$$\tag{A6}$$

4. Open-market operations—equiproportionate reduction in personal and corporate taxes $(dM = - Pdg/r;\ dT_1 = kdT_2$, where k is the constant of tax proportionality; $Pdg = dT_1 + dT_2$, so that $dT_2/dM = - r/1 + k$).

$$\frac{dr}{dM} = \left(\frac{dr}{dM}\right)_{(1)} - \frac{\frac{rm}{1+k}\left[\frac{\partial s}{\partial m}\left(\frac{\partial m}{\partial h} - \frac{\partial m}{\partial y_n}\right) + \left(\frac{\partial s}{\partial h} - \frac{\partial s}{\partial y_n}\right) + k\frac{\partial i}{\partial t_1}\right]}{\Delta P},$$

(A7)

$$\frac{dP}{dM} = \left(\frac{dP}{dM}\right)_{(1)} - \frac{\frac{r}{1+k}\left[\left(\frac{\partial s}{\partial r} - \frac{\partial i}{\partial r}\right)\left(\frac{\partial m}{\partial h} - \frac{\partial m}{\partial y_n}\right) - \frac{\partial m}{\partial r}\left(\frac{\partial s}{\partial h} - \frac{\partial s}{\partial y_n}\right) - \frac{\partial m}{\partial r}\frac{\partial i}{\partial t_1}k\right]}{\Delta}.$$

(A8)

B. Method of comparison

Stability for the system requires that the determinant of the system (Δ in the above derivatives) be greater than zero. In addition to the stability condition we were requiring that the slope of the CC function be positive and the slope of the LL function be negative as follows:

$$\left(\frac{dr}{dm}\right)_{CC} = \frac{-\frac{\partial s}{\partial m}m + \frac{\partial i}{\partial t_1}t_1 + \left(\frac{\partial s}{\partial h} - \frac{\partial s}{\partial y_n}\right)t_2}{\left(\frac{\partial s}{\partial r} - \frac{\partial i}{\partial r}\right)m} > 0,$$

(A9)

$$\left(\frac{dr}{dm}\right)_{LL} = \frac{m + \left(\frac{\partial m}{\partial h} - \frac{\partial m}{\partial y_h}\right)t_2}{\frac{\partial m}{\partial r}m} < 0.$$

(A10)

C. Analysis of various policies

1. Simple money increase. In order to establish a bench mark for comparative purposes we shall evaluate A1 and A2 carefully. The interest in the discussion of A1 is in the determinants of the sign, that is, the direction of the change in the rate of interest. Inspection of the numerator of A2 reveals that the coefficient of t_2 contains the net effect of changes in the price level on the saving function and the coefficient of t_1 contains the net effect of changes in the price level on the investment function, except for an allowance for the absolute magnitude of the changes in h, y_n and t_1. To determine these absolute magnitudes we need only refer to equations 6, 7, and 8 in the model. If we substitute 8 in 6 we get:

$$y_n = d + t_2.$$

(6c)

Now by comparing 6a and 7 it immediately becomes apparent that the magnitude of the absolute change in h and y_n resulting from an increase in P depends on t_2. It is also obvious that the magnitude of the absolute change in t_1 resulting from an increase in P depends on t_1. Hence, given the sign of A10, it is apparent that the sign of A1 depends on whether the shifts in the saving function (leading to lower rates of interest) dominate the shifts in the investment function (leading to higher rates of interest), these shifts being caused by the effect of price changes on the real tax burdens of the public and corporate sectors and, subsequently, on the wealth and human income of the community. Assuming the normal case of A9 > 0 and A10 < 0, it can be shown that A1 < 0.

Substitution of the restrictions imposed on the partial derivatives in A2 immediately shows that A2 > 0 (the expected result). However, the more interesting question is whether the price change is more or less than proportional to the monetary change. The discussion of proportionality of the price change will be facilitated if we invert equation A2 as follows:

$$\frac{dM}{dP} = m + \frac{\left(\dfrac{\partial s}{\partial r} - \dfrac{\partial i}{\partial r}\right)\left(\dfrac{\partial m}{\partial h} - \dfrac{\partial m}{\partial y_n}\right)t_2 - \dfrac{\partial m}{\partial r}\left(\dfrac{\partial s}{\partial h} - \dfrac{\partial s}{\partial y_n}\right)t_2 - \dfrac{\partial m}{\partial r}\dfrac{\partial i}{\partial t_1}t_1}{\left(\dfrac{\partial s}{\partial r} - \dfrac{\partial i}{\partial r}\right) + \dfrac{\partial s}{\partial m}\dfrac{\partial m}{\partial r}}.$$

(A2a)

From A2a it follows that $dP/dM \, M/P \gtreqless 1$ as the numerator of A2a is $\lesseqgtr 0$. Proportionality of the price change to the monetary change cannot be predicted a priori.

We are now prepared to compare the new r and P to the original r and P:

a) $r_1 < r_0$,

b) $P_1 > P_0$,

c) $m_1 \gtreqless m_0$.

To compare cases 2, 3, and 4 with initial equilibrium or simple increase in money we need only determine the signs of the residual fractions since equations A3 – A8 are in terms of A1 and A2.

2. Open-market operations-reductions in corporate taxes

By comparing A3 and A1 it can be shown that the interest will be higher for this case than in the case of simple increase in money. However, it cannot be shown that the rate will be higher than the original equilibrium rate.

Since the numerator of the residual of A4 is always positive, it follows that the price level will be higher than the price level resulting from a simple increase in money. However, it cannot be shown whether $dP/dM \ M/P \gtrless 1$ so that we can conclude nothing concerning the proportionality of the increase in the price level. Hence we reach the following conclusions:

a) $r_1 < r_2 \gtrless r_0$,

b) $P_0 < P_1 < P_2$,

c) $m_0 \gtrless m_2 < m_1$.

3. Open-market operations-reductions in personal taxes. By comparing equation A5 to equation A1, it can be shown that the interest rate will be lower than the rate resulting from a simple increase in money. It will, therefore, be lower than the original equilibrium rate. In addition, a comparison of equations A5 and A3 shows that the personal tax case yields a lower rate of interest than reductions in corporate taxes.

The sign of the numerator of A6 cannot be determined, so that the price level may be higher or lower than the price level resulting from a simple money increase or from open-market operations accompanied by a reduction in corporate taxes. It follows that nothing can be said concerning the proportionality of the price change.

The following are our conclusions:

a) $r_3 < r_1, r_2, r_0$,

b) $P_3 \gtrless P_1, P_2, P_3 > P_0$,

c) $m_3 \gtrless m_1, m_3 \gtrless m_0, m_3 \gtrless m_2$.

4. Open-market operations—equiproportionate reductions in both personal and corporate taxes. Again assuming that A9 > 0 and A10 < 0, it can be shown that the rate of interest for this case will be lower than the rate resulting from a simple increase in money. Therefore, this rate will be lower than the rate in the corporate tax case and the initial equilibrium rate. In addition, by comparing equations A5 and A7 and invoking the normal slopes of the *CC* and *LL* functions we can show that this rate will be higher than the rate associated with case 3, reductions in personal taxes.

The sign of the numerator of A8 cannot be determined (implying that nothing can be said concerning the price-level change relative to the simple-money case). In addition, we cannot say whether this price level will be higher or lower than in any of the other cases. This implies that nothing can be determined concerning the proportionality of the price change.

We conclude:

a) $r_0 > r_1 > r_4 > r_3, r_2 > r_4,$

b) $P_4 > P_0, P_4 \gtreqless P_3, P_2, P_1,$

c) $m_4 < m_0, m_4 \lesseqgtr m_3, m_2, m_1.$

NOTES

1. Almost a decade ago one of the authors greatly profited from a discussion of this topic with Professor George S. Tolley.
2. John Maynard Keynes, *The General Theory of Employment, Interest and Money* (New York: Harcourt, Brace & Co., 1936).
3. A. C. Pigou, *Employment and Equilibrium* (London: Macmillan & Co., 1949).
4. T. Scitovsky, "Capital Accumulation, Employment, and Price Rigidity," *Review of Economic Studies*, VIII (1940–41), pp. 69–88.
5. G. Haberler, *Prosperity and Depression* (Geneva: League of Nations, 1941).
6. Lloyd A. Metzler, "Wealth, Saving, and the Rate of Interest," *Journal of Political Economy*, LIX (April, 1951), p. 113.
7. *Ibid*, p. 98.
8. Robert A. Mundell ("The Public Debt, Corporate Taxes, and the Rate of Interest," *Journal of Political Economy*, LXVIII [December, 1960], pp. 622–7) introduced corporate taxes into Metzler's analysis. However, his model contains only equities that Mundell, in contrast with the more careful usage of Metzler, calls at times "government debt" or "government interest-bearing debt." It might be noted parenthetically that, Mundell's claim notwithstanding, personal taxes are not introduced into his analysis; detailed discussion of this point is relegated to our note 22.
9. Alternatively, such a purchase of bonds would decrease government expenditures while leaving the receipts unaffected, thus leading to a permanent budget surplus that again would affect the rate of interest and the price level.
10. Metzler (*op. cit.*, p. 113) simplifies his task by assuming rigid proportions between real money and other wealth. However, James Tobin ("A Dynamic Aggregative Model," *Journal of Political Economy*, LXIII [April, 1955], p. 105) points out that equilibrium requires "portfolio balance." Frank P. R. Brechling ("Note on Bond-Holding and the Liquidity Preference Theory of Interest," *Review of Economic Studies*, XXIV [June, 1957], pp. 190–97) presents a rigorous analysis of this problem and reaches the same conclusion. Empirical data indicate that the proportion between other wealth and money is not rigid: the wealth elasticity of the demand for money was calculated to be −1.12 in the United States (Martin Bronfenbrenner and Thomas Mayer, "Liquidity Functions in the American Economy," *Econometrica*, XXVIII [October, 1960], p. 817), 0.62 in the United Kingdom (Boris Pesek, "Determinants of the Demand for Money," *Review of Economics and Statistics* [forthcoming], Table 2), and 0.52 in Czechoslovakia (*ibid.*, Table 1).
11. The introduction of an expansion of the money supply by the banking system, affects only the size but not the signs of the changes in the variables considered in this chapter.

12. Variables $r, m, h, y_n, t_1, t_2, g, s, i,$ and P are endogenous; variables $y_h, d, T_1, T_2,$ and M are exogenous. Normally one would state that the nominal value of government interest payments is exogenous and that the taxes necessary to finance these interest payments are endogenous. However, nothing is changed if this classification is reversed, and it proved more convenient to reverse it.

13. Strictly speaking, it might not be justified to deny the presence of the asset demand for money in connection with net human income. However, since human and non-human income are not traded perfectly on the capital market, the change in the asset demand for money that results from a given change in non-human income is necessarily larger than the change resulting from an equal change in human income. Hence, equation 11 remains valid.

14. This can be demonstrated if we differentiate 6 and 7 as follows:

$$dy_n = - dt_1 + dg, \tag{6a}$$

$$dh = - dt_2. \tag{7a}$$

Imposing the condition, derived from equation 8, that

$$dg = dt_1 + dt_2, \tag{8a}$$

on equation 6a gives the following:

$$dy_n = dt_2. \tag{6b}$$

Comparison of 7a and 6b shows that price increases raise net human income and decrease net non-human income by like amounts.

15. This downward shift is the result of assuming that $\partial m / \partial h < \partial m / \partial y_n$, since

$$\frac{\partial m}{\partial P} = \frac{t_2}{P} \left(\frac{\partial m}{\partial h} - \frac{\partial m}{\partial y_n} \right)$$

and, hence,

$$\frac{\partial m}{\partial P} < 0.$$

16. Solely on the basis of geometrical analysis it may appear that a third case is possible: the C^*C^* functions stacked in a reverse order (shifting to the left with each increase in prices) and the CC function positively sloping and cutting the C^*C^* functions from above. The result would then be that an increase in the quantity of money would shift the CC function in the opposite direction to that indicated in Fig. 9.2: many results obtained in this chapter would then become indeterminate. However, mathematical analysis reveals that it is impossible for the CC function to be positively sloping if the C^*C^* functions are stacked in a reverse order: (a) the C^*C^* functions will be stacked in the order indicated in Fig. 9.2 or in the reverse order depending on whether the following total derivative is smaller or greater than zero:

$$\frac{dr}{dP} = \frac{- \dfrac{\partial i}{\partial t_1} t_1 + \dfrac{\partial s}{\partial m} m - \left(\dfrac{\partial s}{\partial h} - \dfrac{\partial s}{\partial y_n} \right) t_2}{P \left(\dfrac{\partial s}{\partial r} - \dfrac{\partial i}{\partial r} \right)}.$$

(b) The *CC* function will be positively or negatively sloping depending on whether the following total derivative is greater or smaller than zero:

$$\frac{dr}{dm} = \frac{\dfrac{\partial i}{\partial t_1} t_1 - \dfrac{\partial s}{\partial m} m + \left(\dfrac{\partial s}{\partial h} - \dfrac{\partial s}{\partial y_n} \right) t_2}{\left(\dfrac{\partial s}{\partial r} - \dfrac{\partial i}{\partial r} \right)}.$$

Since in both equations the denominator is positive, only the numerators need to be considered. For the case mentioned above to exist it would be necessary that *both* numerators be greater than zero. This, however, is impossible because the terms in the two numerators are of equal magnitude but opposite in sign.

17. Metzler, *op. cit.*, p. 101, and Mundell, *op. cit.*, p. 623.
18. The positive slope of the *CC* function requires that the following inequality be satisfied (cf. Appendix, equation A9):

$$\frac{\partial s}{\partial m} m + \left(\frac{\partial s}{\partial h} - \frac{\partial s}{\partial y_n} \right) t_2 > - \frac{\partial i}{\partial t_1} t_1.$$

Since in the United States *both* the quantity of money and the amount of personal taxes are in fact larger than the amount of corporate taxes, this inequality is likely to hold as long as the wealth effect is not inconsequential. If it is, the entire neoclassical full-employment analysis breaks down.

The negative slope of the liquidity preference function *LL* requires that the following inequality be satisfied (cf. Appendix, equation A10):

$$m > - \left(\frac{\partial m}{\partial h} - \frac{\partial m}{\partial y_n} \right) t_2.$$

This inequality, too, is certain to hold today in the United States since (1) the quantity of money is substantially greater than the amount of corporate taxes and (2) the reciprocal of the marginal velocity, which represents a gross overestimate of the term appearing in parenthesis in the above equation, is substantially smaller than 1 (cf. Milton Friedman and David Meiselman, *The Relative Stability of Monetary Velocity and the Investment Multiplier* [A Report to Commission on Money and Credit (New York, 1961)], p. 73).

19. In the Appendix this and all the following conclusions arrived at on the basis of geometrical interpretation of the model are proved rigorously by the use of mathematical analysis. Since the headings in the Appendix are identical to the headings in the main body of the article the reader should find it easy to relate the two.
20. Metzler, *op. cit.*, p. 106: "if the monetary disturbance...consists of an increase...in the quantity of money without any offsetting changes in other assets, then it will not...permanently change the interest rate." Mundell, *op. cit.*, p. 623: "It is easily demonstrated that a simple change in the nominal quantity of money has no effect on the real equilibrium of the system."
21. Metzler, *op. cit.*, p. 108: "According to the system depicted in Figures 4 and 5, however, the security purchases by the central bank will permanently *lower* the equilibrium rate of interest." Mundell, *op. cit.*, p. 625: "Open-market operations combined with corporate income tax reductions *raise* the equilibrium rate of interest."

22. This case cannot be compared with Mundell's case of open-market purchases combined with a reduction in personal taxes in his equities-only model because Mundell's analysis of this case is flawed. He takes into account the effect of a purchase of equities on wealth, but he does not take into account the effect of the simultaneous decrease in personal taxes. This is indicated by the fact that his entire analysis of this case is based on the following effect: "At constant interest rates the real value of earning assets is reduced, and this affects both the capital and the goods markets" (p. 624). In our terms, all he considers are the consequences of a decrease in net non-human income caused by open-market purchases of equities; he ignores the fact that this results in lower personal taxes and consequently in higher net human income and that this higher net human income is bound to affect saving and the demand for money. Formally, he precluded himself from a genuine consideration of the effects of a reduction of personal taxes by writing both his saving equation (p. 622, equation [1]) and his demand for assets equation (p. 622, equation [2]) so that they exclude the level of net human income. In terms of our model, this is equivalent to setting the partial derivatives (b) and (h) in Table 9.1 equal to zero; implicitly, the marginal propensity to consume net human income is assumed to be equal to unity. Under these conditions, any level of personal taxes is consistent with equilibrium; changes in these taxes may be assumed and ignored simultaneously because the model precludes them from affecting anything but the level of consumption.

23. It may still be argued that a decrease in wealth is occurring since a redistribution of income from non-human to human does involve, at least in the public's eyes, a decrease in wealth due to the inability to trade human and non-human wealth on an equal basis. Hence, the rate of interest remains a "real" phenomenon for any change that leaves "total" wealth unaffected.

10 A Note on Permanent Income Theory*

For the deliberations of mortals and timid, an unsure are our plans.
Wisdom 9:14, 17

The permanent income hypothesis (PIH), which employs the concept of permanent income as an independent variable determining consumption and the demand for money, has gained wide influence in economics. Is there any text that does not devote several pages to it? And how many vitae have been enriched by articles exploring it?

Here I shall not criticize the permanent income hypothesis for denying all of human history that tells us of our unceasing and largely futile efforts to pierce the unknown future. Nor shall I, on a lower level of generality, criticize the claim that each man—faced with risks (which have probability distributions) and uncertainties (which do not)—assigns probability distributions to both. Friedman (1957, pp. 23, 25,) obtains a probable future income for each of his remaining forty years (Friedman, 1957, p. 24), and is fool enough to act on it. Instead, on a very pedestrian level, I shall focus on the insoluble empirical problem of not verifying the permanent income hypothesis.

The theory alleges that the demand for money (Friedman, 1969, pp. 122, 124) is determined by

$$M = f[y_p(T)] = f[\beta \int_{-\infty}^{T} e^{\beta(t-T)} y(t)dt] \tag{1}$$

where M denotes money; y_p, permanent income in time T; t, the time of past observed incomes; and β, a calculated statistic that determines the "independent" variable y_p.

---

* From: *Journal of Post Keynesian Economics*, Summer 1979, Fall 1981.

THE DEPENDENT VARIABLE

The permanent income hypothesis does not specify how to measure M. Since the Federal Reserve now publishes six concepts of M (M_1–M_5 and M_{1+}) and three others are waiting in the wings (M_6–M_8), this represents a problem to prospective users of the PIH. Elsewhere, however, the inventor has provided a guideline:

Just where the line should be drawn between assets regarded as money and those regarded as near-monies or simply as "other assets" is not something that can or should be decided either once for all or on the basis of verbal considerations. It must depend on the purpose and on the empirical relevance of a particular distinction for that purpose under specific circumstances, which is to say, on the empirical stability and regularity of relationships between the chosen total and other variables. (Friedman and Schwartz, 1963, p. 650)

Briefly, select the M that correlates well. That this is meant seriously is shown by the fact that this criterion is used explicitly and extensively in a later book by these authors. But this is not the full extent of the leeway claimed for the quantification of M:

The restriction of our attention to these four combinations seems a less serious limitation to us than our acceptance of the common procedure of taking the quantity of money as equal to the aggregate value of the assets it is decided to treat as money. This procedure is a very special case of the more general approach discussed earlier. In brief, the general approach consists of regarding each asset as a joint project having different degrees of "moneyness," and defining the quantity of money as the weighted sum of the aggregate value of all assets, the weights for individual assets varying from zero to unity with a weight of unity assigned to that asset or assets regarded as having the largest quantity of "moneyness" per dollar of aggregate value. The procedure we have followed implies that all weights are either zero or unity. (Friedman and Schwartz, 1970, p. 151)

The authors refer to several attempts in this direction, but as yet do not commit themselves to any single one:

The more general approach has been suggested frequently but experimented with only occasionally. We conjecture that this approach deserves and will get much more attention than it has so far received. The chief problem with it is how to assign the weights and whether the weights assigned by a particular method will be relatively stable for different periods or places or highly erratic. So far there is only the barest beginning of an answer. (Friedman and Schwartz, 1970, p. 152)

This refinement of "the empirical approach" to money can be quantified as follows:

$$M = a_1 C + a_2 DD + a_3 TD + a_4 SL + a_5 MSB + \ldots \qquad (2)$$

(where the mnemotechnical symbols denote currency, demand and time deposits, savings and loan association shares, and deposits in mutual savings banks), with the specification that

$$0 < a_i < \quad (i = 1, 2, ..., n). \tag{3}$$

The set of a's actually used (discussed below) then quantifies the dependent variable, money, out of a huge number of eligible candidates.

THE INDEPENDENT VARIABLE.

The contrast with M, income is given only one value for each period in the official statistics. The PIH gets around this statistical straitjacket by focusing on all the past incomes at once (note the infinity sign in equation 1 above), and by postulating a rate β of decay of memory, or of the significance we assign to past events. The specification of this rate, which enters equation 1 in a complex fashion both as a factor and as an exponent, is

$$0 < \beta < 1. \tag{4}$$

The rate β actually used then quantifies the independent variable out of a huge number of eligible candidates.

EMPIRICAL VERIFICATION OF THE PIH

The computer is fed raw data on the various monies in equation 2 and on GNP, equation 1, and the instruction to select simultaneously for each year one value for M and y_p—using one of the infinite number of sets of a's and β's—which will meet the a priori requirement (and, simultaneously, test *ex post* the hypothesis) of "empirical stability and regularity of relationship between" the two. Only the primitiveness of 1957 computers and the regretted limitation to only four concepts of $M (a_1 - a_4 = 1000, 1100, 1110, 1111)$ explain why initially the PIH yielded merely excellent statistical results. Use of a modern computer and the freedom to employ not just any β but also any set of a's must result in $r = 1$, a perfect correlation.[1] Since one cannot prove a negative, let me offer not a theorem but a law: it is absolutely impossible for the PIH not to be verified. *Ipso facto*, it is not a theory.

DEFENCE OF THE PIH

The author of the theory is not unaware of these technical problems, though he does not exactly stress them:

This weighting pattern has been used for a rather similar problem by Phillip Cagan, namely, to estimate the expected rate of change of prices during hyper-inflations from the time series of past rates of change. The model that led him to his weighting pattern can be readily adapted to the present problem and may perhaps make the use of this pattern seem somewhat less arbitrary than the strictly empirical approach that I have so far followed. (Friedman, 1957, p. 143)

This is like saying that the problems of predicting weather and the path of a bullet are the same. In fact, the two problems could not be more totally dissimilar.

National income is the outcome of innumerable causes and is co-determined by many *uncertainties* that do not have probability distributions: inventions, resource discoveries and unexpected depletions, depressions, Watergates, elections, inflations, income redistributions, revolutions, and wars.

Personal income—and it is this that determines behaviour—is subject to many more uncertainties, many of which are not offsetting in the aggregate. Automobile producers may have buoyant future income expectations, while buggy producers may be complacently extrapolating this year and despairing the next. No weighting of past national incomes can possibly measure these everchanging forces.

In contrast, hyperinflation, it is claimed, is the single-cause outcome of a persistent extreme behaviour (the printing of money) by a known group of policy makers. The *risk* that this group's past behaviour will be an excellent predictor of its future behaviour has a probability close to, if not equal to, unity. (Many social institutions—including prisons—rely on this method.)

Even if the two problems were similar, however, the statement quoted above would not be much of a defence against the anticipated charges of arbitrariness and empiricism in the PIH. In pedagogy, this defence is known as the "Gee, Dad, Phil does it too" gambit.

AD ARGUMENTUM: EMPIRICAL WORK ON PIH IS VALID

Paradoxically, empirical validity is the most damaging—though most totally unreal—possibility facing the PIH. When one looks at what the investigators actually do rather than what they say they do, one realizes that, had the permanent income hypothesis never been enunciated, its testers never would have missed it.

All that has been done is to prove the (unstated) theory that the weighted average of *past* observable GNPs determines *current* consumption and demand for money. In contrast, the PIH claims that it is, instead, the *future* cumulated GNP, of which past GNPs are a proxy, that determines the *current* items. Either the alleged future-past-present link is valid, in which case the PIH is merely one of two equally valid theories, though a circuitous and thus cumbersome supernumerary in the pair; or the alleged unprovable link is not valid, in which case only the former theory is correct.

Let me hasten to the defence of the permanent income hypothesis. All this means is that the empirical work on it cannot be valid. Common sense tells us that, while the known past does constrain us, simultaneously the guessed unknown future goads us on. The theory that the expected future affects our behaviour—given empirical evidence that it is the past that determined practically all of it notwithstanding—cannot be a nullity. But operational content it does not have—nor, I believe, can it ever.

CONCLUSION

The permanent income hypothesis undertook a task that is and will remain impossible: to quantify in one global number[2] a constantly shifting mix of our individual hopes for and fears of the future—a task which generations of historians, philosophers, theologians, psychologists and, until recently, economists, surely view with absolute incredulousness. Nor would any of them pay much attention to such a global number even if it were to become available, for the relationship between future income expectations and current economic behaviour is *not* a single-valued function. High current consumption may be the outcome of either expected explosion or expected implosion of future income; of euphoria or of despair about the future. This psychological flaw aside, in the face of the impossible empirical task of quantifying the independent variable, the usual method of making theory fit the facts simply had to be reversed if anything concrete were to be reported.

Stripped of its empirical plumage, the PIH does nothing more than bind into a self-consciously formal, even torturous, straitjacket the biblical verity taken as the motto of this article. Since the two are perfect substitutes, we shall be better off with the latter, which does not put on scientific airs.[3] I propose that the "theory" of a permanent income be permanently exorcised from economic literature.

NOTES

1. Alternatively stated: given the huge number of M's yielded by all the conceivable sets of a's, and the huge number of GNP's given by all the conceivable β's, the number of permutations of M's and GNPs is astronomical. If one puts an astronomical number of monkeys behind typewriters...
2. Note that I am not questioning the existing valuable measurements of revealed short-term spending plans, which are probably based on a modest version of the adaptive expectations approach to income, employing expectations that keep shifting the lip of a widely flared horn containing all the possible future incomes.
3. Alas, in monetary theory such airs are not uncommon; consider, for example, the billing given to supply-demand "analysis" of the *definition* "1 guinea = 21 shillings," akin to "1 baker's dozen = 13 eggs" (Patinkin, 1965, pp. 699–708):

Accounting prices, confused with money prices, 183–184; defined, 16; indeterminacy of, 38, 42–43, 195, 617–618; lack of operational significance, 16; in Wicksell 586–587 [not there]

Indeterminacy of accounting prices, 38, 42–43, 195, 617–618

Prices, "Accounting," ... defined, 15–16
   See also Accounting prices;

Guinea, 15, 611–612

REFERENCES

Friedman, Milton 1957. *A Theory of the Consumption Function*. Princeton: Princeton University Press.

——— 1969. *The Optimum Quantity of Money and Other Essays*. Chicago: Aldine.

——— and Schwartz, Anna Jacobson 1963. *A Monetary History of the United States 1867–1960*. Princeton: Princeton University Press.

——— 1970. *Monetary Statistics of the United States*. New York: Columbia University Press.

Patinkin, Don 1965. *Money, Interest, and Prices*. New York: Harper and Row.

THE THEORY OF PERMANENT INCOME
*Evangelos O. Simos and John Triantis**

Since Friedman's publications of *Studies in the Quantity Theory of Money* and *A Theory of the Consumption Function*, there has been a considerable interest in the concept of permanent income with the aim of verifying, on empirical grounds, whether permanent income may serve as a better explanatory variable in determining consumption or the demand for money than the conventional Keynesian income. In a recent issue of this journal and in this vein, Boris Pesek (1979, p. 64) has attempted to show "the insoluble empirical problem of not verifying the permanent income hypothesis." Furthermore, based on his analysis, Pesek concludes his short note proposing "that the 'theory' of permanent income be permanently exorcised from economic literature" (p. 69). Unfortunately, this conclusion is based on assumptions made by Pesek, not by Friedman, indicating that Pesek either has not carefully read Friedman's theoretical work or has misinterpreted Friedman's models.

Friedman (1956, 1957, 1959) defines permanent income as the product of and "interest rate" *r* and the stock of wealth *W*. This stock of wealth is interpreted as the present value of anticipated future receipts, from both human and non-human assets, discounted back to the present at a subjective rate of interest whose average value is *r*. Thus permanent income (Y_p) is a theoretical construct which is mathematically expressed by

$$Y_p = rW. \tag{1}$$

It is thus evident that permanent income's empirical counterpart can be found if and only if wealth data, as defined in Friedman's work, are available. As wealth data were not available, Friedman and his adherents estimated permanent income as the weighted average of the present and past values of measured income. In Friedman's words (1959):

In deriving a consumption function from aggregate time-series data, I concluded that an *estimate* [original emphasis] of permanent income—which I called "expected" income—*to distinguish it from the theoretical concept* [emphasis added]—was given by

$$Y_p(T) = \beta \int_{-\infty}^{T} e(\beta - a)(t - T) Y(t)dt. \tag{2}$$

To discount a theory by criticizing an empirical proxy, or in Friedman's words "an estimate," which "should be distinguished from the theoretical concept," is a clear indication of either misunderstanding or misrepresenting well-clarified economic theory. This is evidence, as Pesek argues, "that *the theory* [emphasis added] alleges that the demand for money is determined by [an equation in which his permanent income is defined as in equation 2]."

The purpose of this note is to indicate that Friedman's proxy of permanent income, as described by equation 2, produces the same results in the demand for money model as the theoretical concept of permanent income, equation 1. That is to estimate a demand for money function, we shall utilize three alternative budget constraints: (i) Keynesian income; (ii) permanent income proxied by a weighted average of current and past values of income; and (iii) permanent income measured as the product of a constant (average) interest rate (r) and wealth.

If the results obtained by employing the two concepts of permanent income are identical, though different from those which use the conventional Keynesian income, it seems that Friedman's proxy is not "like predicting weather," while his theoretical model is like "predicting the path of a bullet."

In Table 10.1 we present regression results of the demand for money in logarithmic form for the United States, 1929–69. Both M_1 and M_2 concepts of money, deflated by the GNP price deflator, are used in defining the logarithm of real money balances as the dependent variable. The AAA bond rate is used as the interest rate.

GNP in 1958 dollars was employed for real income. Permanent income is computed as a weighted average of present and past levels of GNP. Following Friedman (1959), the weights starting with the current year and going back in time are: 0.3297, 0.2210, 0.1481, 0.0993, 0.0666, 0.0446, 0.0299, 0.0201, 0.0134, 0.0090, 0.0060, 0.0040, 0.0027, 0.0018, 0.0012, 0.0008, 0.0005, 0.0004, 0.0002, 0.0002, 0.0001, and 0.0001. The sum of these weights equals unity. To compute permanent income for the whole period 1929–69, GNP is extrapolated back twenty-two years using the index of GNP at constant dollars published recently by Maddison (1977).

The series of wealth, which in Friedman's theoretical work is the sum of human and non-human capital, is taken from Kendrick's study (1976). His estimates of total capital are generated by the following categories of investment expenditures: (i) Tangible non-human investment. This type of expenditure constitutes what is traditionally considered investment in physical capital. (ii) Tangible human investment. These expenditure estimates measure the costs of producing the physical human being. They cover the average variable costs of raising children to working age, that is, age fourteen. To avoid double counting in (ii), expenditures on education and health care are separately estimated and not included in rearing costs. (iii) Investment in research and development. These estimates comprise all the forms of R & D outlays. (iv) Intangible human investment. These series comprise (a) education,

Table 10.1:   Empirical results of the US demand for money, 1929–69[*]

$\log (M_i/P) = \text{constant} + \beta_1 \log (r) + \beta_2 \log (X_j) + u$
$i = 1,2. \quad j = 1,2,3.$

Definition of money	Constant term	Budget Constraint Variable (X_j)				R^2	SEE	DW
		log (r)	log (Y)	log (Y_p)	log(W)			
M_1	1.848 (2.72)	−0.213 (−2.15)	0.525 (4.63)			0.990	0.0433	1.884
	−0.404 (−0.58)	−0.354 (−3.85)		0.957 (7.86)		0.991	0.0403	1.900
	−3.169 (−1.65)	−0.251 (−2.26)			0.978 (4.21)	0.987	0.0485	1.898
M_2	0.546 (2.54)	−0.222 (−3.65)	0.833 (21.62)			0.989	0.0431	1.954
	0.143 (0.56)	−0.264 (−4.28)		0.922 (19.78)		0.993	0.0360	1.777
	−3.865 (−4.58)	−0.296 (−3.22)			1.122 (10.68)	0.988	0.0450	1.775

Note: t ratios below coefficient estimates.
M_1 = currency plus demand deposits.
$M_2 = M_1$ plus time deposits.
P = GNP price deflator.
$X_1 = Y$, real GNP
$X_2 = Y_p$, proxied as a weighed average of current and past real GNP.
$X_3 = W$, wealth, human plus non-human real capital.

[*]Corrected for autocorrelation using the Cochrane-Orcutt technique.

consisting of expenditures on formal, informal, and special education, as well as the several cost components of employee training; (b) medical care, covering expenditures on health and safety adjusted to reflect medical outlays designed to increase future productive capacity; (c) mobility, comprising job search and hiring, frictional unemployment, and migration costs. Based on these categories of investment expenditures, the corresponding series of total capital stock are also available in Kendrick's study, and those estimates have been employed in our study as wealth.

The coefficients of log (Y_P) and log (W) using either M_1 or M_2 are not statistically different than one at the five per cent level. Since in the theoretical model (equation 1) permanent income is the product of a constant interest rate and wealth, this finding implies that the permanent income elasticity of the demand for money is unitary whether permanent income is proxied using equation 2 or permanent income is computed as the sum of expected yield of all the assets that make up wealth discounted by an overall rate of return.[1] The income elasticity of real money balances is, however, less than one, using the conventional income concept, indicating the differences between the Keynesian and Friedmanian models of the demand for money.

In conclusion, the results indicate that the proxy of permanent income used in many empirical studies on consumption and demand for money functions has been a good one. Recent estimates of wealth, defined in a similar way to Friedman's theoretical model, produce results identical to those utilizing the proxy. It could therefore be inferred that it is better that the exorcists, rather than the permanent income hypothesis, "be permanently exorcised."

NOTES

[*] Evangelos O. Simos is Assistant Professor of Business and Economics at the University of New Hampshire. John Triantis is an economist employed by AT&T Long Lines.
1. Since $Y_p = rW$ (equation 1), the elasticity of real money balances with respect to wealth ($e_{m,w}$) is identical to the elasticity of real money balances with respect to permanent income (e_{m,Y_p}), i.e.,

$$\frac{d(M/P)}{dW} \frac{W}{(M/P)} = \frac{d(M/P)}{dY_p} \frac{Y_p}{(M/P)},$$

given that $Y_p = rW$, where r = constant.

REFERENCES

Friedman, M. 1956. *Studies in the Quantity Theory of Money*, Chicago: University of Chicago Press.
———— 1957. *A Theory of the Consumption Function*. Princeton: Princeton University Press.
———— 1959. "The Demand for Money: Some Theoretical and Empirical Results." *Journal of Political Economy*, August 1959, 67, pp. 327–51.
Kendrick, J. 1976. *The Formation and Stocks of Total Capital*. New York: Columbia University Press.
Maddison, A. 1977. "Phases of Capitalists Development." *Banca Nazionale de Lavoro, Quarterly Review*, 121, June 1977, pp. 103–38.
Pesek, B. 1979. "A Note on the Theory of Permanent Income." *Journal of Post Keynesian Economics*, Summer 1979, 1, pp. 64–69.

REPLY BY
Boris P. Pesek

Friedman's theoretical concept of permanent income is—I agree—the present value of anticipated *future receipts* times the current rate of interest; his empirical "proxy" for it is the weighted sum of *past receipts*. A key point in my paper is that there is no relationship between the two. The authors do not argue the issue; they merely assert it by using the term "proxy." Denial of the *empirical* proposition that the output of steel is a good proxy for the output of cheese hardly merits the charge that such denial "is a clear indication of either misunderstanding or misrepresenting well-clarified economic theory".

Friedman's theoretical concept of wealth is—I agree—the present value of anticipated *future receipts*; Kendrick's measure is the cumulated value of *past investment* costs. Let me suggest that there is no relationship between the two. [1] The authors do not claim it; they merely assert it by giving to these two totally different concepts of wealth the common name "wealth."

After sweeping the two key *logical* problems under the rug, the authors make an *empirical* comparison of the performance of (1) current income, (2) the weighted sum of past GNPs, and (3) the cumulated sum of significant fractions of past GNPs. Thereby they furnish an excellent illustration of my claim that:

When one looks at what the investigators do rather than what they say they do one realizes that, had the permanent income hypothesis never been enunciated, *its testers would never have missed it.* (1979a, p. 68)

It might be stressed that my note is in full agreement with the currently so strong "rational expectations hypothesis"—that the consumers try to act on the basis of their estimates as to what the future will bring—and that it would be irrational to base these on the past: on weighted averages of past incomes or, as in the above note, on historical costs of current wealth. How to measure the future, *that's* the question. Without an answer to it, there is no "permanent income theory."

As far as the empirical part of the paper is concerned (where current demand for money is made to depend not on the future but on the past), let me suggest that the results reported for M_2 are worthless:

Two products entering M_1 ... have one key theoretically predicted and empirically confirmed characteristic: negative interest elasticities of demand. In M_2–M_5 more and more products are added ... with the opposite key characteristic. Thus, the functions dealing the M_2–M_5 yield "elasticities" ... that are nothing more than *haphazard* averages of two elasticities with opposite signs, determined by rapidly changing weights attached to them; e.g., only from 1950 to 1977 the ratio of $[M_1]$ to [time deposits] has exploded from $177/$59 to $344/$542. (Chapter 4, p. 86)

With one "elasticity" in each M_2 equation a meaningless number, the other cannot be any better.[2] The estimates for M_1, are, I believe, only of mild interest. Our journals are full of such equations, showing that in an interconnected economy everything moves with everything else: few of them have added to our predictive power.

Besides, all three equations dealing with M_1 are theoretically suspect. I can think of no economic rationale for the claim that current demand for money depends on GNPs received in the past fifteen years or on all past expenditures on capital. Dependence on current GNP is no less suspect. From 1964 to 1980 the transaction efficiency of demand deposits has risen from 37.9–42.3 to 202 (see turnover data in *Federal Reserve Bulletins*). Would any price theorist accept the claim of a stable demand function in the case of a factor of production the efficiency of which has risen fivefold?

NOTES

1. The correctness of both my propositions seems self-evident: consider the effect of expectations of (e.g., and *only* e.g.) higher energy costs, or a sharp growth in taxes, or of war on each item in the two pairs.
2. As I reported in Chapter 2, I am extremely sceptical of empirical research. Here is another example:
   (a) *All* theories show that M_1 and M_2 minus M_1 are negatively and positively related to the rate of interest.
   (b) When the authors add M_2 minus M_1 to M_1, two interest elasticities out of three become more strongly negative than those of M_1!

REFERENCES

Pesek, B.P. 1979a. "A Note on the Theory of Permanent Income." *Journal of Post Keynesian Economics*, Summer 1979(6), 1, pp. 64–9.

———— 1979b. "Modern Bank Deposits and the Theory of Optimum Undefined Money." In M.B. Ballabon, (ed.), *Economic Perspectives*. New York: Hardwood Academic Publishers.

Part Three:
Monetary Policy

11 Statement of Boris P. Pesek, University of Wisconsin-Milwaukee*

I. QUESTIONS ON MONETARY POLICY GUIDELINES

Question 1a. Do you believe that a program coordinating fiscal, debt management, and area monetary policies should be set forth at the beginning of each year for the purpose of advancing the goals of the Employment Act?

Expenditure decisions are—or should be—based primarily on the intrinsic merits of the program that they are to finance. By and large, to change them to fit the needs of an anticyclical policy involves waste, and is not practical to boot. An expenditure program which cannot justify itself on its own merits should not be accepted merely because the economy needs stimulation; a meritorious program should not be cut—and probably cannot be cut—merely because the economy is overheated. *Tax* decisions are more subject to manipulation guided by the needs of an anticyclical policy. Yet, the restraint provided by the acceptable size of, and changes in, national debt make it impossible to manipulate taxes as freely as an anticyclical policy might demand. Since the key consideration facing Congress in the case of fiscal policy is the difficult issue of the intrinsic merits of any specific action, there is a long lag between the time at which a fiscal policy is proposed and the time at which it becomes enacted.

The problem facing the Federal Reserve System that controls *monetary policy* is completely different. An action that expands or contracts the monetary base has no intrinsic merits of its own which would have to be carefully investigated. In the case of monetary policy, anticyclical effects of any action taken are the sole criterion. A counterpart of this

* From: *Compendium on Monetary Policy, Guidelines, and the Federal Reserve Structure.*
Committee on Banking and Currency, US House of Representatives, 1968.

fact is that monetary policy may be adopted and changed very rapidly, as the economic scene unfolds.

Thus, I would conclude that fiscal policy is—unfortunately but inevitably—quite rigid within any fiscal year and not very flexible even in the course of transition from one fiscal year to the next. To impose on the monetary policy the requirement that it be coordinated with the fiscal policy at the beginning of each year would place monetary policy in the same straitjacket. Rather than to facilitate the achievement of the goals of the Employment Act, it would hamper it. It would tie the agile to the lame.

Question 1b. Alternatively, should we treat monetary and fiscal policies as independent, mutually exclusive stabilization policies?

In the light of the foregoing, this does not appear to be a meaningful question. We have two levers which we may use to stabilize our economy: fiscal policy and monetary policy. One of the levers, controlling fiscal policy, must be frozen in any given position for the duration of one fiscal year. The other lever, controlling monetary policy, may be moved by the Federal Reserve Board as frequently as appears necessary. Thus, monetary measures can and should be used to overcome or to compensate for rigidities in fiscal policy, as the need to do so becomes apparent in the course of the fiscal year.

Question 2. If you believe a program should be specified, do you believe that the President should be responsible for drawing up this program, or alternatively, should such responsibility be dispersed between the Federal Reserve System and agencies responsible to the President?

Since I do not believe so, it is not possible for me to answer this question

Question 3-1. Should monetary policy be used to try to achieve the goals of the Employment Act via interventions of money supply (defined as desired) as provided in H.R.11, or alternatively should H.R.11 be amended to make some other variable or variables the immediate target of monetary policy: for example, interest rates, bank credit, liquidity, high-powered or base-money, total bank reserves, excess reserves, and free reserves?

(a) High-powered money, base money, total reserves, excess reserves, free reserves

There is a general agreement among economists that what co-determines spending by consumers and businesses is the stock of money in public hands; not any single component of it (such as high-powered money), nor any of the several Reserve concepts. Changes in the various Reserve concepts merely measure the looseness of the links between any policy action undertaken by the Federal Reserve System and its outcome, the stock of money in public hands. If the powers of the Federal Reserve System were inadequate, an increase (decrease) in the reserve base, excess reserves, or free reserves which is accompanied by no change in the money stock could be taken as evidence that the Federal Reserve System "meant well" but failed for reasons beyond its control. However, there is overwhelming evidence that the Federal Reserve System does have adequate powers to overcome any slippage that may occur within the banking system. Under these conditions, to focus attention on reserves rather than on the stock of money itself can only confuse our efforts to judge the wisdom of any policy followed by the Federal Reserve System. In public affairs, good intentions are unimportant; it is the results which count. Thus, H.R.11 is entirely correct when it proposes to judge the actions of the Federal Reserve System on the basis of the level and changes in the stock of money in public hands.

(b) Bank credit, liquidity
"Bank credit" contains time deposit credit over which the Federal Reserve System has next to no control. "Liquidity" is an ill-defined term that contains, presumably, all short-term or marketable debt certificates issued by banks, corporations, Federal, State, and local governments; again, the Federal Reserve System has no control over this item. To make the Federal Reserve System responsible for variables over which it has no control seems entirely inappropriate.

(c) Interest rates
Just as a driver of a car has a policy tool—the gas pedal—which he uses to achieve his purpose—the speed of his car—so the Federal Reserve System has a policy tool, the stock of money, which it uses to achieve the national purpose of high levels of income and employment. Interposed between the tools of control and results obtained, there is a number of intermediate indicators. In the case of a car, these are the various gauges showing, e.g., oil pressure or temperature of the engine. In the case of national economy, these are items such as the total volume of credit or changes in it, or the interest rates. *If* we were sure that the initial impulse—money—becomes converted to its end product—income and employment level—only through lending and never through direct spending, and *if* we were sure that the lending rate (the interest rate) is determined solely by supply factors and is completely unaffected by demand factors, then it would make little difference whether we evaluate the activities of the Federal Reserve System on the basis of data on the money stock or on the basis of data on interest rates.

However, the two conditions stated above are not satisfied. Increased money supply may and does enter the spending stream not only through lending but also through direct spending. For instance it is perfectly possible that an open market purchase of my US bond will cause me to buy a car with the proceeds. By observing an increase in the money stock, we shall conclude that the FRS engaged in an expansionary policy. In contrast, by looking at the constant level of interest rates we shall get the false impression that the FRS took no action. The second "if" listed above is not satisfied either. An expansionary monetary policy may be pushing interest rates down by making credit more easily available; however, it is perfectly possible that at the same time the demand function for loans will be shifting upward. In that case, the *net* change will be an increase in the rate of interest. By looking at the money stock, we will correctly conclude that the FRS is following an expansionary monetary policy; by looking at the level of the interest rates, we shall falsely conclude that the FRS is following a contractionary policy.

Just as I would advise a driver to concentrate on his gas pedal and speedometer and merely throw an occasional glance at the secondary gauges on his instrument panel, so I would advise the FRS to concentrate on the money supply and on the rate of growth of income and employment while giving to the unreliable intermediate indicators only secondary attention. As long as the primary goal (full employment) is satisfied, the level of interest rates is—relatively—unimportant. In contrast, it will not help the Nation very much if the interest rates are moving in the "right" direction while income and employment are falling. Once again, I feel that H.R. 11 correctly focuses attention on the money stock and correctly relegates interest rates to a secondary position.

Question 3-2. Define, as desired, the money supply.

At the present time, there are two approaches to the task of defining the money supply. An extremely influential one is "*the empirical approach*" that denies that economic theory is able to provide *a priori* specifications for the item called "money." The necessary consequence of this denial is that empirical workers lack criteria that would enable them to look at the great variety of assets held by the public and separate those which qualify from those assets which do not so qualify. If the theoretical construct *money* cannot be expressed in operational terms, empirical research which would relate money to income, employment, and the price level becomes impossible.

Unfortunately, those who deny economic theory the ability to work out operational specifications for the item called money refuse to draw this inescapable conclusion. Instead, they argue that one should (a) offer a theoretical hypothesis that money co-determines income, employment, and prices, (b) correlate all possible conglomerates of assets with income or prices, and (c) give, *ex post*, to that conglomerate that correlates best the honorific name "money."[1] This leads to two basic difficulties.

First, any and every monetary theory becomes incontrovertible. Suppose that one economist's monetary theory leads him to believe that money is *inversely related* to income. Surely, there must be some conglomerate of assets (i.e., inferior goods) which will show a strong inverse relationship with income. If this conglomerate is then defined, *ex post*, as "money," monetary theory of the first economist is confirmed. At the same time, a second economist's monetary theory may cause him to believe that there is *no relationship* between money and income. There must be some conglomerate of assets which will not correlate well with income; if this conglomerate is called, *ex post*, "money," monetary theory of the second economist will also rest on solid empirical evidence. Finally, a third economist may have a monetary theory telling him that there is a strong *positive relationship* between money and income. Once again, there must exist some conglomerate of assets held by the public which yields strong positive correlation with income. If this conglomerate is then, *ex post*, called "money," monetary theory of the third economist will be confirmed as well. As this discussion indicates, the empirical approach to defining money makes it possible for us to be faced by three, completely contradictory, monetary theories and forces us to agree that all three theories are correct and that none is false. Surely, this is an intolerable situation.

And yet, the above-described possibilities are not purely hypothetical; they give vent to a worry that is not an idle one. When economists evaluate, for instance, the period between 1929 and 1939 they do reach the conclusion that monetary policy did not matter if "money" is defined as currency and demand deposits, and that monetary policy was highly effective when time deposits are added to these two items.[2] When the empirical approach to money denies that economic theory is able to provide us with an operational definition of money, it deprives us—simultaneously—of any possibility to decide whether an increase in money hinders, has no effect, or fosters economic growth. As Harry G. Johnson put it:

[The issue] as to what money is ... is an important question both for theory and for policy. Obviously, there is no point in monetary theory if we cannot define what it is that we are theorizing about.[3]

There is a second difficulty with this "empirical approach" to the definition of money. Once we declare all assets eligible for the money club and leave it to a computer to decide which items do or do not qualify for membership (i.e., which items do or do not correlate well with income), the chosen total may or may not contain items that the public considers to be money and that the Federal Reserve System is able to control. This is not an idle worry either. A researcher of the Federal Reserve Bank of Chicago—who takes the empirical approach seriously —recently concluded that his statistical evidence "casts doubt on the conventional wisdom of automatically including currency and demand deposits in any definition of money supply."[4] Obviously, the "empirical approach" leads to, and permits, the absurd conclusion that a $5 bill in my pocket or a $5 demand deposit is not "money." Since it is the volume of these two items (currency and demand deposits) that the Federal Reserve System controls, it then follows that, whatever the FRS may be controlling, it is not money; that whatever policy the FRS may be pursuing, it is not monetary policy. And, finally, whatever the Committee on Banking and Currency may be concerned with is neither money nor monetary policy, since currency is not "money." Again, as Harry G. Johnson put it when completing the sentence just quoted:

There is no point in talking about monetary policy if whatever money is, is something the Central Bank cannot get a grip on. The issues here are therefore deeper than might appear at first sight.[5]

The second approach to the definition of money, which may be called "*the theoretical approach*," agrees that this issue is deep indeed. It insists that what is or is not money must be decided by economic theory and not by a computer spewing correlations between all sorts of ad hoc aggregates and income. A distinguished British economist, Sir John Hicks, recently concluded that an asset qualifies as "money" only if it performs the functions as a means of payment.[6] On this side of the Atlantic, this writer in association with T. R. Saving reached the same conclusion: "It is not an arbitrary decision whether we stress, or discover what is money, the role resources play as a medium of exchange or a store of value. Economic theory forces a decision, and forces it to be made in favor of the medium of exchange role."[7] From this, then, follows that any definition of money supply must not aim for consistency in *names* of items entering the money supply but for consistency in one specific *function*. Even though the name "gold" is the same, gold coin serving as a medium of exchange is money and gold ornament is not; even though the name "time deposit" is the same, in the twenties time deposits served as a medium of exchange and thus were money and in the sixties they do not serve as a medium of exchange and thus are not money. On this basis I would suggest that the only theoretically defensible definition of money at the present time contains (1) currency in public hands, (2) demand deposits in public hands, and (3) travellers' cheques in public hands.

How does this theoretical concept of money relate to the definition of money used by the Federal Reserve System? In the period prior to 1933, not very well. Before the passage of the Banking Act of 1933, demand deposits served partly as a medium of exchange and partly only as a store of value, held because this asset paid interest. Similarly, time deposits and savings deposits were transferable by check and thus served, partly, as a medium of exchange. [8] After 1933, Congress greatly simplified this situation and, since then, our theoretical concept of money coincides very closely with the concept of money used by the Federal Reserve System. At the present time, there are only two major shortcomings, one of which cannot be eliminated without Congressional action.

(a) Travellers' cheques

Indirect evidence indicates that since 1933 the significance of travellers' cheques grew very rapidly. For the holders, travellers' cheques are just as good as cash. When a consumer exchanges his currency or his demand deposit money for travellers' cheques, surely he has not reduced his holdings of a medium of exchange. In essence, such transaction is no different from one in the course of which a consumer, prior to 1914, exchanged his demand deposit money for National Banknotes. And, just as National Banknotes were produced by commercial banks on the basis of fractional reserves and thus represented a net expansion of the money supply, so there is no doubt that travellers' cheques are produced on the basis of fractional reserves and thus represent a net expansion of the nation's money supply. The only difference is that our Congress did classify National Banknotes as money and rigidly regulated their production while it does not classify travellers' cheques as money and thus enables this money to escape any regulation whatever.

I respectfully submit that our Congress should acknowledge that travellers' cheques represent a new type of money. Until abuses appear, there seems to be no need to introduce reserve requirements or to subject financial institutions producing travellers' cheques to the same tight regulation to which commercial banks as producers of demand deposit money are subjected. However, the volume of money consisting of travellers' cheques is treated, by the financial institutions producing this money, as a trade secret. This makes our data on the money supply incomplete, and perhaps seriously so. Surely, travellers' cheques must be introducing a strong seasonal element into our money supply. Makers of monetary policy must rely on evidence which is incomplete and therefore their ability to follow a correct monetary policy is being hampered.

In pursuance of its constitutional right and responsibility to regulate money, our Congress should pass legislation requiring full disclosure, at regular and frequent intervals, of the volume of travellers' cheques held by the public.

(b) Demand deposits held by the US Treasury

Reserves which must be held to support monies produced by the US Treasury, the Federal Reserve System, and commercial banks are—and properly so—excluded from our official measure of the quantity of money. They are viewed as "inputs" which make the final outputs of some other money possible. As immobilized inputs or "frozen assets" they cannot affect the spending decisions of our Government, consumers, and business enterprises. Federal Reserve statisticians extended this decision to exclude reserves to demand deposits held by the US Treasury. This, I submit, is an error. Demand deposit holdings of the US Treasury are not immobilized reserves. Their level is likely to affect spending and borrowing decisions of the US Treasury, just as the level of demand deposits held by, say, General Motors is likely to affect spending and borrowing decisions of that corporation. In a recently published book, I argued this case as follows:

Finally, the Government statisticians also subtract from the net US money supply the Treasury holdings of demand deposit money produced by commercial banks. This subtraction appears to us to be on extremely weak footing. These holdings are clearly not (1) legally required reserves making the production of Treasury's money possible or (2) business-required reserves resulting from the Treasury's money-producing activity. They are *not* an input that is necessary to make the Treasury's money production possible. As table 11.1 shows, in some months they are much *bigger* than the total Treasury output of currency; is a mountain giving birth to a molehill? Clearly, these money holdings result soley from the fact that the US Treasury is not just a money producer but also (actually, mainly) the financial agent for the huge economic operation of the US Government. In other words, these holdings are not different from the holdings of, for instance, General Motors. They are here to finance expenditures on goods and services: If they grow, the US Treasury will—just as will General Motors—surely take steps to draw them down, and if they fall off, the US Treasury will surely take steps to replenish them. They will reduce them by additional spending, tax reductions (which General Motors cannot do), or debt reductions; they will replenish them by a reduction of spending, tax increases (which General Motors cannot do), or debt increases. In either case, economic variables are bound to be affected. In contrast, there are no such effects if the Treasury coins an extra billion dollars and then puts this money aside for emergency. *These* latter inventories are clearly the result of the fact that the Treasury, in addition to being the disbursing agent for the Government, is in the money-producing business.

This view of Treasury holdings of demand deposit money is, actually shared by

Table 11.1: *US Government demand deposits, 1966*

[In millions of dollars]	
Jan. 26	3,930
Feb. 23	5,440
Mar. 30	5,120
Apr. 27	5,030
May 25	7,780
June 30	11,005
July 27	6,180
Aug. 31	4,720
Sept. 28	6,000
Oct. 26	4,720
Nov. 30	3,810
Dec. 28	5,130

Source: Federal Reserve Bulletin, March 1967, p. 408.

the Treasury itself. It states:

"Every operating enterprise—governmental or private, corporate or individual —must maintain a cash balance. A basic common purpose of this cash is to provide a cushion for meeting current obligations, because receipts never precisely match disbursements in timing and amount ... The Federal Government is no exception in this regard: The fixed policy is to maintain a cash operating balance no larger than required in its particular circumstances. Federal receipts do not come into the Treasury in an even flow.

Thus, as far as we can see, the reduction of the US money supply by the size of the (working) balances of commercial bank money held by the Treasury is not warranted.[9]

Question 3-B. Should the guidelines of monetary policy be specified in terms of some index of ... economic activity, or alternatively, in terms of the target variable's value or growth?

I do not see that it is possible to specify *one single* target variable as the question implies. The Federal Reserve System must control the quantity of money to achieve some acceptable compromise values for a *number* of variables. Income and employment are, obviously, crucial targets. Yet, price stability must be also striven for. Finally, the international balance of payments is surely a variable that may not be ignored without grave consequences. As long as nobody is able to agree on acceptable tradeoffs (how much unemployment for how much of price stability, how much of a loss of national income shall we tolerate in exchange for a smaller gold outflow, etc.), no sharply defined set of objectives can be imposed upon the Board of Governors of the Federal Reserve System.

Question 3-C. For only those persons who recommend that some index of economic activity be used to guide the monetary authorities in controlling the target variable: Should we use a leading (forward looking), lagging (backward looking) or coincident indicator of economic activity?

Question 3-D. For only those persons who recommend that the guidelines be put in terms of the target variable's value or growth: Should the same guidelines be used each year into the foreseeable future, or alternatively, should new guidelines be issued at the beginning of each year conditioned on expected private investment, government spending, taxes, et cetera?

Question 3-E. For only those persons who recommend that the guidelines be put in terms of the target variable's value or growth and who also recommend that the same guidelines be used year after year into the foreseeable future: What band of values or range of growth do you recommend?

Question 3-F. For all those persons recommending that the guidelines be put in terms of the target variable's value or growth. ... Under what circumstances, if any, should the monetary authorities be permitted during the year to adjust the target variable so that it exceeds or falls short of the band of values or range of growth defined by the guidelines issued at the beginning of the year?

Since I do not feel it possible to specify a single target variable or a defined mix of target variables to guide FRS decisions, I feel unable to answer these questions which are, explicitly, directed at those who do feel able to offer such a guide.

Question 4. Given the Goals of the Employment Act, what can debt management do to help their implementation?

Since my work is concentrated on money, I hesitate to speak on debt management.

Question 5-A. Do you see any merit in using open market operations for defensive purposes ... What risks and costs, if any, must be faced and paid if open market operations are used to counteract transient factors?

A highly influential view has it that monetary policy is incapable of eliminating transient fluctuations in income and employment. When we try to discover the basis for this view, we face two issues:

(a) What is the lag between a Federal Reserve policy that makes an increase in money possible and an actual increase in money?
(b) What is the lag between an actual increase in money and an increase in the public's spending?

In a widely quoted study Thomas Mayer concluded that "an expansionary policy ... takes seven months to reach 50-per cent level [of effectiveness] and 10 months to reach 75-per cent level." [10] This study is a very convenient tool for illustrating empirical and theoretical difficulties that plague our efforts to quantify the effectiveness of monetary policy in the short run. I shall discuss it in some detail not because I would want to single out my good and respected friend, Thomas Mayer, for criticism, but because his article enables me to pinpoint some basic shortcomings that one may find in almost *any* study that attempts to explore this topic. What is the basic method used by Mayer to reach the melancholy conclusion that monetary policy is ineffective? The author, *first*, computes the shares of various assets that we find as an average bank's portfolio. *Second*, he estimates with great care the time lag that separates a policy of monetary ease from actual spending on goods and services. *Third* and finally, he calculates the average time lag by using, as weights, the portfolio shares calculated in step one. If, for instance, 20 per cent of a bank's portfolio consists of mortgages and if residential construction involves a nine month delay between easing of credit and construction starts, he concludes that 20 per cent of monetary policy will become effective only after nine months.

This method has numerous shortcomings which I consider to be very serious:

(1) The study implicitly assumes that the entire increase in money resulting from open market operations takes the form of demand deposits, which are the only item reflected in the banks' portfolio. Yet, the money expansion process contains the public's desired currency-demand deposit ratio as one of the key variables. Thus, if the FRS increase the size of its portfolio by, say, $1 billion, initially only $770 million of the new money produced should become demand deposits and $230 million should turn out to be currency. Since Mayer does not consider the effect of an increase in currency on output, Mayer's conclusion leaves the effect of some 23 per cent of the actual increase in money unaccounted for.

(2) The study ignores the fact that the banks' total portfolio is composed of two subportfolios: the one based on demand deposits and the one based on time deposits. Banking laws and prudent business practices enable banks to hold the more long term assets (e.g., mortgages) the more time deposits they do hold. Thus, the average structure of the banks' portfolio—which forms the basis of Mayer's study—is *not* the structure that is based on demand deposits alone and thus cannot form the basis for our estimate of the consequences of an FRS action that enables the banks to produce more demand deposits.

(3) The study implicitly assumes that commercial banks' average and marginal portfolio purchases are identical. If, e.g., banks hold on the average 28 per cent of their assets in residential construction portfolio, and if construction starts occur six to eight months after easing of credit, Mayer assumes that the banks will hold $280 million out of $1 billion of potential credit idle until the residential-construction sector asks for these funds. This is in conflict with any rational business behaviour. Banks surely should be expected to try to lend newly available loanable funds to those sectors able to make use of these funds immediately. This accomplished, they should be expected to start to readjust the structure of the increment to their total portfolio to the structure of their total portfolio. In other words, one would expect the increment to banks' lending power to be concentrated, at first, on sectors which are willing and able to make use of credit "at once" (according to Mayer, consumer credit). As time passes, some of these assets should become retired and be made available to the sector standing next on the list of agility of response; etc. This profit-maximizing bank behaviour would completely destroy the validity of Mayer's estimates of the length of the lag between initiation of monetary policy and its effectiveness.

(4) But, it may be argued, how do we know that the bankers are trying to maximize profits? Perhaps they don't, and in that case it is perfectly possible that a banker discovers today that he is able to make additional loans but will wait for the next six or twelve months before doing so. However, there is empirical evidence that may be used to throw light on this problem. If bankers actually do behave in this irrational manner, we should see a reflection of this behaviour in the behaviour of excess reserves. If the estimated time lags are relevant, we should see that open market operations cause excess reserves to jump up almost by the same amount. Then, over a period of twenty-one months (at the end of which monetary policy according to Mayer becomes fully effective) these excess reserves should be falling until they become exhausted entirely. In reality, however, data on excess reserves show an extraordinary smooth series: the bankers seem to be able to convert an increase in their ability to lend into actual lending with an extraordinary speed.

(5) If so, then the only explanation that would support the frequently made claim that monetary policy works very slowly is that the consumers and business borrow today but spend the process only four, nine, or twenty months from now. Once again, this type of behaviour cannot be reconciled with our standard assumption that consumers and business enterprises act in a rational manner. Why borrow today if the proceeds are to be spent only six or twenty-one months from today? I am not aware of any empirical evidence that would indicate that consumers and business enterprises actually do behave in this irrational manner. In the

case of consumer expenditures, this is obvious: credit is arranged at the time of purchase. In the case of business enterprises, all available evidence indicates that while the issue of financing is discussed with the banks when a project starts to be considered, actual borrowing occurs at the time when funds are actually needed to pay suppliers.

If the currently fashionable view that monetary policy works extremely slowly is to be taken seriously, we need some analysis that would reconcile this view with the known behaviour of excess reserves. And, in addition, we need much more evidence than is currently available about the time that elapses between *the moment* at which a consumer of a business firm borrows from a bank (and starts paying interest charges) and *the moment* at which the proceeds of borrowing are spent. Until then, our knowledge of the paths and of the speed of the money-propagation process will remain extremely rudimentary. So rudimentary that a confident answer to question 5-A simply cannot be given.

Question 5-B: Do you believe that monetary policy can be effectively and efficiently implemented solely by open market operations?
If we want the FRS to change the quantity of money and have no other effect on the economy, the answer surely must be an affirmative one.
Question 5-C: For what purposes, if any, should (a) rediscounting, (b) changes in reserve requirements, and (c) regulation Q be used?

(a) Rediscounting
The current practice seems to be to use rediscounting to aid banks which find themselves in difficulties. Vague information available indicates that supervision of credit extended is quite strict and becomes more so after, say, two months. Such emergency aid to individual banks can do no overall harm and may do some good.

I am opposed, however, to the current tendency of the Board to make it much easier for commercial banks to make use of their rediscounting privileges. For reasons which have never been adequately explained, the Board seems to be anxious to borrow trouble. At the present time, there are several loose links in the chain that connects any action taken by the Board with the stock of money in public hands. Indeed, the Board frequently points out these loose links and argues that it should not be blamed if a specific policy—say, an open market operation—fails to change the money stock in the desired direction. If, henceforth, the right to rediscount is substantially strengthened, the Board will add *another* loose link to the chain that connects any action taken by the Board with the stock of money in public hands. Increased ability of the banks to borrow from the FRS will greatly increase the ability of commercial banks to neutralize policy measures taken by the Board. Should the Board persist in its new policy, which is bound to make it much more difficult for the Board to perform the task entrusted to it by Congress, serious consideration should be given to new legislation which would substantially tighten up the rules governing banks' ability to borrow from the Federal Reserve System.

(b) Reserve requirements
Changes in the reserve requirements are a blunt policy instrument which is being used by the Federal Reserve System only infrequently. It seems desirable, however, to keep this instrument in the FRS armoury.

(c) Regulation Q
As most professional economists, I consider the law that enables the Federal Reserve System to fix the maximum rate of interest that our savers are able to obtain from commercial banks, savings and loan institutions, and other financial institutions as utterly inequitable. In a recently published book, I have argued this case as follows:

Extraneous rule: maximum interest rate paid

There is, however, one major rule for which there is no justification: it involves the legislation that fixes the maximum interest rate that the commercial bankers (and, since the fall of 1966, savings and loan associations and mutual savings banks) are permitted to pay to those who lend money to them. The alleged reason for the institution of the maximum is the necessity to control the volume of credit, protect the banks' profits, and thus protect them from the temptation to engage in unsound and risky high-yield investment. The argument about the volume of credit is irrelevant and discriminatory. If it is desirable to control the terms at which people rent their property to others, then equity requires that *all* such credit be regulated: money credit passing through financial intermediaries just as house credit passing through real estate firms, or car credit passing through car rental agencies, or money credit passing through the bond market. The argument that commercial banks must be protected from a competitive "profit squeeze" and the resulting recklessness through the control of prices they pay to savers is no more adequate. It can easily be shown to be logically inconsistent and in contradiction to a wealth of available empirical evidence.

(a) If it is desirable to control the small fraction of the bankers' costs consisting of interest payments to savers, it should be equally desirable to control the 60 or 70 per cent of the bankers' costs consisting of wages, supplies of materials, rents, and so on. Because they *all* determine the extent of the profit squeeze facing the banker, why single out the savers for discriminatory treatment?

(b) Until 1966 there existed a huge sector of financial institutions that prospered and that had a record of safety just as excellent as the commercial banking sector: the sector of financial intermediaries represented by savings and loan associations and mutual savings banks. Yet, this sector did not enjoy and, clearly, did not need the protection given to commercial banks against competition for the saver's dollars.

Unfortunately, however, the notion that all financial intermediaries should gain the advantage of not having to pay the competitive market rate of interest to savers gained the upper hand in the fall of 1966, and the interest-fixing legislation, instead of being scrapped as clearly superfluous, has been extended to all the above-named financial intermediaries. The only exception was granted to those who open a time deposit account of $100,000 or more. [11]

There is no doubt that regulation Q should be scrapped. For obvious reasons, this cannot be done overnight. The best procedure would be to order the Federal Reserve System to increase the maximum permissible interest rate by one quarter of one per cent annually until the maximum permissible rate reaches ten per cent per annum.

Question 5-D. Is there any merit in requiring the Federal Reserve Board to make detailed quarterly reports?

I believe that actions speak louder and clearer than words. Whatever the FRS does is easy to discover by anyone who cares to study the *Federal Reserve Bulletin.* I would expect that any explanation of the reasons for action would be so opaque as to be worthless.

Question 5-E. What costs and benefits would accrue if representatives of the Congress, the Treasury, and the Council of Economic Advisors were observers at Open Market Committee Meetings?

In view of my answer to question 5-D, I can see no benefits. The cost would consist of the value of the time that the observers would spend in these meetings.

II. APPRAISAL OF THE STRUCTURE OF THE FEDERAL RESERVE

H.R.11 provides for the following structural changes in the Federal Reserve System:

1. Retiring Federal Reserve bank stock;

2. Reducing the number of members of the Federal Reserve Board to five and their terms of office to no longer than five years;

3. Making the term of the Chairman of the Board coterminous with that of the President of the United States;

4. An audit for each fiscal year of the Federal Reserve Board and the Federal Reserves banks and their branches by the Comptroller General of the United States; and

5. Funds to operate the Federal Reserve System to be a appropriated by the Congress of the United States.

Respondents were instructed:

Please comment freely on these several provisions. In particular, it would be most helpful if you would indicate any risks involved in adopting these provisions and discuss whether their adoption would facilitate the grand aim of H.R.11, which is to provide for coordination by the President of monetary and fiscal policies.

(1)   There is great merit in the proposal that would require our Federal Reserve System to retire its debts to member banks. The present law forces the Federal Reserve System to borrow money from commercial banks and to pay to these banks interest in return. This is, clearly, wasteful since the FRS—as any other central bank—has the power to produce money at next to zero cost. Why, then, require it to borrow this money from commercial banks at the cost of six per cent per annum? Also, why should the commercial banks be able to receive this income while the rest of the private sector is able to obtain from the Government interest rates, determined by market forces, which are frequently lower than is the rate paid by the Federal Reserve System?

(2)-(3) It appears desirable to give to the members of the Board long tenure. The problems that they are facing are complex ones and require, I believe, long apprenticeship. To remove members of the Board too frequently appears wasteful. Also, I believe that there is great merit in insulating the Federal Reserve System from short-term political influences. Short tenure would increase the danger that the members of the Board will tend to follow policy which is popular rather than "right."

(4)   Unless positive evidence of wrongdoing is available (and I am not aware of any) there seems to be no justification for making our Federal Government even bigger than it is at the present time. Surely, to require the Comptroller General to audit the FRS would require that we devote additional resources to a superfluous task.

(5)   The power of the purse string is the power of control. Since it appears highly desirable to insulate every central bank, including the Federal Reserve System, from short-run political influences, I would consider it most undesirable to endow Congress with the power to appropriate funds needed for the operation of the Federal Reserve System.

NOTES

1. Milton Friedman and Anna Jacobson Schwartz, *A Monetary History of the United States, 1867–1960.* Princeton: Princeton University Press, 1963, p. 650.

2. Milton Friedman and David Meiselman, "The Relative Stability of Monetary Velocity and the Investment Multiplier in the United States, 1897–1958," In B. Fox and E. Shapiro, *Stabilization Policies*. Englewood Cliffs, N.J.: Prentice-Hall, 1963, p. 244.
3. Harry G. Johnson, *Essays in Monetary Economics*. London: George Allen & Unwin, Ltd., 1967, p. 95.
4. George G. Kaufman, "A Staff Memorandum: More on Empirical Definition of Money," Research Department, Federal Reserve Bank of Chicago, April 1968, p. 6 (mimeo).
5. Johnson, *op. cit.*, p. 95.
6. Sir John Hicks, *Critical Essays in Monetary Theory*. Oxford: The Clarendon Press, 1967, pp. 18–37.
7. Boris P. Pesek and Thomas R. Saving, *Money, Wealth, and Economic Theory*. New York: Macmillan Co., 1967, 170–1.
8. For statistical method of allocating the total market value to components, see *ibid.*, pp. 188–97.
9. Boris P. Pesek and Thomas R. Saving, *The Foundations of Money and Banking*. New York: Macmillan Co., 1968, pp. 224–5.
10. Thomas Mayer, "The Inflexibility of Monetary Policy," *The Review of Economics and Statistics*, Vol. XL., November 1958, p. 370.
11. Pesek and Saving, *Foundations*, pp. 138–9.

12 There is Another Bank Reform in the Wings*

1. "DEPOSITORY REFORM ACT OF 1980" AND MY CREDENTIALS

In many of my writings (e.g., 1979) I kept warning against the permission to pay interest on chequable demand deposits and the permission of chequability of interest-earning time deposits. With overwhelming professional support (based on a different theory), the Depository Institutions Deregulation and Monetary Control Act of 1980 has been passed. All my dire predictions—and more—have been fulfilled:

a. The benefits to the consumer are nil. The Act has not changed the total amount of interest that banks are able to pay. The sole difference is that before the Act the consumers had the choice of *either* receiving only transaction services (on demand deposits) *or* only interest income on their savings (time deposits). After the Act, they became able to stop "wasting shoeleather" by fusing the two. They now receive the same amount of interest as before on a new joint product, a sickly offspring of two healthy parents.

b. Private costs to the consumers are heavy. In our Condominium Association, members started, as I predicted, to waste shoeleather by paying their dues not when convenient but when least costly. The never-considered *net* change in demand for shoeleather is unpredictable *a priori.* What interest they gain on their NOW accounts is more than offset by the association's loss on our money market funds. But, even if there were no net loss, our dues have to be increased. This is equivalent to business firms' increases in prices. It would be interesting to know by how much late payments caused by the reform have fostered inflation.

---

* From: *The Journal of Post Keynesian Economics*, Spring 1982.

c. Public costs are staggering. As the constantly changing kaleidoscope of official measures of M's shows, data on bank deposits before and after 1980 ceased to be—as predicted—comparable. Empirical monetary research will have to start from scratch. Without econometric evidence, only rudimentary policy recommendations can be made.

What is worse: data on bank deposits after 1980 are not comparable from month to month and thus are worthless. Each bank with a NOW or ATF account sets it own "minimum balance" (roughly equivalent to the former time deposits) and sets its own system of penalties and incentives voluntarily to exceed this minimum balance. With only demand deposits spendable, time depositors *had* to put the banker (and us) on notice about a change in their spending plans; not now with NOW. To use a metaphor, before 1980 demand deposits with an annual velocity (in FRS terms, "turnover") of over 200 were akin to scotch; time deposits with annual velocity of three were akin to soda. After 1980, each bank now markets its own—changeable—mix of scotch-and-soda, with the proportions unknown even to the bank since a great deal is left to the depositors' discretion. To aggregate the individual gallons marketed (into "the money") is an exercise in futility: the sum tells us nothing about the alcoholic (inflationary) content of the brew. We have ceased to know *what is.*

And we have ceased to be able to make even the most rudimentary predictions of *what will be.* We used to know analytically the signs (negative and positive, respectively) and, empirically, the sizes of interest elasticities of demand for demand and time deposits. Predictions could be based on this. Now the sign of the elasticity of demand for the mix of the two is analytically unpredictable; the size of the average of the two former elasticities is empirically unknown. And, with the structure of the mix constantly changing, it is probably unknowable.[1]

Since mid-1980 we don't know where we are and cannot predict where we are going: a most disturbing fact to the whole business community. No wonder Friedman (1981) finds our economy's "aberrant behavior" for which he cannot find any "reasonable explanation" (after having tried eight pre-1980 rules.) Never before—I believe—has a branch of economics so unanimously and so long propagated a policy without the slightest consideration of its consequences. "No need for it": reward of virtue—of any *laissez-faire* measure—is predestined.

Despite the current fashion of "deregulation" huge growth of non-bank intermediation (with even department stores getting into the act), introduction of what are in essence non-bank checking accounts (e.g., CMA of Merrill Lynch), advances in electronic handling and transmission of data, these and many other forces spoke in favour of draconian additional regulations. Regulations essential to leave unimpaired the economically vital duty of the government "To coin money [and] regulate the value thereof, ..." imposed on it by the Constitution. Wisely, *two* tasks are here imposed. It is futile to keep control of the monetary base and give up control of its value: to permit financial and formerly non-financial institutions to reprocess this "base" into thousands of disparate rubber bands.

2. PROPOSED "DEPOSITORY REFORM ACT OF 1982(?)"

Press reports indicate that yet another "Reform Act"—containing measures which I have also vigorously criticized—is now upon us: "Events have happened much more rapidly than I have thought possible," said Senator Jake Garn (Rep., Utah), Chairman of the Banking Committee (*The Wall Street Journal*, September 15, 1981, p. 8). A major feature is to be the total elimination of the now vanishing restrictions on the territorial limits imposed upon banks. And, a few days later it was reported that Chairman Volker supports "emergency legislation" permitting bank holding companies to buy SLAs, even across state boundaries (*Chicago Tribune*, October 2, 1981, p. 2, section 2). These would be other tragic errors.

Monetary theorists are, correctly, in favour of one national financial market because it fosters national efficiency. A myopic small banker in North Dakota will invest poorly locally, while Bank of America is aware of the splendid investment opportunities that beckon in Texas. *Laissez faire* in banking will correct this.

The trouble is that savers do not give a hoot about nationally efficient allocation of their (and I stress, *their*) savings. And since these are their savings, the principle of consumers' sovereignty tells us that they have a perfect right not to give a hoot and establish for themselves institutions that violate the rules of *laissez faire* which, in this case, would (paradoxically) result in central planning overriding their own personal interests and decisions. Just as there is a Keynesian federal income multiplier, so there is a state and local multiplier. A dollar of North Dakota's savings spent in Texas will have its ripple effect *there*. Technically, North Dakota's LM function shifts to the origin, and Texas' LM shifts away from it.[2] The consequences of this on income and employment in Texas and North Dakota are obvious. After the local banker has been replaced with a national banker, many a saver in North Dakota who used to get inefficiently low interest on his savings out of a positive income will discover that he now may obtain Texas-sized interest on his savings out of his zero income.

Consumers cannot make rational decisions unless they know both microeconomic facts (interest rates differential) *and* macroeconomic facts (sizes of state and local income multipliers). To deny them the latter is to mislead them into irrational regulatory and lending decisions. Dakota's savers, if informed about the IS-LM analysis, would never select a National Bank promising high yield (along with unemployment); they would always select a Local Bank promising low yield (and employment). Of course, many an informed consumer may even then decide "Let George do it." This is always a problem when a collectivity's good clashes with individual gain. A unit banking system is a neat solution of this problem. A unit banker is familiar with business in his area and ignorant about business elsewhere. He invests the savers' money in the region in which he and they live and thus recycles it. He keeps the regional LM function and employment at a higher level than a national banker would. Protection of him is well within the Constitutional power of Congress "to regulate commerce ... among the several States ..."

Were we to live in a *laissez-faire* system, ignorant Dakotans would be punished for their ignorance, and economically educated Dakotans, for their short-sighted greed. They would be forced to move to Texas. For better or worse, we do not live in such a system. But, in some cases introduction of some *laissez-faire* measure (always analyzed on the basis of macroeconomically patently false "*ceteris paribus*") into a non *laissez-faire* world gets us not a partial improvement but further deterioration in the allocation of resources:

a. Federally financed unemployment and welfare benefits will replace the local monies that the local banker has previously distributed with reasonable efficiency.

b. We shall get some new "Depressed Areas Redevelopment Act" by which federal bureaucrats will try to replace the vanished competent local banker.

c. Ultimately, the savers will discover the root of the evil. They will insist, as our black citizens have correctly insisted (to the despair of all right-thinking theorists), on a "Community Reinvestment Act of 1977." It requires banks to put some money back into areas where it came from.[3]

National banks will hate to be forced to do what a local banker has loved to do, and will do as little of it as they can get away with. And, they will casually write off losses the size of which would have spelled ruin to a local banker; thus, they will have more losses. They will put in less money, less efficiently. And, losses may even come handy as an argument that the act that they don't want to work is unworkable. Finally, inter-area tensions (with obvious racial content in many cases) will be increased as depositors start to feel that "their" bank is forced into low-yield investments.

CONCLUSION

It is ironical that vocal proponents of "stable and predictable monetary environment" are simultaneously proponents of the massive Reform Act imposed in 1980, and of still more reforms. Even *if* they were all beneficial, they would be—as most reforms are—destabilizing even in the most tranquil times. In our distressed times, the battle cry "Don't just stand there, undo something" imperils the whole reform movement.

What is worse, the just discussed reforms would not be beneficial even in tranquil times: they are unambiguously harmful. Monetary and banking theorists could not have done better if somebody had paid them to destroy monetary statistics and our ability to predict effects of monetary policies, this accomplished, they are now busy on an effort to create pockets of depressed areas all around the country. Given our knowledge that prices are rigid downward in depressed areas and flexible upward in booming areas, this is simultaneously another effort to accelerate inflation.

NOTES

1. Note the $M2$ has suffered from the same inscrutability from 1933 on (Pesek, 1981). But, those who knew it could help themselves, by disaggregating into its two scrutable components: $M1$ and the rest. Now NOW and ATF have made $M1$ also inscrutable. *The Wall Street Journal* editorial (October 5, 1981, p. 22) quotes its foremost expert's belated recognition of this predicted effect. It recommends that we focus on $M2$ alone. Makes sense: with *all* M's now inscrutable, why not go by seniority?
2. T. R. Saving's and my analysis of "feedbacks" (1968, pp. 152–7, 173–5) has been totally ignored. As a result, banking theorists feel free to offer policies based on what is—in our terms—the unsupported assertion that all state and local feedbacks and thus the Keynesian multipliers are zero.
3. Strife is already starting, though in forms different from those foreseen above. The Attorney General in Iowa is suing (economically correctly) major banks and money market funds distributors for engaging in illegal interstate banking, and thereby siphoning money out of Iowa (see *Chicago Tribune*, October 9, 1981).

REFERENCES

Friedman, M. 1981. "The Experts Speak Out." *Newsweek*, September 21, p. 39.

Pesek, B. P. 1979. "Modern Bank Deposits and the Theory of Optimum Undefined Money." In M. G. Ballabon, (ed.), *Economic Perspectives.* New York: Hardwood Academic Publishers.

———— 1981. "Reply." *Journal of Post Keynesian Economics*, Fall 1981, 4(1), pp. 157–8.

———— 1968. and Saving, T. R. *The Foundation of Money and Banking.* New York: Macmillan Co.

Acknowledgments

I am grateful for permissions to reprint in this volume a number of essays and portions of books:

Giornale degli Economisti e Annali di Economia
The MacMillan Company
Harwood Academic Publishers
The Journal of Finance
The Canadian Journal of Economics
The Journal of Economic Literature
Quarterly Review of Economics and Business
Journal of Political Economy and The University of Chicago Press
Journal of Post Keynesian Economics and M. E. Sharpe, Inc.

(In the last two cases the copyright owner is not the Journal but publisher.)

Name Index

Subject Index